William Stainton Moses

Spirit Teachings

William Stainton Moses

Spirit Teachings

ISBN/EAN: 9783337003609

Printed in Europe, USA, Canada, Australia, Japan

Cover: Foto ©Thomas Meinert / pixelio.de

More available books at **www.hansebooks.com**

SPIRIT TEACHINGS

THROUGH THE MEDIUMSHIP OF

WILLIAM STAINTON MOSES

(*M.A., OXON.*),

AUTHOR OF "PSYCHOGRAPHY," "SPIRIT IDENTITY," "HIGHER ASPECTS OF
SPIRITUALISM," "PERSONAL REMINISCENCES OF EPES SARGENT,"
"SPIRITUALISM AT THE CHURCH CONGRESS," ETC., ETC.

Memorial Edition.

LONDON:
LONDON SPIRITUALIST ALLIANCE, LTD.
110, ST. MARTIN'S LANE, LONDON, W.C.

1898.

PREFACE.

THIS reprint of the Memorial Edition of "Spirit Teachings received through the mediumship of the late Mr. Stainton Moses, M.A. (Oxon.), has, in compliance with the urgent request of many friends, been issued by the London Spiritualist Alliance, Ltd., 110, St. Martin's Lane, London, W.C.

1898.

BIOGRAPHY OF W. STAINTON MOSES.

WILLIAM STAINTON MOSES was born at the village of Donnington, in Lincolnshire, on the fifth of November, 1839. His father, William Moses, was the Head Master of the Grammar School, and his mother the daughter of Thomas Stainton, of Alford, Lincolnshire. His education was commenced at the school of which his father was Principal, and was afterwards continued with a private tutor, who, impressed by his great abilities, strongly urged Mr. Moses to send his son to a public school. His advice was acted upon, and in August, 1855, young Stainton Moses, then in his 16th year, was placed at the, Grammar School at Bedford. Here he remained for nearly three years, winning golden opinions from all the masters on account not only of his brilliant abilities but also of his conspicuous industry, regularity, and general attention to all his duties. In one term alone he carried off four prizes; and shortly before he left he was elected to one of the two exhibitions which had been founded in connection with the school. On leaving, he received from the Head Master testimonials of the most flattering nature, speaking in high terms of the very rapid progress he had made in all departments of study, and also of the uniform excellence and correctness of his school conduct.

From Bedford Stainton Moses went to Exeter College Oxford, which he entered at the commencement of Michaelmas term, 1858. His college life was in every way as successful as his school life had been, and great hopes were formed by all connected with him that at the end of his Oxford career he would take the highest honours open to him. This, however, was not to be—overwork gradually told upon him, but he refused to rest or in any way relax his studies; and so, sad to relate, on the very day before the commencement of his last examination his health gave way completely, and he broke down, absolutely worn out in mind and body. For some time he was very ill, but on regaining convalescence he was ordered abroad. He spent nearly a year travelling on the Continent with friends, and, with a view to complete restoration, he visited many different scenes and climates. St. Petersburg was the farthest limit of his wanderings, and on his return journey he lingered for six months at the old Greek Monastery of "Mount Athos." Curiosity apparently guided him thither, and his strong desire for rest and meditation doubtless impelled him to remain for so long a time in that remote, old-world spot. Many years afterwards he learned from Imperator, his controlling spirit, that he had been influenced even then by his unseen guides, who had impressed him to go to "Mount Athos" as part of his spiritual training

At the age of 23, Stainton Moses returned to England and took his degree, leaving Oxford finally in the year 1863. Though much improved in health by his foreign travel, he was not yet strong; so, acting on the advice of his doctor, who insisted on a quiet rural life, he accepted a curacy at Maughold, near Ramsey, Isle of Man. Here he remained for nearly five years, and succeeded during that period in gaining the affection and esteem of all his parishioners. The Rector, a very old and infirm man, was practically unable to render any assistance in the work of the parish, so that the whole of the duties connected with the church and the district devolved upon Stainton Moses. During his stay at Maughold, a severe epidemic of small-pox broke out in the village and surrounding neighbourhood; and it was then that the utter fearlessness of his nature was strikingly manifested. There was no resident doctor in the district, but having at different times acquired some little knowledge of medicine, Stainton Moses was enabled to minister to a certain extent to the bodily necessities of his parishioners, as well as to their spiritual needs. Day and night he was in attendance at the bedside of some poor victim who was stricken by the fell disease, and in one or two cases when, after an unsuccessful struggle with the enemy, he had soothed the sufferer's dying moments by his ministrations, he was compelled to combine the offices of priest and grave-digger, and conduct the interment with his own hands. Such was the panic, inspired by the fear of infection, that it was sometimes found impossible to induce men to dig graves for the dead bodies of the victims, or even to remove the coffins containing them. But through all this terrible time Stainton Moses never flinched, and, notwithstanding the threefold nature of the duties thus compulsorily thrust upon him, he was fortunate in escaping the malady, and though he steadily remained at his post single-handed, from the commencement to the end of the outbreak, he was spared any uneasiness on the score of his own health. It may be readily imagined how greatly he endeared himself to all those around him by his courageous devotion and strong sense of duty during such an anxious and critical period; but the feelings which he inspired in his parishioners, and everyone with whom he came in contact at Maughold, will be best appreciated by a perusal of the address presented to him on relinquishing his curacy there. It reads as follows:—

"REV. AND DEAR SIR,—We, the undersigned parishioners of Maughold, are much concerned to learn that it is your intention shortly to resign the position which you have for some years past so usefully and honourably occupied amongst us. We beg to assure you that your labours have been greatly appreciated in the parish. The longer we have known you, and the more we have seen of your work, the greater has our regard for you increased. The congregations at both the churches under your charge are very different in numbers to what they were some time ago. The schools have been better looked after; the aged and infirm have been visited and comforted; and the poor have been cheered and helped by your kindness and liberality. By your courteous demeanour, by your friendly intercourse, and by your attention to the duties of the parish generally, you have greatly endeared yourself to us all; and not least to our respected and venerable Vicar, whose hands we are well satisfied you have done all you possibly could to strengthen. We cannot but feel that your loss will be a very serious one to the parish, and we should be glad if you could see your way to remaining some time longer with us. By reconsidering your determination and consenting to remain, you would place us under a deep debt of gratitude and obligation."

Here follow the signatures of the Rector and Churchwardens, also of fifty-four of the principal inhabitants of the district. Such a document, spontaneously presented, speaks for itself. However, in spite of the unanimous wish of the inhabitants that he should remain, Stainton Moses found that the work of looking after two parishes, practically single-handed, made too great demands upon his health, and so in the spring of 1868 he reluctantly relinquished his charge at Maughold, and accepted the curacy of St. George's, Douglas, Isle of Man. Here he first met Dr. and Mrs. Stanhope Speer, and the acquaintance thus commenced soon ripened into an intimacy which was destined to exercise a very important influence upon the future of the three persons concerned. Very soon after taking up his duties at St. George's, Stainton Moses was laid up with a sharp attack of congestion of the liver, which confined him to his bed for some little time. Dr. Speer attended him through this illness (although he had retired from active practice for some years), and was successful in effecting a complete cure. In September of 1869 Stainton Moses left Douglas, where he had made a great impression by his preaching and ministrations among the poor of the parish, and took up the post of *locum tenens* at Langton Maltravers, in Dorsetshire. Here he remained for two months, when he was transferred to a curacy in the diocese of Salisbury, the last ecclesiastical appointment he held.

At this time he was troubled by an affection of the throat, which rapidly became worse, and necessitated a complete rest, and the relinquishing of all public speaking and preaching. Acting, therefore, upon medical advice, Stainton Moses gave up his curacy, and came to London with the intention of turning his attention to tuition. This practically severed his connection with the Church. Had his health permitted him to follow his original career, he would no doubt have attained a distinguished position, as he was a powerful and original preacher, a successful organiser, and an earnest and efficient worker among the poor.

On coming to London Stainton Moses stayed with Dr. and Mrs. Speer for nearly a year, during which time he superintended privately the education of their son, the present writer. About the close of 1870 or the beginning of 1871, he obtained the appointment of English Master in University College School, which position he held until 1889. Little need be said of his work there, further than that as long as his health permitted it was always done well. As one of the English masters in a great school, his opportunities of influencing the boys under his charge, in respect of literary taste and style, were considerable; and of those opportunities he made good use. Many will remember his excellent suggestions, and kindly criticisms of their essays. A portion of his work consisted of preparing a class for the Matriculation of the University of London. The peculiarly crabbed philological and historical knowledge required for that examination was uncongenial to Stainton Moses's mind, as in literature he liked to have a free hand ; yet the work was done, and done well, and during the years he spent at the school he embodied in a manuscript volume a vast number of valuable notes bearing upon this subject.

Even more striking than his success as a master was the personal influence exercised by him over his pupils. One of the peculiar institutions at University College School is that by which a certain number of boys are especially attached to certain senior masters, with whom they can take counsel and from whom they can seek advice in all matters pertaining to their well-being, moral, intellectual, and physical. Over the boys thus placed under his immediate care the strong personality of Stainton Moses had an enormous influence, often extending over a period long subsequent to their leaving school. Many a time in after life his advice has been sought by old pupils on important matters, and whenever he felt he could help them it was always a real pleasure to him to do so to the best of his ability. His geniality, his knowledge of the world and of men, his invariable straightforwardness and kindness, all combined to strengthen the affectionate regard in which he was held by those boys who had the good fortune to be under his especial supervision. On resigning his post through ill-health the Council of University College passed a resolution conveying to Stainton Moses their best thanks for his long and valuable service to the school, and a special letter of affectionate regret was also sent to him signed by twenty-eight of his colleagues. Of his capacity for imparting his ideas to others I can speak from a personal experience extending over seven years, during which period our relations as master and pupil were continuous and unbroken. Nothing could have been kinder or more convincing than his method of imparting knowledge and information; nothing clearer or more helpful than his manner of explaining all difficulties; and no trouble was too great for him to take in smoothing away all obstacles to a clear understanding of the matter in hand.

It was during Stainton Moses's visit to Dr. Speer in 1870 that the subject of Spiritualism was first brought prominently before him. For some time he and Dr. Speer had been in the habit of discussing various topics bearing upon religious belief. Both were gradually drifting into an unorthodox, almost agnostic, frame of mind, and both were becoming more and more dissatisfied with existing doctrines, and longing for absolute truth as regards the future life, and for some demonstration of the certainty of immortality. To obtain any proof of such immortality founded upon a strictly scientific basis seemed impossible, and Dr. Speer was rapidly becoming a materialist of the most hard and fast nature. A note received by him from Stainton Moses, together with a copy of W. R. Greg's "Enigmas of Life," may prove interesting to those who would fain have some inkling of the inner working of these two friends' minds, at a time when the old faith had lost its hold upon them, and they were standing upon the brink of a newer Revelation:—

"MY DEAR FRIEND,—You and I have tackled some 'Enigmas of Life' together, and if we have not always solved them, we have generally agreed in our opinion respecting them. I offer you the opinions of a great thinker, which will be, in their outcome, very similar to what we have thought out for ourselves. And if the half century, during which your life here has lasted, leaves much unknown, and much that even another such period will not unravel, I hope at least that during such part of it as we are here together we may continue to talk and speculate together.—Your sincere friend, W. S. M."

It will be interesting to note the circumstances under which, during this visit to Dr. Speer, the subject of Spiritualism pressed itself upon Stainton Moses's attention. Mrs. Speer had been confined to her room by illness for three weeks, during which period she had occupied herself in reading Dale Owen's "The Debatable Land." It interested her much, and on being able to rejoin the family circle she asked Stainton Moses to read the book, and endeavour to discover whether there was any truth in the experiences therein narrated. Though at that time he took no interest in Spiritualism, regarding it merely as trickery and fraud, yet he promised Mrs. Speer to go into the matter with the view of ascertaining whether there might be some germs of truth underlying the mass of jugglery and imposture; and so began those astounding experiences of his, which, commencing at that time, extended over a period of more than twenty years. In those days, although dissatisfied with the cut-and-dried doctrines of the Church, and with the manner in which its teachings were expounded from the pulpit and elsewhere, Stainton Moses was, nevertheless, immensely interested in all religious subjects, and his reading of everything that bore upon them was enormous. No book, pamphlet, or magazine likely to throw any light upon the questions which perplexed him was overlooked, and even after his regular intercourse with the unseen world had commenced he did not entirely give up his faith in the Church without an arduous and prolonged struggle. The reality of the struggle may be clearly discerned in the pages of "Spirit Teachings," and in his other automatic writings; but when he had fully satisfied himself of the reality of those "Teachings," and of the truthfulness and integrity of his spirit-guides, his faith never faltered, and his zeal in the prosecution of the work entrusted to him never flagged. Previous to his own development as a medium, Stainton Moses had been present at various sittings with other mediums. Mrs. Speer having been so immensely impressed by her perusal of the "Debatable Land" he determined to read it for himself, and in consequence became almost as anxious as she was for fuller information. This was the more curious as, only a month before, he had tried in vain to read Lord Adare's record of private séances with D. D. Home, but, as he said himself, it had absolutely no interest for him. His first noteworthy experiences were with Lottie Fowler, in the spring of 1872; and soon afterwards Dr. Speer—although at that time regarding the whole subject of Spiritualism as "stuff and nonsense"—was persuaded to join him in a visit to the medium Williams. They went several times, and were soon convinced that there was *some* force outside the medium at work—in which conviction they were much strengthened by a remarkable séance held shortly afterwards in Dr. Speer's house, when Williams was again the medium.

About this time Stainton Moses's own mediumistic powers began to be developed. It is unnecessary to give a detailed description of that development, as a full and exhaustive account may be found in Mrs. Speer's "Records," which have lately appeared in *Light*; but I think that some of my own recollections of the séances, at which I had the privilege of being present during the last two years of Stainton Moses's active mediumship may be of some interest. At any rate they will place on record the impressions of another witness, and may possibly be of service as bearing additional testimony to the wonderful powers of the medium, and the absolute reality of the phenomena given through him.

It is important to note that at these séances no less than ten different kinds of manifestations took place, with more or less frequency. On occasions when there were fewer varieties we were usually told that the conditions were not good. When they were favourable the manifestations were more numerous, the raps more distinct, the lights brighter, and the musical sounds clearer. The various occurrences may be briefly enumerated as follows:—

1. Great variety of raps, often given simultaneously, and ranging in force from the tapping of a finger-nail to the tread of a foot sufficiently heavy to shake the room. Each spirit *always* had its own distinctive rap, many of them so peculiar as to be immediately recognisable; and these sounds often took place in sufficient light for the sitters to see each other's features, and—I suppose more important—hands. Raps also were frequently heard on the door, sideboard, and wall, all some distance removed from the table at which we sat; these raps could not possibly have been produced by any human agency; of that I satisfied myself in every conceivable way.

2. Raps which answered questions coherently and with the greatest distinctness, and also gave messages, sometimes of considerable length, through the medium of the alphabet. At these times all the raps ceased except the one identified with the communicating spirit, and perfect quiet prevailed until the message had been

delivered. We could almost always tell immediately with which spirit we were talking, owing to the perfectly distinct individuality of each different rap. Some of the higher spirits never manifested by raps at all, after the first few séances, but announced their presence by a note of music, or the flash of a light; but among those who did manifest in the usual way it would be difficult to forget Rector's heavy and ponderous tread, which shook the whole room with its weight, while it appeared to move slowly round the circle.

3. Numerous lights were generally visible to all the sitters. These lights were of two different kinds—objective and subjective. The former usually resembled small illuminated globes, which shone brightly and steadily, often moved rapidly about the room, and were visible to all the sitters. A curious fact in connection with these lights always struck me, viz., that looking on to the top of the table one could see a light slowly ascending from the floor, and to all appearance passing out *through* the top of the table—the table itself apparently not affording any obstacle to one's view of the light. It is a little difficult to explain my meaning exactly, but had the top of the table been composed of plain glass, the effect of the ascending light, as it appealed to one's organs of vision, would have been pretty much the same as it was, seen through the solid mahogany. Even then, to make the parallel complete, it would be necessary to have a hole in the glass top of the table, through which the light could emerge. The subjective lights were described as being large masses of luminous vapour floating round the room and assuming a variety of shapes. Dr. Speer and myself, being of entirely unmediumistic temperaments, were only able to see the objective lights, but Mr. Stainton Moses, Mrs. Speer, and other occasional sitters frequently saw and described those which were merely subjective. Another curious point in relation to the objective lights was that, however brightly they might shine, they never, unlike an ordinary lamp, threw any radiance around them, or illuminated the smallest

portion of the surrounding darkness—when it *was* dark —in the slightest degree.

4. Scents of various descriptions were always brought to the circle—the most common being musk, verbena, new-mown hay, and one unfamiliar odour, which we were told was called spirit-scent. Sometimes breezes heavy with perfume swept round the circle; at other times quantities of liquid musk, &c., would be poured on to the hands of the sitters, and also, by request, on to our handkerchiefs. At the close of a séance scent was nearly always found to be oozing out of the medium's head, and the more frequently it was wiped away the stronger and more plentiful it became.

5. The musical sounds, which were many and varied, formed a very important item in the list of phenomena which occurred in our presence. Having myself had a thorough musical education, I was able to estimate at its proper value the importance of these particular manifestations, and was also more or less in a position to judge of the possibility or impossibility of their being produced by natural means, or through human agency. These sounds may, roughly speaking, be divided into two classes—those which obviously proceeded from an instrument—a harmonium—in a room, whilst the hands of all the sitters were joined round the table; and those which were produced in a room in which there was no instrument of any kind whatever. These latter were, of course, by far the most wonderful. As regards the musical sounds produced in the room in which there was no instrument, they were about four in number. First, there were what we called "The Fairy Bells." These resembled the tones produced by striking musical glasses with a small hammer. The sounds given forth were clear, crisp, and melodious. No definite tune was ever played, but the sounds were always harmonious, and at the request of myself, or any other member of the circle, the "bells" would always run up or down a scale in perfect tune. It was difficult to judge where the sound of these "fairy bells" came from,

but I often applied my ear to the top of the table, and the music seemed to be somehow *in* the wood—not underneath it, as on listening *under* the table the music would appear to be above. Next we had quite a different sound—that of a stringed instrument, more nearly akin to a violoncello than anything else I have ever heard. It was, however, more powerful and sonorous, and might perhaps be produced by placing a 'cello on the top of a drum, or anything else likely to increase the vibration. This instrument was only heard in single notes, and was used only by one spirit, who employed it usually for answering questions—in the same way that others did by raps. The third sound was an exact imitation of an ordinary handbell, which would be rung sharply by way of indicating the presence of the particular spirit with whom it was associated. We naturally took care to ascertain that there was *no* bell of any kind in the room at the time. Even if there had been, it would have been a matter of some difficulty to ring it all round the walls and even up to the ceiling, and this particular sound proceeded indifferently from all parts of the room. Lastly, we had a sound of which it is exceedingly difficult to offer an adequate description. The best idea of it I can give is to ask the reader to imagine the soft tone of a clarionet gradually increasing in intensity until it rivalled the sound of a trumpet, and then, by degrees, diminishing to the original subdued note of the clarionet until it eventually died away in a long drawn-out melancholy wail. This is a very inefficient description of this really extraordinary sound, but as I have in the whole course of my experience never heard anything else at all like it, it is impossible to give to those who have *not* heard it a more accurate idea of what it was like. As was the case with the two previous sounds I have described, it was always associated with one spirit. It is a noteworthy fact that in no case did the controlling agencies produce more than single notes or at best isolated passages. This they accounted for as due to the peculiarly unmusical organisation of the medium. At any rate, the production of these sounds was wonderful enough in itself, as I over and over again satisfied myself fully that there were no materials in the room which could in any way assist in the making of any kind of musical tones; and the clarionet and trumpet sound was one that I should be utterly at a loss to give at all an adequate imitation of, whatever materials might be at my disposal. Before I joined the circle several other musical sounds were frequently heard, and all were given with greater variety, both of manipulation and tone; but as I am now only giving a brief epitome of what actually happened under my own observation, I refrain from alluding to occurences which took place when I was not present.

6. Direct writing was often given, sometimes on a sheet of paper placed in the centre of the table, and equidistant from all the sitters; at other times one of us would place our hands on a piece of paper previously dated and initialled, and usually a message was found written upon it at the conclusion of the séance. We usually placed a pencil upon the paper, but sometimes we only provided a small piece of lead—the results being the same in both cases. Usually, the writing took the form of answering questions which we had asked, but sometimes short, independent communications were given, and also messages of greeting.

7. Movements of heavy bodies, such as tables and chairs, were by no means infrequent. Sometimes the table would be tilted up at a considerable angle; at other times the chairs of one or more of the sitters would be pushed more or less forcibly away from the table, until they touched the wall behind; or the table would move away from the sitters on one side, and be propelled irresistibly against those on the other, compelling them to shift their chairs in order to avoid the advance of so heavy a piece of furniture. The table in question, at which we usually sat, was an extremely weighty dining-table made of solid Honduras mahogany, but

at times it was moved with much greater ease than the combined efforts of all the sitters could accomplish; and these combined efforts were powerless to prevent it moving in a certain direction, if the unseen force willed it to do so. We frequently tested the strength of this force by trying to check the onward movement of the table, but without success.

8. The passage of matter through matter was sometimes strikingly demonstrated by the bringing of various articles from other rooms, though the doors were closed and bolted. Photographs, picture-frames, books, and other objects were frequently so brought, both from rooms on the same floor and from those above. How they came through the closed doors I cannot say, except by some process of de-materialisation, but come they certainly did, apparently none the worse for the process, whatever it might have been.

9. The direct spirit voice, as opposed to the voice of a spirit speaking through the medium while in a state of trance, was very seldom heard, and never with any clearness or distinctness. But occasionally it was attempted, and by listening carefully we could distinguish one or two broken sentences which were hissed out in a sort of husky whisper. These sounds generally seemed to be in the air above us, but they were produced with evident difficulty, and there being so many other methods of communication, the direct voice was essayed but seldom.

10. The inspirational addresses given by various spirits through Stainton Moses when in an entranced condition have been so thoroughly dealt with by Mrs. Speer in her "Records" that I can add nothing as regards the *matter* thus expounded. Touching the *manner* of these addresses (one or more of which we had at almost every séance) I can only say that they were delivered in a dignified, temperate, clear and convincing tone, and that though the voice proceeded from the medium, it was always immediately apparent that the personality addressing us was *not* that of the medium. The voice was different, and the ideas were often not in

accordance with those held at the time by the medium. An important fact, too, was that although many spirits exercised this power of control, the voice which spoke was always different; and in the case of those spirits which controlled regularly we came to know perfectly well which intelligence was communicating, by the tone of the voice and the method of enunciation.

So far, in this enumeration of the various phenomena, I have spoken *generally* of the manifestations which usually occurred at most of our sittings, but in conclusion I will give two particular instances, one of direct writing, and one of identity, both of which I think are interesting, and which certainly impressed me considerably. On one occasion we were told to cease for a time, and resume the séance later on. I asked the communicating intelligences if they would during the interval give me a sample of direct writing under test conditions. Having received an affirmative reply, I procured a piece of my own note-paper, and, unknown to the other members of the circle, I dated and initialled it, and also put a private mark in a corner of the sheet. The others having retired from the dining to the drawing room, I placed my piece of paper with a pencil under a table in the study, and having thoroughly searched the room I barred the shutters, bolted and locked the door, and put the key in my pocket. I did not lose sight of the door until I re-entered, when to my great satisfaction I found a message clearly written on the paper. As we had not been sitting in the study, and as I can positively aver that no one entered the room after I had left it until I myself unlocked the door, I have always considered this particular instance of direct spirit writing as a most satisfactory and conclusive test. The other occurrence which I consider specially worthy of mention took place as follows. We were sitting one night as usual, and I had in front of me, with my hand resting upon it, a piece of note-paper, with a pencil close by. Suddenly Stainton Moses, who was sitting exactly opposite me, exclaimed, " There is a very bright column of light behind you." Soon afterwards he said that the column of light had developed into a spirit-form. I asked him if the face was familiar to him, and he replied in the negative, at the same time describing the head and features. When the séance was concluded I examined my sheet of paper, which my hand had never left, and found written on it a message and signature. The name was that of a distinguished musician who died in the early part of the present century. I purposely refrain from specifying him, as the use of great names very frequently leads to results quite different from those intended. However, now comes the most extrordinary part of the affair. I asked Stainton Moses—without, of course showing him the written message—whether he thought he could recognise the spirit he saw behind my chair if he saw a portrait of him. He said he thought he could, so I gave him several albums, containing likenesses of friends dead and alive, and also portraits of various celebrities. On coming to the photograph of the composer in question he at once said, without hesitation, "That is the face of the spirit I saw behind you." Then, for the first time, I showed him the message and signature. I regarded the whole incident as a very fair proof of spirit identity, and I think that most people would, at any rate, consider the occurrence one of interest.

During the time of Stainton Moses's active mediumship, he was often busily engaged in assisting in the formation of various societies, whose primary object was the investigation of Spiritualism and other occult, though kindred, subjects. He took part in the establishment of the British National Association of Spiritualists in 1873. He was also connected with the Psychological Society of Great Britain, which was inaugurated in April, 1875, and of the Council of that Society he was one of the original members. In 1882, Stainton Moses took an active interest in the formation of the Society for Psychical Research; and in 1884 he established "The London Spiritualist Alliance," and became its first President, which post he filled up to the time of his death. For the last few years of his life, he added to his other duties the editorship of *Light*, and though his active mediumship, as regards physical phenomena, had then almost entirely ceased, yet his power of automatic writing remained with him to the end. For the last three or four years of his life he suffered from failing health, and many successive attacks of influenza gradually undermined a constitution which had never been conspicuously robust. Though he gradually became worse he was never supposed to be in any real danger, and when the end came on September 5th, 1892, it was a terrible shock to all those who knew him, and who realised what a loss to themselves personally, and to the cause of Spiritualism generally, his death would prove.

Far more interesting to those who knew him intimately was Stainton Moses's personality than his life. The latter, as all who read this brief sketch will readily see for themselves, was, with the exception of the wonderful spiritual experiences so indissolubly linked with it, unmomentous and uneventful. But his individuality and force of character were immense; his ability was quite out of the common; and more than all, the versatility of his talents was perhaps one of his most striking features. No study was too dry or uninteresting for him to master, no subject so apparently unimportant and unworthy his attention but he would easily acquire an intelligent conception of its details. And this applies equally to the whole range of more or less trivial matters which make up the sum total of nineteenth-century every-day life, as well as to those deeper and more serious subjects which, being akin to his own especial one, naturally engrossed most of his attention. From the time that he first began to realise of what vast importance it was to establish the possibility of communion with the world of the future, to the end of his life, his zeal in proving the truth of his teachings never failed. In spite of the demands made upon his time by school and press work, he contrived to bestow an immense amount of energy upon his Spiritualistic researches; his enormous correspondence with thousands of inquirers all over the world affording quite sufficient material to occupy the life of any ordinary man. But in this as in everything else he was conscientious to the last degree, and never considered time wasted that was expended in answering the queries and solving, to the best of his ability, the doubts of earnest seekers after truth. A certain proportion of his time was devoted to visiting many of the most important people in the country—important both socially and politically—and also those who were distinguished for their eminence in the scientific, literary, and artistic world. During the lifetimes of such people their names cannot be divulged, but it is not too much to say that Stainton

Moses had interviews, more or less frequently, with most of the illustrious personages of his day; and all who took any interest in the phenomena of Spiritualism, whatever their position or attainments, were alike anxious to hear his opinions and experiences of that subject on which none were so well qualified to speak as himself.

Apart from Spiritualism, Stainton Moses possessed in his own character a rare combination of remarkable qualities, not often met with in the same individual. He had the keenest sense of justice and equity, his judgment was invariably sound and discreet, and in addition to all this, no man ever possessed a kinder heart or livelier sympathies, or was more ready to assist with counsel or advice those who came to him for either. Notwithstanding his varied spiritual experiences, unique in themselves, he was never puffed up by them in the smallest degree, and though impatient of mere frivolous or ignorant opposition, he would never refuse to join issue in friendly argument with any opponent—however much beneath his attention. In these various encounters, Stainton Moses's clear understanding and extremely logical habits of mind enabled him to score heavily and with decisive effect off those antagonists who sometimes had the temerity to attack him with very little reason and still less knowledge. His crushing rejoinder to Dr. Carpenter, who some eighteen or twenty years ago lectured at the London Institution on the "Fallacies of Modern Spiritualism," will probably be still remembered by a good many people as a striking instance of logical reasoning and effective sarcasm, which, significantly enough, was never answered. Considering the then unpopular nature of the subject which he had so unmistakably made his own, and of the conclusions which he deduced from a close and systematic study of the same, it is a matter to be wondered at that he was not more often attacked by narrow-minded religious bigots, pseudo-scientists, and superficial penny-a-liners. But however this may be, the fact remains that with a few insignificant exceptions he was *not* so attacked; when he was, his power of showing up the weakness of his opponent's case and ignorance of the matters on which he presumed to dogmatise was only equalled by the polite ridicule and quiet satire which he was always ready to bring to bear upon the author of any unprovoked piece of aggressive meddling.

It was a noteworthy feature about Stainton Moses, that in spite of his being compulsorily drawn in many ways into a conspicuously public position, no man ever hated publicity more than he did. Retiring and modest by nature, he detested the making of speeches, delivering of addresses, presiding over meetings, and other similar functions for which the singularity of his powers and the extent of his knowledge naturally marked him out as being eminently fitted. Though richly endowed with gifts sufficient to stamp him in any age as a leader of men, his own inclinations would, had he been untrammelled by force of circumstances, have led him to prefer a life of studious ease and unostentatious retirement. But this was not to be; so he trod his allotted path with zeal, courage, and discretion; did his duty with an utter abnegation of self; and died at his post in the prime of manhood, carrying with him to the grave the affectionate regard and esteem of hundreds who will cherish the memory of his friendship as one of their most precious legacies.

It is quite impossible within the limits of a short biography like the present to do more than present a brief sketch of the character of Stainton Moses; but I should like to once more insist upon the entirely admirable ingredients of which that character was composed, and I might fill volumes in dilating upon his utter absence of pride, fanaticism, arrogance, or conceit; upon his love of truth, purity, and integrity; and upon his absolute fearlessness, generous large-heartedness, and wholly sympathetic friendship. But of what avail? He has crossed the bar, and gone from our *mortal* vision for ever. And whatever I could say in his praise would not heighten the affection and esteem of those who knew him; and those who did not would gain but a poor idea of his worth and talents from any paltry efforts of mine. So let us gain what benefit we can from the words of those inspirational teachings which he has left behind, and to which this short memoir is intended to serve as a humble introduction, and then, for a time at any rate, let us re-echo the old formula, *Requiescat in Pace.*

CHARLTON TEMPLEMAN SPEER.

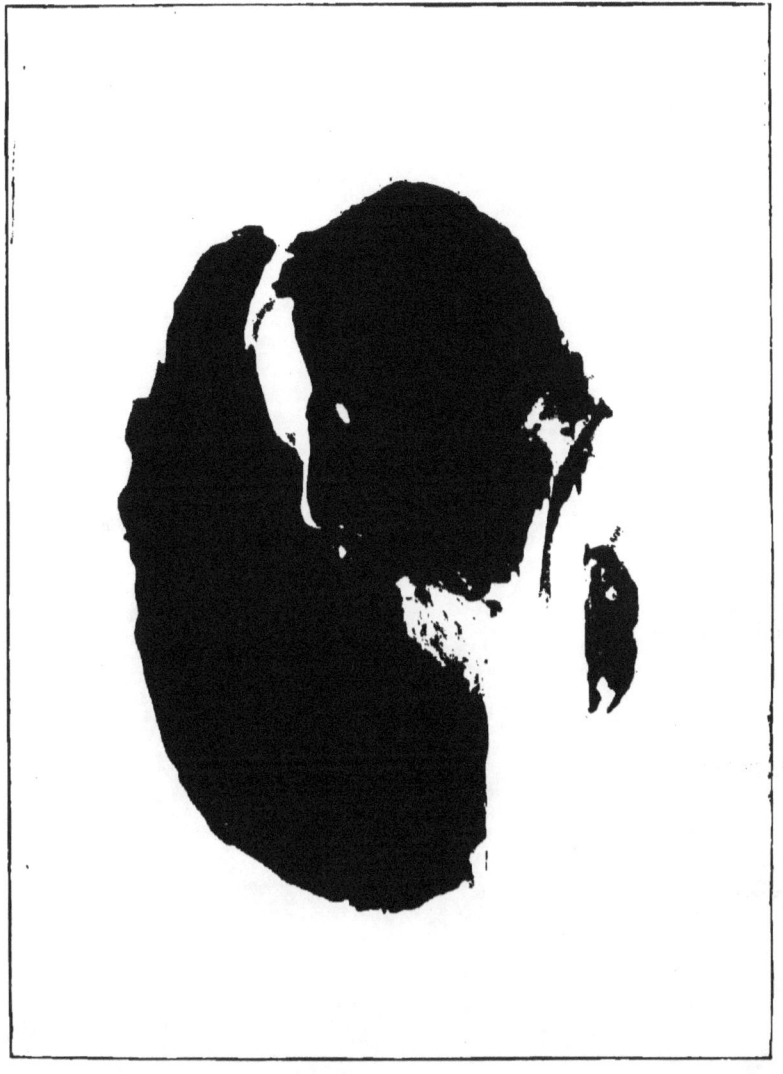

W. STAINTON MOSES.

FROM A PHOTOGRAPH TAKEN AFTER DEATH BY TUOHY, BEDFORD.

PREFACE TO THE MEMORIAL EDITION.

This Edition of "Spirit Teachings" is issued by the Council of the London Spiritualist Alliance in affectionate memory of their friend, Mr. W. Stainton Moses, to whom the Alliance owed its existence, and who was its first and only President from its formation in 1884 to the time of his decease on September 5th, 1892. Anxious to show their loving regard for one with whom it had been their pleasure and privilege to co-operate in the work which was so dear to him, and to which he gave so large a portion of his very busy life, the Council have concluded that the fittest memorial to his worth, and to the value of his labours, would be the re-issue of the book which he himself regarded as the most generally useful of his publications. Others, no doubt, have each a special interest of its own; but "Spirit Teachings" —revealing as it does the struggles of a robust mind against new phases of thought, and its gradual acceptance, as truth, of what was at first suspected and feared as dangerous heresy— will always possess a peculiar charm for the many who, in these days of intellectual daring, having become impatient of old creeds, are striving for greater liberty and clearer light. The Council, therefore, trust that the re-publication of "Spirit Teachings" will meet with a very general acceptance.

By the kindness of Mr. Charlton T. Speer, who enjoyed the close personal friendship of Mr. Stainton Moses, they are able to include in the volume a valuable biographical notice, which cannot but add greatly to the interest of the work.

Signed on behalf of the Council of the London Spiritualist Alliance,

E. DAWSON ROGERS,
President.

110, ST. MARTIN'S LANE, LONDON, W.C.

PREFACE TO FIRST EDITION.

SOME apology may be deemed necessary for the publication of this book. My excuse is to be found in the following facts.

When these communications first saw the light they attracted a large amount of attention, and brought me much correspondence. Many found in them words which were suitable to their own experience, and more or less helpful to themselves. It seemed that no case is quite singular, and that the record of my own spiritual education was not merely of private application.

Since that time many requests have been made for the publication of these Teachings in a connected form. The compliance, however, did not rest with me, and it is only lately that I have been enabled to present the complete series, duly revised, by the same method as was originally employed in writing them, and arranged in such order as was possible with so disconnected a mass. For these are but specimens taken from a great bulk, and from them are excluded some of the most striking by reason of their purely personal application.

They are now strung together on a thread that is strong enough, perhaps, to hold them together in some sort of relation. But no attempt of mine can even faintly reproduce their force and coherence when originally given. They must go forth, a curious record of an educational influence brought to bear from without and unsought on a mind that endeavoured strenuously to sift and probe what was said. They pretend to no dogmatic authority, to no literary completeness. They will be to each reader only what he makes them.

(M.A. OXON.).

CORRECTION.—The word "*voice*" in the 20th line of page 24 is a misprint for "*rice*."

INDEX.

PREFACE, ... iv

INTRODUCTION.

The method by which the messages were received (1)—The character of the writing (2)—The communicating spirits (3)—The circumstances under which the messages were written (4)—How far were they tinged by the mind of the medium? (5)—Power of controlling by will the production of writing (6)—These communications mark a period of spiritual education (7)—And, though to him who received them of great value, are published with no such claim on others (8), ... 1-8

SECTION I.

Special efforts to spread progressive truth at this special epoch thwarted by the Adversaries (9)—Obstacles in the way—The efforts now made greater than men think (10)—Revelation: its continuity—Its deterioration in men's hands—The work of destruction must precede that of construction (11)—Spirit-guides: how given—Spirits who return to earth—The Adversaries and their work (12)—Evil—The perpetuation of the nature generated on earth—The growth of character (13)—Each soul to his own place, and to no other—The Devil (14), . 9-14

SECTION II.

The true philanthropist the ideal man—The notes of his character (15)—The true philosopher—The notes of his character—Eternal life—Progressive and contemplative—God, known only by his acts (16)—The conflict between good and evil (a typical message of this period)—These conflicts periodic, especially consequent on the premature withdrawal of spirits from the body: *e.g.*, by wars, suicide, or by execution for murder—The folly of our methods of dealing with crime (17)—Of herding criminals together and hanging the worst of them—Remedial methods preferable (18)—For in sending a spirit prematurely forth from its body with rage and vengeance, we send him with enlarged opportunity to work mischief—We do this in the name of God, of whom we have a very false conception (19)—Pity and Love are more potent than Vengeance—The sublimity of the idea of God revealed in Spirit-Teaching compared with the old idea (20, 21), ... 15-21

SECTION III.

Physical results of the rapid writing of the last message: headache, and great prostration—Explanation (22)—Punitive and remedial legislation—Asylums and their abuses—Mediums in

INDEX.

madhouses (23)—Obsessing spirits living over again their base lives vicariously (24)—Children in the spirit-world: their training and progress—Love and knowledge as aids—Purification by trial—Motives that bring spirits to earth again (25)—Return to earth not the only mode of progression—States of probation or purgation, and spheres of contemplation (26)—Spheres and states within them—The descent of spirit through hoice of evil (27)—Its hatred of good and gradual assumption of materiality till it sinks lower and lower (28)—The Unpardonable Sin (29), ... 22-30

SECTION IV.

Time: April and May, 1873—Facts of a minute nature given through writing, all unknown to me (31)—Spirit reading a book and reproducing a sentence, through the writing, from Virgil and from an old book, Rogers' Antipopopriestian—Experiment reversed (33), ... 31-33

SECTION V.

Mediumship and its varieties—The physical medium (34)—Clairvoyants—Recipients of teaching, whether by objective message or by impression—The mind must be receptive, free from dogmatism, inquiring, and progressive (35)—Not positive or antagonistic, but truthful and fearless (36)—Selfishness and vaingloriousness must be eradicated—The self-abnegation of Jesus Christ (37)—A perfect character, fostered by a secluded life, the life of contemplation (39), - 34-39

SECTION VI.

The Derby Day and its effects spiritually (40)—National Holidays, their riot and debauchery—Spirit photographs and deceiving spirits (41)—Explanation of the event: a warning for the future (42)—Passivity needed: the circle to be kept unchanged: not to meet too soon after eating (43)—Phosphorescent lights varying according to conditions (44)—The marriage bond in the future state (45)—The law of Progress and the law of Association (46)—Discrepancies in communications (47), . . . 40-47

SECTION VII.

The Neo-Platonic philosophy—Souffism—Extracts from old poets, Lydgate, and others written—Answers to theological questions (48)—The most difficult to approach are those who attribute everything to the devil—The pseudo-scientific man of small moment (49)—The ignorant and uncultured must bide their time—The proud and arrogant children of routine and respectability are passed by—The receptive are too often cramped by a human theology which stifles true religious instincts (50)—They are armed at all points, and their honest but mistaken arguments are very saddening—Reason, the final Court of Appeal (51)—How far does Reason prove us of the devil, and our creed diabolic (52) 48-52

INDEX.

SECTION VIII.

The writer's personal beliefs and theological training—A period of great spiritual exaltation (53)—The dual aspect of religion—The spirit-creed respecting God—The relations between God and man (54)—Faith—Belief—The theology of spirit (55)—Human life and its issues—Sin and its punishment—Virtue and its reward—Divine justice (56)—The spirit-creed drawn out—Revelation not confined to Sinai—No revelation of plenary inspiration (57)—But to be judged by reason (58), - - - - - - - 53-58

SECTION IX.

The writer's objections—The reply: necessary to clear away rubbish—The atonement (60)—Further objections of the writer—The reply (61)—The sign of the cross—The vulgar conception of plenary inspiration (62)—The gradual unfolding of the God-idea (63)—The Bible the record of a gradual growth in knowledge easily discernible (64)—The inspiration divine, the medium human—Hence each finds in the Bible the reflex of his own mind—And so the Bible becomes an armoury for all (65)—And too much stress is laid on isolated texts, and words and phrases (66)—At variance with these views, spirits endeavour to eradicate what is so false as not to be put right, otherwise they take existing opinions and mould them into closer semblance of truth (67)—So theological views are toned down, not eradicated—Opinions are spiritualised (68)—In this way has this teaching been given—How the sign of the cross can be prefixed to it (69-71), - - - - - - - - - - 59-71

SECTION X.

Further objections of the writer—The reply (72)—A comparison between these objections and those which assailed the work of Jesus Christ (73)—Spiritualised Christianity is as little acceptable now (74)—The outcome of spirit-teaching—How far is it reasonable?—An exposition of the belief compared with the orthodox creed (75-79), - - - - - - - - 72-79

SECTION XI.

The powerful nature of the spiritual influence exerted on the writer—His argument resumed (80)—The rejoinder—No objection to honest doubt (81)—The decision must be made on the merits of what is said, its coherence, and moral elevation (82)—The almost utter worthlessness of what is called opinion—Religion not so abstruse a problem as man imagines (83)—Truth the appanage of no sect—To be found in the philosophy of Athenodorus, of Plotinus, of Algazzali, of Achillini (84)—To whom earth-opinions are of little moment now—All may work in such work as this, and there is no discrepancy (85)—Every statement made, scrupulously exact, though some may have been distorted

In transit (86)—This attempt to teach is one of many made to many different minds (87)—The prospects of acceptance and rejection (88-89)—The position assigned to Jesus the Christ (90-91), ... 80-91

SECTION XII.

The writer's difficulties—Spirit identity—Divergence among spirits in what they taught (92)—The reply—The root-error is a false conception of God and His dealings with man—Elucidation at length of this idea (93-97)—The devil—Risk of incursion of evil and obsession applies only to those who, by their own debased nature, attract undeveloped spirits (99), ... 92-100

SECTION XIII.

Further objections of the writer, and statement of his difficulties (101)—The reply—Patience and prayerfulness needed—Prayer (103)—Its benefits and blessings—The spirit-view of it (104-108) —A vehemently-written communication—The dead past and the living future (106-107)—The attitude of the world to the New Truth (108-109), ... 101-109

SECTION XIV.

The conflict between the writer's strong opinions and those of the Unseen Teacher (110)—Difficulties of belief in an Unseen Intelligence—The battle with intellectual doubt (111)—Patience needed to see that the world is craving for something real in place of the creed outworn (112)—The result of the contention was that the writer, having carried his point, was lifted out of the personal dispute about the Messenger into a grasp of the dignity and beauty of the message—Statement of his mental condition (113)—His own contention (114, 115)—The reiterated claim to be an enunciation of a Divine Message (116)—Spirit intercourse governed by laws—No proper care of mediums (117, 118), ... 110-118

SECTION XV.

The religious teaching of Spiritualism—Deism, Theism, Atheism (119) —No absolute Truth—A motiveless religion not that of Spirit-teaching—Man, the arbiter of his own destiny—Judged by his works; not in a far hereafter, but at once—A definite, intelligible system—The greatest incentive to holiness and deterrent from crime (120-122)—Spiritualism not bad in the mass—Hard for those who are in the midst to judge—Means are adapted to ends—A multiplicity of minds are being operated on by methods best adapted to reach them, hence the apparent din and confusion (123-125)—The question of Evil—Popular Spiritualism —Not only a profoundly external revelation, but assurance of reunion, a gospel of consolation (126-128), ... 119-128

INDEX.

SECTION XVI

The summing up—Religion has little hold of men, and they can find nothing better—Investigation paralysed by the demand for blind faith (129)—A matter of geography what form of religious faith a man professes—No monopoly of truth in any (130)—This geographical sectarianism will yield to the New Revelation (131)—Theology a bye-word even amongst men—Life and Immortality (133), - - - - - - - - - 129-132

SECTION XVII.

The request of the writer for independent corroboration, and further criticism (134)—The reply—Refusal—General retrospect of the argument—Temporary withdrawal of Spirit-influence to give time for thought (134-136)—Attempts at establishing facts through another medium futile (137)—"You cannot have mathematical proof" (138)—"I and my Father are one" explained in reference to the Divinity of Christ (139)—Further message from IMPERATOR during my absence from home, and more evidence of identity (139, 140)—Advice to review patiently the past, and seek composure (140, 141), - - - - 134-141

SECTION XVIII.

Difficulty of getting communications when it was not desired to give them—The mean in all things desirable (142)—The religion of body and soul—Spiritualising of already existing knowledge (143)—Cramping theology worse than useless—Such are not able to tread the mountain-tops but must keep within their walls, not daring to look over (144)—Their father's creed is sufficient for them, and they must gain their knowledge in another state of being (145)—Others do not think at all: they want things settled for them—With all these we have nothing to do, for nothing can be done—The way to know of the things of spirit is free, and that man who struggles up to light gains more than he does who lets others do his thinking for him (147)—That is now being done for Christianity that Jesus did for Judaism: it is being Spiritualised (148)—Christ was the Great Social Reformer, teaching liberty without license, elevating man, and living among the common people—We declare truths identical with those preached then (149, 150)—The spiritual return of Christ (151), - - - - - - - 142-151

SECTION XIX.

Outline of the religious faith here taught—God and man (153)—The duty of man to God, his fellow, and himself (154)—Progress, Culture, Purity (155)—Reverence, Adoration, Love (156)—Man's Destiny (157)—Heaven, how gained (158)—Helps: communion with Spirits (159)—Individual belief of little moment—Religion of acts and habits which produce character, and for which in result each is responsible—Religion of body and soul (160), - - - - - - - - - - 152-161

INDEX.

SECTION XX.

More evidence of identity of spirits communicating—Perplexity caused by a name, written psychographically, being wrongly spelt: explanation (163)—The writer's disturbed and anxious state reacting on the communications—Doubt and its effects (165)—No use to maintain a dogmatic attitude against facts—The trustful spirit—Advice as to the future—Withdrawal of further communication (166-169), ... 162-169

SECTION XXI.

The writer's condition, a personal explanation (170-171)—The reply: reiterated advice to ponder on the past and seek seclusion (172)—Final address by IMPERATOR, retrospective, and closing for the time the argument: October 4, 1873 (172-177), - - - 170-177

SECTION XXII.

IMPERATOR'S despairing view of his work (178-181)—A striking case of identity (181)—Personal explanation of the writer (183), - 178-183

SECTION XXIII.

Progressive Revelation (184)—The chain of spiritual influence from Melchizedek, through Moses, Elijah, to the Mount of Transfiguration, and the Apocalyptic Vision (185-187)—The Pentateuch (188)—Abraham not on the highest plane—Translations of Enoch and Elijah (189)—Legendary Beliefs in the Sacred Records to be carefully discriminated (190-193), - - - 184-193

SECTION XXIV.

The intervening period between the records of the Old and New Testaments—A period of darkness and desolation, the night succeeding a day of revelation (194-195)—The internal craving for advanced truth corresponds to external revelation (196-197)—Points to be considered in the records of the Old Testament of the life of Christ for the writer's own instruction—A glimpse of the method of guidance exercised over him (198, 199), - - 194-199

SECTION XXV.

Pursuing his studies on the lines indicated the writer found evidence of the work of various hands in the Mosaic Records—A message thereupon, and a dissertation on the danger of quoting isolated texts, and relying on the plenary inspiration of a translation (200-202)—The compilation in Ezra's day—The Elohistic and Jehovistic legends—The Canon of the Old Testament, how settled (203)—Daniel, a great seer (204)—The progressive idea of God in the Bible developed and elucidated (204-206), . . 200-206

SECTION XXVI.

Changes in the communications—A retrospect marking the close of another phase in the writer's relations to his Teachers (207-209)

INDEX.

—The writer's mental state, and the various phenomena that were presented, bearing on the attempts to lift him into a more passive condition (210)—Music—Autographs of two celebrated composers authenticating a communication (211), - - - 207-211

SECTION XXVII.

India as the cradle of races and religions—A communication from PRUDENS (212-214)—The man crushed by a steam-roller who communicated immediately after death (*vide* Spirit-Identity, app. iii., p. 103): explanations (215, 216), - - - - 212-216

SECTION XXVIII.

A communication in hieroglyphics by an old Egyptian (217)—Particulars about Egyptian theology, and its relation to Judaism (218-220)—The prophet of Ra, at On, who lived 1630 B.C. (220) The religion of daily life as exemplified in Egypt (221)—The trinity (223-224)—India and Egypt (225)—Progress in religious knowledge not necessarily connected with any special belief (226)—General judgment—The fulness of spirit (227-229), - 217-229

SECTION XXIX.

Danger of deception by personating spirits—A case in point, and an emphatic warning on the subject (230)—The adversaries—Obsessing spirits—The earth-bound and undeveloped—Temptation by them (231)—The danger from these to those on whom they are able to fasten most real and terrible (232)—Civilisation and its results—Christianity as in England—Missionaries to the heathen—Our great cities, foul, weltering masses of vice and cruelty (233)—The atmosphere of them intolerable to spirit (234)—The other side not dwelt on now, but conspicuous exceptions admitted—These causes hamper the good, and swell the army of the adversaries, one of whose ready devices is to personate truthful spirits, and so to introduce doubt and fraud (235-237) — The phenomenal illusory — The spiritual real — Higher revealings wait for those who can hear (239)—How to know a personating spirit (240)—The subject to be approached with care, whereas it is recklessly and idly meddled with (241, 242)—Frolicsome spirits, not evil, but sportive, foolish, with no sense of responsibility (243) — Avoid the personal element as far as possible (244), - - - - - - 230-244

SECTION XXX.

Easter Day Teaching (1874), ... 245-249
,, ,, ,, (1875), ... 249-255
,, ,, ,, (1876), ... 255-259
,, ,, ,, (1877), ... 259-268

Specimens of various teachings given on anniversaries, to which spirits always seem to pay great regard.

SECTION XXXI

A photograph at Hudson's, and a communication thereupon (269)—Suicide and its consequences (270-272)—The story of a wasted life, selfish and useless—A stagnant life breeds corruption (273)—Experiences of the Spirit when the cord of earth-life was severed—Remorse the road to progress—Work the means of progression (274)—Help from Spirit-ministers—The fire of purification (275)—Selfishness and sin bring misery and remorse—And thus sore judgment—No paraphernalia of assize (276)—Man makes his own future, stamps his own character, suffers for his own sins, and must work out his own salvation (277)—The threefold life of meditation and prayer: worship and adoration: conflict (278)—Accountability (279), ... 269-279

SECTION XXXII.

It is necessary that afflictions come—A period of conflict is a period of progress (280)—Revelation overlaid bit by bit—Then comes the question, What *is* Truth?—The answer in a new revelation—Esoteric at first, then adapted to general needs (281)—All cannot know truth in the same degree—Truth is many-sided—The purest truth must not be proclaimed on the house-top, or it becomes vulgarised (282)—The pursuit of Truth for its own sake the noblest end of life (283)—Having passed the Exoteric, it is well to dwell on the Esoteric (284)—Loving Truth as a Deity, following it careless whither it may lead (285), . . 280-285

SECTION XXXIII.

Further evidences of Spirit-Identity—John Blow—Extracts from ancient chronicles—Norton, the Alchymist—Specimens from a large number (286, 287)—Charlotte Buckworth and the verification of the story concerning her (288, 290)—Conclusion, . 286-291

SPIRIT-TEACHINGS.

INTRODUCTION.

THE communications which form the bulk of this volume were received by the process known as Automatic or Passive Writing. This is to be distinguished from Psychography. In the former case, the Psychic holds the pen or pencil, or places his hand upon the Planchette, and the message is written without the conscious intervention of his mind. In the latter case, the writing is direct, or is obtained without the use of the hand of the psychic, and sometimes without the aid of pen or pencil.

Automatic Writing is a well-known method of communication with the invisible world of what we loosely call Spirit. I use that word as the most intelligible to my readers, though I am well aware that I shall be told that I ought not to apply any such term to many of the unseen beings who communicate with earth, of whom we hear much and often as being the *reliquiæ* of humanity, the *shells* of what once were *men*. It is no part of my business to enter into this moot question. My interlocutors call themselves Spirits, perhaps because I so called them, and Spirits they are to me for my present purposes.

These messages began to be written through my hand just ten years since, March 30, 1873, about a year after my first introduction to Spiritualism. I had had many communications before, and this method was adopted for the purpose of convenience, and also to preserve what was intended to be a connected body of teaching. The laborious method of rapping out messages was manifestly unfitted for communications such as those which I here print. If spoken through the lips of the medium in trance, they were partially lost, and it was, moreover, impossible at first to rely upon such a measure of mental passivity as would preserve them from admixture with his ideas.

I procured a pocket-book, which I habitually carried about with me. I soon found that writing flowed more easily when I used a book that was permeated with the psychic aura, just as raps come more easily on a table that has been frequently used for the purpose, and as phenomena occur most readily in the medium's own room. When Slade could not get messages on a new slate, he rarely failed to get one on his own seasoned one. I am not responsible for the fact, the reason for which is sufficiently intelligible.

At first the writing was very small and irregular, and it was necessary for me to write slowly and cautiously, and to watch the hand, following the lines with my eye, otherwise the message soon became incoherent, and the result was mere scribble.

In a short time, however, I found that I could dispense with these precautions. The writing, while becoming more and more minute, became at the same time very regular and beautifully formed. As a specimen of caligraphy, some of the pages are exceedingly beautiful. The answers to my questions (written at the top of a page) were paragraphed, and arranged as if for the press : and the name of God was always written in capitals, and slowly, and, as it seemed, reverentially. The subject-matter was always of a pure and elevated character, much of it being of personal application, intended for my own guidance and direction. I may say that throughout the whole of these written communications, extending in unbroken continuity to the year 1880, there is no flippant message, no attempt at jest, no vulgarity or incongruity, no false or misleading statement, so far as I know or could discover; nothing incompatible with the avowed object, again and again repeated, of instruction, enlightenment, and guidance by Spirits fitted for the task. Judged as I should wish to be judged myself, they were what they pretended to be. Their words were words of sincerity, and of sober, serious purpose.

The earliest communications were all written in the minute characters that I have described, and were uniform in style, and in the signature, "Doctor, the Teacher": nor have his messages ever varied during all the years that he has written. Whenever and wherever he wrote, his handwriting was unchanged, showing, indeed, less change than my own does during the last decade. The tricks of style remained the same, and there was, in short, a sustained individuality throughout his messages. He is to me an entity, a personality, a being with his own idiosyncrasies and characteristics, quite as clearly defined as the human beings with whom I come in contact, if, indeed, I do not do him injustice by the broad comparison.

After a time, communications came from other sources, and these were distinguished, each by its own handwriting, and by its own peculiarities of style and expression. These, once assumed, were equally invariable. I could tell at once who was writing by the mere characteristics of the caligraphy.

By degrees I found that many Spirits, who were unable to influence my hand themselves, sought the aid of a Spirit "Rector," who was apparently able to write more freely, and with less strain on me, for writing by a Spirit unaccustomed to the work was often incoherent, and always resulted in a serious drain upon my vital powers. They did not know how easily the reserve of force was exhausted, and I suffered proportionately.

Moreover, the writing of the Spirit who thus became a sort of amanuensis was fluent and easy to decipher, whereas that of many Spirits was cramped, archaic in form, and frequently executed with difficulty, and almost illegible. So it came to pass, that, as a matter of ordinary course, Rector wrote: but, when a Spirit came for the first time, or when it was desired to emphasise a communication, the Spirit responsible for the message wrote for himself.

It must not be assumed, however, that all messages proceeded from one solitary inspiration. In the case of the majority of the communications printed in this volume this is so. The volume is the record of a period during which "Imperator" was alone concerned with me; though, as he never attempted writing, Rector acted as his amanuensis. At other times, and especially since that time, communications have apparently proceeded from a company of associated Spirits, who have used their amanuensis for the purpose of their message. This was increasingly the case during the last five years that I received these communications.

The circumstances under which the messages were written were infinitely various. As a rule, it was necessary that I should be isolated, and the more passive my mind the more easy was the communication. But I have received these messages under all sorts of conditions. At first they came with difficulty, but soon the mechanical method appeared to be mastered, and page after page was covered with matter of which the specimens contained in this book will enable the public to judge.

What is now printed has been subjected to revision by a method similar to that by which it was first written. Originally published in the *Spiritualist* newspaper, the messages have been revised, but not substantially altered, by those who first wrote them. When the publication in the *Spiritualist* was commenced I had no sort of idea of doing what is now being done. Friends desired specimens to be published, and the selection was made without any special regard to continuity. I was governed only by a desire to avoid the publication of what was of personal interest only: and I perforce excluded much that involved allusion to those still living whom I had no right to drag into print. I disliked printing personal matter relating to myself: I had obviously no right to print that which concerned others. Some of the most striking and impressive communications have thus been excluded: and what is printed must be regarded as a mere sample of what cannot see the light now, and which must be reserved for consideration at a remote period when I and those concerned can no longer be aggrieved by its publication.

It is an interesting subject for speculation whether my own thoughts entered into the subject-matter of the communications. I took extraordinary pains to prevent any such admixture. At first the writing was slow, and it was necessary for me to follow it with my eye, but even then the thoughts were not my thoughts. Very soon the messages assumed a character of which I had no doubt whatever that the thought was opposed to my own. But I cultivated the power of occupying my mind with other things during the time that the writing was going on, and was able to read an abstruse book, and follow out a line of close reasoning, while the message was written with unbroken regularity. Messages so written extended over many pages, and in their course there is no correction, no fault in composition, and often a sustained vigour and beauty of style.

I am not, however, concerned to contend that my own

mind was not utilised, or that what was thus written did not depend for its form on the mental qualifications of the medium through whom it was given. So far as I know, it is always the case that the idiosyncrasies of the medium are traceable in such communications. It is not conceivable that it should be otherwise. But it is certain that the mass of ideas conveyed to me were alien to my own opinions, were in the main opposed to my settled convictions, and, moreover, that in several cases information, of which I was assuredly ignorant, clear, precise, and definite in form, susceptible of verification, and always exact, was thus conveyed to me As at many of the séances spirits came and rapped out on the table clear and precise information about themselves, which we afterwards verified, so on repeated occasions was such information conveyed to me by this method of automatic writing.

I argue from the one case to others. In one I can positively assert and prove the conveyance of information new to me. In others I equally believe that I was in communication with an external intelligence that conveyed to me thoughts other than my own. Indeed, the subject-matter of many of the communications printed in this volume will, by its own inherent quality, probably lead to the same conclusion.

I never could command the writing. It came unsought usually: and when I did seek it, as often as not I was unable to obtain it. A sudden impulse, coming I knew not how, led me to sit down and prepare to write. Where the messages were in regular course, I was accustomed to devote the first hour of each day to sitting for their reception. I rose early, and the beginning of the day was spent, in a room that I used for no other purpose, in what was to all intents and purposes a religious service. These writings frequently came then, but I could by no means reckon on them. Other forms of spirit-manifestation came too: I was rarely without some, unless ill-health intervened, as it often did of late years, until the messages ceased.

The particular communications which I received from the spirit known to me as IMPERATOR, mark a distinct epoch in my life. I have noted in the course of my remarks the intense exaltation of spirit, the strenuous conflict, the intervals of peace that I have since longed for, but have seldom attained, which marked their transmission. It was a period of education in which I underwent a spiritual development that was, in its outcome, a very regeneration. I cannot hope, I do not try, to convey to others what I then experienced. But it may possibly be borne in upon the minds of some, who are not ignorant of the dispensation of the Spirit in their own inner selves, that for me the question of the beneficent action of external Spirit on my own self was then finally settled. I have never since, even in the vagaries of an extremely sceptical mind, and amid much cause for questioning, ever seriously entertained a doubt.

This introduction has become autobiographical in a way that is extremely distasteful to me. I can only plead that I have reason to know that the history of the pleading of Spirit with one struggling soul has been helpful to others. It is unfortunately necessary for me to speak of myself in order to make what follows intelligible. I regret the necessity, and acquiesce in it only from the conviction that what I record may be of use to some to whom my experiences may come home as typical. I presume that no two of us ever struggle up to light by precisely similar methods. But I believe that the needs and difficulties of individual souls have a family likeness, and it may be in the future, as I am thankful to know that it has been in the past, serviceable to some to learn by what methods I was educated.

Besides this—the subject matter of these communications, and their bearing educationally on myself—the form and manner of their delivery is of infinitely small importance. It is their intrinsic claim, the end disclosed, the inherent and essential truth that they contain, which marks their value. To many they will be utterly valueless, because their truth is not truth to them. To others they will be merely curious. To some they will be as an idle tale. I do not publish them in any expectation of general acceptance. I shall be quite content that they be at the service of any who can find them helpful.

M. A. (Oxon.)

March 30, 1883.

SECTION I.

[After a conversation on this special epoch in the world's history, and its characteristics, it was written]:—

Special efforts are being made now to spread a knowledge of progressive truth: efforts by the messengers of God, which are resisted, now as ever, by the hosts of the adversaries. The history of the world has been the story of the struggle between the evil and the good; between God and goodness on the one side, and ignorance, vice, and evil—spiritual, mental, and corporeal—on the other side. At certain times, of which this is one, extraordinary efforts are made. The army of the messengers of God is massed in greater force: men are influenced: knowledge is spread: and the end draws nigh. Fear for the deserters, the half-hearted, the temporisers, the merely curious. Fear for them: but fear not for the cause of God's truth.

> *Yes. But how are many doubting souls to know what is God's truth? Many look anxiously, but cannot find.*

None anxiously look who do not find in the end, though they may have long to wait—yes, even till they reach a higher sphere of being. God tries all: and to those only who are fitted is advanced knowledge granted. The preparation must be complete before the step is gained. This is an unalterable law. Fitness precedes progression. Patience is required.

> *Yes. The obstacles from internal dissension, from the impossibility of bringing home evidence to many, from prejudice, from many other causes, seem almost invincible.*

——To you. Why interfere with that which is God's work? Obstacles! You know not what they are compared with what we have had to endure in times past. Had you lived on earth in the later days of Rome's imperial sway, when everything spiritual had fled in horror from a realm steeped in debauchery, sensuality, and all that is base and bad, you would have known then what the banded powers of darkness can effect. The coldness was the coldness of despair: the darkness was the gloom of the sepulchre. The body, the body was all: and the guardians fled in dismay from a scene on which they could not gaze, and whose pangs they could not alleviate. Faithlessness there was indeed, and worse. The world scorned us and our efforts, laughed at all virtue, derided the Supreme, mocked at immortality, and lived but to eat and drink and wallow in the mire—the degraded, down-stricken animals they had made themselves. Ah, yes! say not that evil is invincible when the power of God and of his Spirits has prevailed to cleanse even such a sink as that.

> [More was said as to the repeated failure of plans for man's benefit through his ignorance and obstinacy. I asked if this were to be another failure.]

God is giving far more than you think. In all parts are springing up centres from which the truth of God is being poured into longing hearts, and permeating thinking minds. There must be many to whom the gospel given of old is satisfying yet, and who are not receptive of further truth. With these we meddle not. But many there are who have learned what the past can teach, and who are thirsting for further knowledge. To these it is given in such measure as the Most High sees fit. And from them it flows to others, and the glorious tidings spread until the day comes when we shall be called on to proclaim them from the mountain top! and lo! God's hidden ones shall start up from the lowly places of the earth to bear witness to that which they have seen and known: and the little rills that man has heeded not shall coalesce, and the river of God's truth, omnipotent in its energy, shall flood the earth, and sweep away in its resistless course, the ignorance and unbelief, and folly and sin which now dismay and perplex you.

This New Revelation of which you speak: is it contrary to the Old? Many are exercised on that point.

Revelation is from God: and that which He has revealed at one time cannot contradict that which He has revealed at another, seeing that each is, in its kind, a revealing of truth, but of truth revealed in proportion to man's necessities, and in accordance with his capacities. That which seems contradictory is not in the Word of God, but in the mind of man. Man was not content with the simple message. He has adulterated it with his glosses, overlaid it with his deductions and speculations. And so, as years go by, it comes to pass that what came from God is in no sense what it was. It has become contradictory, impure, and earthy. When a further revelation comes, instead of fitting it reasonably, it becomes necessary to clear away much of the superstition that has been built on the old foundations; and the work of destruction must precede the work of addition. The revelations are not contradictory; but it is necessary to destroy man's rubbish before God's truth can be revealed. Man must judge according to the light of reason that is in him. That is the ultimate standard, and the progressive soul will receive what the ignorant or prejudiced will reject. God's truth is forced on none. So for a time, during the previous processes, this must be a special revelation to a special people. It has ever been so. Did Moses obtain universal acceptance even amongst his own people? Did any of the seers? Did Jesus even? Did Paul? Did any reformer in any age, amongst any people? God changes not. He offers, but he does not force acceptance. He offers, and they who are prepared receive the message. The ignorant and unfit reject it. It must be so; and the dissensions and differences which you deplore are but for the sifting of the false from the true. They spring from unworthy causes, and are impelled by malignant spirits. You must expect annoyance, too, from the banded powers of evil. But cast your eyes beyond the present. Look to the far future, and be of good courage.

Touching Spirit-guides. How are they appointed?

Spirit-guides are not always attracted to those whom they direct, though this is usually the case. Sometimes they are selected for their own fitness. They are naturally apt to teach. Sometimes they are charged with a special commission. Sometimes they are picked because they are able to supply what is wanting in the characters which they train. Sometimes they themselves select a character which they wish to mould. This is a great pleasure to the higher spirits. Sometimes they desire, for their own spiritual progress, to be attached to a soul, the training of which is irksome and difficult. They toil upward along with the soul. Sometimes they are attracted by pure affinity, or by the remains of earth-love. Very frequently, when there is no special mission for the soul, the guides are changed as the soul progresses.

Who are the Spirits who return to earth? Of what class?

Principally those who are nearest to the earth, in the three lower spheres or states of being. They converse most readily with you. Of the higher spirits, those who are able to return are they who have what is analogous to mediumistic power on earth. We cannot tell you more than that we higher spirits find it very difficult to find a medium through whom we can communicate. Many spirits would gladly converse, but for the want of a suitable medium, and from their unwillingness to prolong their research for one, they will not risk the waste of time. Hence, too, communications vary much at times. Communications which you discover to be false are not always wilfully so. As time goes on we shall know more of the conditions which affect communication.

You have spoken of adversaries. Who are they?

The antagonistic spirits who range themselves against our mission; who strive to mar its progress by counterfeiting our influence and work, and by setting men and other spirits against us and it. These are spirits who have chosen the evil, have put aside promptings and influences of good, and have banded themselves under the leadership of intelligence still more evil to malign us and to hamper our work. Such are powerful for mischief, and their activity shows itself in evil passions, in imitating our work, and so gaining influence over the deluded, and most of all, in presenting to inquiring souls that which is mean and base, where we would tenderly lead to the noble and refined. They are the foes of God and man; enemies of goodness; ministers of evil. Against them we wage perpetual war.

It is very startling to hear of such a powerful organisation of evil. There are some, you know, who deny the existence of evil altogether, and teach that all is good though disguised.

Alas! alas! most sad is the abandonment of good and choice of evil. You wonder that so many evil spirits obstruct. Friend, it is even so, and it is not astonishing. As the soul lives in the earth-life, so does it go to spirit-life. Its tastes, its predilections, its habits, its antipathies, they are with it still. It is not changed save in the accident of being freed from the body. The soul that on earth has been low in taste and impure in habit, does not change its nature by passing from the earth-sphere, any more than the soul that has been truthful, pure, and progressive, becomes base and bad by death. Wonderful that you do not recognise this truth! You would not fancy a pure and upright soul degenerating after it has passed from your gaze. Yet you fable a purification of that which has become by habit impure and unholy, hating God and goodness, and choosing sensuality and sin. The one is no more possible than the other. The soul's character has been a daily, hourly growth. It has not been an overlaying of the soul with that which can be thrown off. Rather it has been a weaving into the nature of the spirit that which becomes part of itself, identified with its nature, inseparable from its character. It is no more possible that that character should be undone, save by the slow process of obliteration, than that the woven fabric should be rudely cut and the threads remain intact. Nay more. The soul has cultivated habits that have become so engrained as to be essential parts of its individuality. The spirit that has yielded to the lusts of a sensual body becomes in the end their slave. It would not be happy in the midst of purity and refinement. It would sigh for its old haunts and habits. They are of its essence. So you see that the legions of the adversaries are simply the masses of unprogressed, undeveloped spirits, who have banded together from affinity against all that is pure and good. They can only progress by penitence, through the instruction of higher intelligences, and by gradual and laborious undoing of sin and sinful habit. There are many such, and they are the adversaries. The idea that there is no such thing as evil, no antagonism to good, no banded company of adversaries who resist progress and truth, and fight against the dissemination of what advantages humanity, is an open device of the evil ones for your bewilderment.

Have they a Chief—a Devil?

Chiefs many who govern; but not such a Devil as theologians have feigned. Spirits, good and bad alike, are subject to the rule of commanding Intelligences.

SECTION II.

[The answers given in this section are from the same source. The conversation commenced by some questions as to what the life of spirit showed to be most serviceable work in the training school of life here. Much was made of the heart as well as of the head, and the orderly development of the whole powers of body, and intellect, and affection was insisted on. It was said that want of balance was a great cause of retrogression, or of inability, at any rate, to progress.

I suggested the Philanthropist as the man who came nearest to the ideal. The reply was] :—

The true philanthropist, the man who has the benefit and progress of his fellows most at heart, is the true man, the true child of the Almighty Father, who is the great Philanthropist The true philanthropist is he who grows likest God every hour. He is enlarging by constant exercise the sympathies which are eternal and undying, and in the perpetual exercise of which man finds increasing happiness. The philanthropist and the philosopher, the man who loves mankind, and the man who loves knowledge for its own sake, these are God's jewels of priceless value, and of boundless promise. The one, fettered by no restrictions of race or place, of creed or name, embraces in his loving heart the whole brotherhood of humanity. He loves them as friends, as brethren. He asks not what are their opinions, he only sees their wants, and in ministering to them progressive knowledge he is blest. This is the true philanthropist, though frequently the counterfeit, who loves those who think with him, and will help those who fawn on him, and give alms, so the generous deed be well known, robs the fair name of philanthropy of that all-embracing beneficence which is its true mark.

The other, the philosopher, hampered by no theories of what ought to be, and what therefore must be—bound by no subservience to sectarian opinion, to the dogmas of a special school, free from prejudice, receptive of truth, whatever that truth may be, so it be proven—he seeks into the mysteries of Divine wisdom, and, searching, finds his happiness. He need have no fear of exhausting the treasures, they are without end. His joy throughout life shall be to gather ever richer stores of knowledge, truer ideas of God. The union of those two—the philanthropist and the philosopher—makes the perfect man. Those who unite the two, progress further than spirits who progress alone.

"His life," you say. Is life eternal?

Yes; we have every reason to believe so. Life is of two stages—progressive and contemplative. We, who are still progressive, and who hope to progress for countless myriads of ages (as you say), after the farthest point to which your finite mind can reach, we know naught of the life of contemplation. But we believe that far—far in the vast hereafter—there will be a period at which progressive souls will eventually arrive, when progress has brought them to the very dwelling-place of the Omnipotent, and that there they will lay aside their former state, and bask in the full light of Deity, in contemplation of all the secrets of the universe. Of this we cannot tell you. It is too high. Soar not to such vast heights. Life is unending, as you count it, but you are concerned with the approach to its threshold, not with the inner temple.

Of course. Do you know more of God than you did on earth?

We know more of the operations of His love—more of the operations of that beneficent Power which controls and guides the worlds. We know of Him, but we know Him not; nor shall know, as you would seek to know, until we enter on the life of contemplation. He is known to us only by His acts.

[In further conversation I alluded again to the conflict between good and evil; and a long answer to my question, or, rather, to what was in my mind, was written. The storm was spoken of as one that would rage, with intervals of lull, till some ten or twelve years had passed, when a period of repose would ensue. This is almost the only case I have noted in which a prophecy was ventured upon. Though the ideas in the message have since been conveyed repeatedly, and with more precision and power, I leave it untouched to show the character of the teaching at the time.]

What you hear are the first mutterings of a conflict which will be long and arduous. Such are of periodical occurrence. If you could read the story of the world with spirit-sight, you would see that there have always been periodic battles between the evil and the good. There have recurred seasons when undeveloped intelligences have had predominance. Especially are such seasons consequent on great wars among you. Many spirits are prematurely withdrawn from the body. They then pass before they are fit; and at the moment of departure they are in evil state, angry, blood-thirsty, filled with evil passion. They do mischief great and long in after-life.

Nothing is more dangerous than for souls to be rudely severed from their bodily habitation, and to be launched into spirit-life, with angry passions stirred, and revengeful feelings dominant. It is bad that any should be dismissed from earth-life suddenly, and before the bond is naturally severed. It is for this reason that all destruction of bodily life is foolish and rude: rude, as betokening a barbarous ignorance of the conditions of life and progress in the hereafter; foolish, as releasing an undeveloped angry spirit from its trammels, and enduing it with extended capacity for mischief. You are blind and ignorant in your dealings with those who have offended against your laws and the regulations, moral and restrictive, by which you govern intercourse amongst yourselves. You find a low and debased intelligence offending against morality, or against constituted law. Straightway you take the readiest means of aggravating his capacity for mischief. Instead of separating such an one from evil influence, removing him from association with sin, and isolating him under the educating influence of true purity and spirituality, where the more refined intelligences may gradually operate and counteract the baleful power of evil and evil ministrations, you place him in the midst of evil associations, in company with offenders like himself, where the very atmosphere is heavy with evil, where the hordes of the undeveloped and unprogressed spirits most do congregate, and where, both from human associates and spirit influence, the whole tendency is evil.

Vain and short-sighted and ignorant folly! Into your dens of criminals we cannot enter. The missionary spirits pause and find their mission vain. The good angels weep to find an associated band of evil—human and spiritual—massed against them by man's ignorance and folly. What wonder that you have gathered from such experience the conviction that a tendency to open crime is seldom cured, seeing that you yourselves are the plainest accomplices of the spirits who gloat over the fall of the offender. How many an erring soul—erring through ignorance, as frequently as through choice—has come forth from your jails hardened and attended by evil guides you know not, and can never know. But were you to pursue an enlightened plan with your offenders, you would find a perceptible gain, and confer blessing incalculable on the misguided and vicious.

You should teach your criminals: you should punish them, as they will be punished here, by showing them how they hurt themselves by their sin, and how they retard their future progress. You should place them where advanced and earnest spirits among you may lead them to unlearn their sin, and to drink in wisdom: where the Bands of the Blessed may aid their efforts, and the spirits of the higher spheres may shed on them their benign and elevating influence. But you horde together your dangerous spirits. You shut them up, and confine them as those who are beyond hope. You punish them vindictively, cruelly, foolishly: and the man who has been the victim of your ignorant treatment pursues his course of foolish, suicidal sin, until in the end you add to the list of your foolish deeds this last and worst of all, that you cut him off, debased degraded, sensual, ignorant, mad with rage and hate, thirsting for vengeance on his fellows: you remove from him the great bar on his passions, and send him into spirit-life to work out without hindrance the devilish suggestions of his inflamed passions.

Blind! blind! you know not what you do. You are your own worst enemies, the truest friends of those who fight against God, and us, and you.

Ignorant no less than blind! for you spend vast trouble to aid your foes. You cut from a spirit its bodily life. You punish vengefully the erring. You falsely arrogate to yourselves the right by law divine to shed human blood. You err, and know not that the spirits you so hurt shall in their turn avenge themselves upon you. You have yet to learn the earliest principles of that Divine tenderness and pity which labours ever through us to rescue the debased spirit, to raise it from the depths of sin and passion, and to elevate it to purity and progress in goodness. You know naught of God when you do such deeds. You have framed for yourselves a God whose acts accord with your own instincts. You have fabled, that He sits on high, careless of His creatures, and jealous only of His own power and honour. You have fabricated a monster who delights to harm, and kill, and torture: a God who rejoices in inflicting punishment bitter, unending, unmitigable. You have imagined such a God, and have put into His mouth words which He never knew, and laws which His loving heart would disown.

God—our God Good, Loving, Tender, Pitiful—delighting in punishing with cruel hand His ignorantly-erring sons! Base fable! Base and foolish fancy, produced of man's cruel heart, of man's rude and undeveloped mind. There is no such God! there is none. He has no place with us: none, save in man's degraded mind.

Great Father! reveal Thyself to these blind wanderers, and teach them of Thyself. Tell them that they dream bad dreams of Thee, that they know Thee not, nor can know till they unlearn their ignorant conceptions of Thy Nature and Thy Love.

Yes, friend, your jails and your legalised murder, the whole tenor of your dealings with criminals, are based on error and ignorance.

Your wars and your wholesale murderings are even more fearful. You settle your differences with your neighbours, who should be your friends, by arraying against each other masses of spirits—we see not the body; we care only for the spirit temporarily clothed with those human atoms—and those spirits you excite to full pitch of rage and fury, and so you launch them, rudely severed from their earth-bodies, into spirit life. You inflame their passions, and give them full vent. Vengeful, debased, cruel, earth-bound spirits throng around your earth-sphere, and incite the debased who are still in the body to deeds of cruelty and lust and sin. And this for the satisfying of ambition, for a passing fancy, for an idle princely whim, for lack of something else to occupy a king.

Ah! friend, you have much, very much to learn: and you will learn it by the sad and bitter experience of undoing hereafter that which you have now done. You must learn the golden lesson, that Pity and Love are truer wisdom than vengeance and vindictive punishment; that were the Great God to deal with us as you deal with your fellows, and as you have falsely fabled that He will, you would be justly sent to your own imagined hell. You must know of God, and of us, and of yourselves, ere you can progress and do our work instead of our adversaries'.

Friend, when others seek from you as to the usefulness of our message, and the benefit which it can confer on those to whom the Father sends it, tell them that it is a Gospel which will reveal a God of tenderness and pity and love, instead of a fabled creation of harshness, cruelty, and passion. Tell them that it will lead them to know of Intelligences whose whole life is one of love and mercy and pity and helpful aid to man, combined with adoration of the Supreme. Tell them that it will lead man to see his own folly, to unlearn his fancied theories, to learn how to cultivate his intelligence that it may progress, to use his opportunities that they may profit him, to serve his fellow-men, so that when they and he meet in the hereafter, they may not be able to reproach him that he has been, so far as he could, a clog and an injury to them. Tell them that such is our glorious mission; and if they sneer, as the ignorant will, and boast of their fancied knowledge, turn to the progressive souls who will receive the teaching of wisdom: speak to them the message of Divine truth that shall regenerate and elevate the world: and for the blind ones pray that, when their eyes are opened, they may not despair at the sight which they shall see.

SECTION III

[The intensity with which the above message was written out was something quite new to me. The hand traversed sheet after sheet of my book, tracing the most minute characters, always emphasising the name of God with capitals, and paragraphing and keeping a margin, so that the writing struck the eye as a beautiful piece of caligraphy. The hand tingled, and the arm throbbed, and I was conscious of waves of force surging through me. When the message was done, I was prostrate with exhaustion, and suffered from a violent headache at the base of the brain. On the next day I asked the cause, and the following message was given, but much more quietly]:—

Your headache was the result of the intensity of the power, and the rapidity with which it was withdrawn from you. We could not write on such a subject without displaying eagerness: for it is one of most vital concern to those to whom we are sent. We would fain impress on you the paramount importance of obeying ever those unalterable laws which God has laid down for you, and which you violate at your own peril.

Wars are but the product of your lust for gain, your ambition, your angry, proud, vengeful passions. And what is the product? God's fair works destroyed and trampled under foot: the lovely and peaceful results of man's industry destroyed: the holy ties of home and kindred severed: thousands of families plunged into distress: rivers of blood shed wantonly: souls unnumbered rent from their earth-body to rush unprepared, uneducated, unpurified into the life of spirit. Bad, all bad! earthy! evil sprung from earth, and resulting in misery. Till you know better than this, your race will progress but slowly; but you are perpetually sowing seed which produces a crop of obstacles to our work.

Much there is in social knowledge, and in the conduct of State affairs that you must unlearn: much that is to be added to your knowledge.

For instance, you legislate for the masses, but you deal only with the offender. Your legislation must be punitive, but it should be remedial too. Those whom you think insane you shut up fast lest they should injure others. A few years ago, and you tortured them, and filled your madhouses with many whose only crime it was to differ from the foolish notions of their fellows, or to be—as many were, and are, whom you have thought mad—recipients of undeveloped spirit influence. This you will one day know to your sorrow—that to leave the beaten track is not always evidence of a wandering mind; and to be the vehicle of spirit-teaching is not proof of a mind unhinged. From many the power of proclaiming their mission has been taken away, and it has been falsely said that we have filled the asylums, and driven our mediums to madness, because blind and ignorant men have chosen to attribute insanity to all who have ventured to proclaim their connection with us and our teaching. They have decided, forsooth, that to be in communion with the world of spirit is evidence of madness; therefore, all who claim to be are mad, and consequently must be shut up within the madhouse. And because by lying statements they have succeeded in affixing the stigma, and in incarcerating the medium, they further charge on us the sin they have invented of driving our mediums to madness.

Were it not ignorance, it would be blasphemy. We have brought nought but blessing to our friends. We are to them the bearers of Divine Truth. If man has chosen to attract by his evil mind and evil life congenial spirits who aggravate his wickedness, on his head be the sin. They have but tended the crop which he has already sown. He was mad already; mad in neglect of his own spirit and body; mad in that he has driven far from him the holy influences. But *we* deal not with such. Far more mad indeed are those besotted drunkards whom you deem not mad. To spirit-eye there is no more fearful sight than those dens of wickedness and impurity where the evil men gather to steep their senses in oblivion, to excite the lustful and sensual passions of their debased bodies, to consort with the degraded and the impure, and to offer themselves the ready prey of the basest and worst spirits who hover around and find their gratification in living over again their bodily lives. These are dens of basest, most hideous degradation; a blot on your civilisation, a disgrace to your intelligence.

What do you mean by living over again their base lives?

These earth-bound spirits retain much of their earthy passion and propensity. The cravings of the body are not extinct, though the power to gratify them is withdrawn. The drunkard retains his old thirst, but exaggerated; aggravated by the impossibility of slaking it. It burns within him, the unquenched desire, and urges him to frequent the haunts of his old vices, and to drive wretches like himself to further degradation. In them he lives again his old life, and drinks in satisfaction, grim and devilish, from the excesses which he causes them to commit. And so his vice perpetuates itself, and swells the crop of sin and sorrow. The besotted wretch, goaded on by agencies he cannot see, sinks deeper and deeper into the mire. His innocent wife and babe starve and weep in silent agony, and near them hovers, and over them broods the guardian angel who has no power to reach the sodden wretch who mars their lives and breaks their hearts.

This we shadow forth to you when we tell you that the earth-bound spirit lives again its life of excess in the excesses of those whom it is enabled to drive to ruin. The remedy is slow, for such vices perpetuate themselves. It can only be found in the moral and material elevation of the race; in the gradual growth of purer and truer knowledge; in advanced education, in its widest and truest sense.

This would prevent obsession such as you picture?

Yes, in the end: and nothing else will, so long as you keep up the supply at the rate you now do.

Do children pass at once to a high sphere?

No: the experience of the earth-life cannot so be dispensed with. The absence of contamination ensures a rapid passage through the spheres of purification, but the absence of experience and knowledge requires to be remedied by training and education, by spirits whose special care it is to train these tender souls, and supply to them that which they have missed. It is not a gain to be removed from earth-life, save in one way—that misuse of opportunities might have entailed greater loss and have more retarded progress. The soul that gains most is the soul that keeps ever before it the work that has been allotted to it, which has laboured zealously for its own improvement and the benefit of its fellows, which has loved and served God, and has followed the guidance of its guardians. This is the soul which has least to unlearn, and which progresses rapidly. All vanity and selfishness in every form, all sluggishness and indolence, all self-indulgence mars progress. We say nought of open vice and sin, nor of obstinate refusal to learn and to be taught. Love and knowledge help on the soul. The child may have the one qualification; it cannot have the other save by education, which is frequently gained by its being attached to a medium, and living over the earth-life again. But many a child-spirit leaves the earth-life pure and unsullied who would have been exposed to temptation and grievous trial; and so it gains in purity what it has lost in knowledge. The spirit who has fought and won is the nobler one. Purified by trial, it rises to the sphere set apart for the proven souls. Such experience is essential; and for the purpose of gaining it many spirits elect to return to earth, and, by attaching themselves to a medium, gain the special phase of experience which they need. To one it is the cultivation of the affections that is necessary; to another the experience of suffering and sorrow; to another mental culture; to another the curbing and restraining of the impulses of the spirit, evenness of balance. All who return, save those who, like ourselves, are charged with a mission, have an object to gain: and in being associated with us and with you they gain their progress.

This is the one desire of spirit. More progress! More knowledge! More love! till the dross is purged away, and the soul soars higher and yet higher towards the Supreme.

Return to earth is not the only method of progression.

No: nor even the usual one. We have with us many schools of instruction: and we do not employ a second time one that has proved a failure.

[Some further conversation having taken place respecting the home and occupation of Spirit, I enquired, not getting much information that I could assimilate, whether the writer knew anything of states of being outside of his own, or rather above it; and whether he knew of states of being inferior to that of incarnation on this earth. In reply, it was affirmed that spirits had no power to take in so vast a prospect as the range of spiritual existence: and that their knowledge was barred by the gulf fixed between what were called spheres of probation, or sometimes of purgation, in which the soul was developed and perfected, and the spheres of contemplation into which it then passed, never (except in rare cases) to return. It was said]:—

The passage from the highest of the seven spheres of probation, to the lowest of the seven spheres of contemplation, is a change analogous to what you know as death. We hear little from beyond, though we know that the blessed ones who dwell there have power to help and guide us even as we watch over you. But we know nothing by experimental knowledge of their work, save that they are occupied with nearer views of the Divine perfection, in closer contemplation of the causes of things, and in nearer adoration of the Supreme. We are far from that blissful state. We have our work yet to do; and in doing it we find our delight. It is necessary for you to remember that spirits speak according to their experience and knowledge. Some who are asked abstruse questions give replies according to the measure of their knowledge, and are in error. But do not, therefore, blame them. We believe that we state what is accurate when we say that your earth is the highest of seven spheres; that there are succeeding the earth-life seven spheres of active work, and succeeding these, seven spheres of Divine contemplation. But each sphere has many states. We have said something to you of the reasons why the voluntary degraded souls sink until they pass the boundary beyond which restoration becomes hard. The perpetual choosing of evil and refusing of good breeds necessarily an aversion to that which is pure and good, and a craving for that which is debased. Spirits of this character have usually been incarned in bodies where the animal passions had great sway. They began by yielding to animal desires, and ended by being slaves of the body. Noble aspirations, godlike longings, desire for holiness and purity, all are quenched, and in place of spirit the body reigns supreme, dictating its own laws, quenching all moral and intellectual light, and surrounding the spirit with influences and associations of impurity. Such a spirit is in perilous case. The guardians retire affrighted from the presence; they cannot breathe the atmosphere which surrounds it; other spirits take their place; spirits who in their earth-life had been victims to kindred vices. They live over again their earthly sensual lives, and find their gratification in encouraging the spirit to base and debasing sin. This tendency of bodily sin to reproduce itself is one of the most fearful and terrible of the consequences of conscious gross transgression of nature's laws. The spirit has found all its pleasure in bodily gratifications, and lo! when the body is dead, the spirit still hovers round the scene of its former gratifications, and lives over again the bodily life in the vices of those whom it lures to sin. Round the gin-shops of your cities, dens of vice, haunted by miserable besotted wretches, lost to self-respect and sense of shame, hover the spirits who in the flesh were lovers of drunkenness and debauchery. They lived the drunkard's life in the body, they live it over again now, and gloat with fiendish glee over the downward course of the spirit whom they are leagued to ruin. Could you but see how in spots where the vicious congregate the dark spirits throng, you would know something of the mystery of evil. It is the influence of these debased spirits which tends so much to aggravate the difficulty of retracing lost steps, which makes the descent of Avernus so easy, the return so toilsome. The slopes of Avernus, are dotted with spirits hurrying to their destruction, sinking with mad haste to ruin. Each is the centre of a knot of malignant spirits, who find their joy in wrecking souls and dragging them down to their own miserable level.

Such are they who gravitate when released from the body to congenial spheres below the earth. They and their tempters find their home together in spheres where they live in hope of gratifying passions and lusts, which have not faded with the loss of the means of satisfying their cravings.

In these spheres they must remain subject to the attempted influence of missionary spirits, until the desire for progress is renewed. When the desire rises, the spirit makes its first step. It becomes amenable to holy and ennobling influence, and is tended by those pure and self-sacrificing spirits whose mission it is to tend such souls. You have among you spirits bright and noble, whose mission in the earth-life is among the dens of infamy and haunts of vice, and who are preparing for themselves a crown of glory, whose brightest jewels are self-sacrifice and love. So amongst us there are spirits who give themselves to work in the sphere of the degraded and abandoned. By their efforts many spirits rise, and when rescued from degradation, work out long and laborious purification in the probation spheres, where they are removed from influences for evil, and entrusted to the care of the pure and good. So desire for holiness is encouraged and the spirit is purified. Of the lower spheres we know little. We only know vaguely that there are separations made between degrees and sorts of vice. They that will not seek for anything that is good, that wallow in impurity and vice, sink lower and lower, until they lose conscious identity, and become practically extinct, so far as personal existence is concerned; so at least we believe.

Alas! alas! sad and sorrowful is the thought. Mercifully, such cases are rare, and spring only from deliberate rejection by the soul of all that is good and ennobling. This is the sin unto death of which Jesus told His followers; the sin against the Holy Spirit of God of which you are told. The sin, viz., of rejecting the influences of God's holy angel ministers, and of preferring the death of vice and impurity to the life of holiness and purity and love. It is the sin of exalting the animal to the extinction of the spiritual; of degrading even the corporeal; of cultivating sensual earthly lusts; of depraving even the lowest tastes; of reducing the human to the level of the lowest brute. In such the Divine essence is quenched; the baser elements are fostered, forced, developed to undue excess. They gain absolute sway, they quench the spirit, and extinguish all desire for progress. The vice perpetuates itself, and drags the wretch who has yielded himself to the animal enjoyments further and further from the path of progress, until even the animal becomes vitiated and diseased; the unhealthily stimulated passions prey on themselves; and the voice of the spirit is heard no more. Down must the soul sink, down, and yet down further and further until it is lost in fathomless obscurity.

This is the unpardonable sin. Unpardonable, not because the Supreme will not pardon, but because the sinner chooses it to be so. Unpardonable, because pardon is impossible where sin is congenial, and penitence unfelt.

Punishment is ever the immediate consequence of sin; it is of its essence, not arbitrarily meted out, but the inevitable result of the violation of law. The consequences of such transgression cannot be altogether averted, though they may be palliated by remorse, the effect of which is to breed a loathing for sin and a desire for good. This is the first step, the retracing of false steps, the undoing of error, and by consequence, the creation in the spirit of another longing. The spiritual atmosphere is changed, and into it good angels enter readily and aid the striving soul. It is isolated from evil agencies. Remorse and sorrow are fostered. The spirit becomes gentle and tender, amenable to influences of good. The hard, cold, repellant tone is gone, and the soul progresses. So the results of former sin are purged away, and the length and bitterness of punishment alleviated. This is true for all time.

It was on this principle that we told you of the folly which dictates your dealings with the transgressors of your laws. Were we to deal with offenders so, there would be no restoration, and the spheres of the depraved would be crowded with lost and ruined souls. But God is wiser, and we are His ministers.

SECTION IV.

[The above are selections from a great number of messages which were written during April and May, 1873. By this time the writing had become easy and fluent, and there was, apparently, less difficulty in finding appropriate words.

Already several facts and precise records of the life of some spirits had been given. For instance, on May 22nd, I was writing on quite another subject when the message broke off, and the name of Thomas Augustine Arne was written. It was said that he had been brought into relation with me through his connection with a son of Dr. Speer's, a pupil of mine, who displayed great musical ability.

I was at this time greatly impressed with the character of the automatic writing and with the information given. I inquired at once if I could ascertain from Arne, through the medium of the spirit DOCTOR, who was writing, any precise facts as to his life. The request was at once complied with, there being no interval between my question and the reply. The date of his birth (1710); his school (Eton); his instructor in the violin (Festing). His works, or at any rate some eight or nine of them; the fact that "Rule Britannia" was contained in the masque of Alfred ; and a number of other minute particulars were given without the least hesitation. Profoundly astonished at receiving such a mass of information, foreign not only to my mind in its details, but utterly foreign to my habit of thought—for I know absolutely nothing about music, and have read nothing on the subject—I inquired how it was possible to give information so minute. It was said to be extremely difficult, possible only when an extremely passive and receptive state in the medium were secured. Moreover, spirits were said to have access to sources of information so that they could refresh their imperfect recollection.

I asked how? By reading; under certain conditions, and with special end in view; or by inquiry, as man does, only to spirits it would be more difficult, though possible.

Could my friend himself so acquire information? No; he had too long left the earth, but he mentioned the names of two spirits accustomed occasionally to write, who could perform this feat. I asked that one of them should be brought. I was sitting waiting for a pupil in a room, not my own, which was used as a study, and the walls of which were covered with bookshelves.

The writing ceased, and after an interval of some minutes, another kind of writing appeared. I inquired if the newly arrived spirit could demonstrate to me the power alleged.]

Can you read?

No, friend, I cannot, but ZACHARY GRAY can, and RECTOR. I am not able to materialise myself, or to command the elements.

Are either of those spirits here?

I will bring one by and by. I will send . . . . RECTOR is here.

I am told you can read. Is that so? Can you read a book?

[Spirit hand-writing changed.]

Yes, friend, with difficulty.

Will you write for me the last line of the first book of the Æneid?

Wait——"*Omnibus errantem terris et fluctibus æstas.*"

[This was right.]

Quite so. But I might have known it. Can you go to the book-case, take the last book but one on the second shelf, and read me the last paragraph on the ninety-fourth page? I have not seen it, and do not even know its name.

"I will curtly prove, by a short historical narrative that popery is a novelty, and has gradually arisen or grown up since the primitive and pure time of Christianity, not only since the apostolic age, but even since the lamentable union of kirk and the state by Constantine."

> [The book on examination then proved to be a queer one called "*Roger's Antipopopriestian,* an attempt to liberate and purify Christianity from Popery, Politikirkality, and Priestrule." The extract given above was accurate, but the word "narrative" was substituted for "account."]

How came I to pitch on so appropriate a sentence?

I know not, my friend. It was by coincidence. The word was changed by error. I knew it when it was done, but would not change.

How do you read? You wrote more slowly, and by fits and starts.

I wrote what I remembered, and then I went for more. It is a special effort to read, and useful only as a test. Your friend was right last night: we can read, but only when conditions are very good. We will read once again, and write, and then impress you of the book:—"Pope is the last great writer of that school of poetry, the poetry of the intellect, or rather of the intellect mingled with the fancy." That is truly written. Go and take the eleventh book on the same shelf. [I took a book called *Poetry, Romance, and Rhetoric.*] It will open at the page for you. Take it and read, and recognise our power, and the permission which the great and good God gives us, to show you of our power over matter. To Him be glory. Amen.

> [The book opened at page 145, and there was the quotation perfectly true. I had not seen the book before; certainly had no idea of its contents.]

SECTION V.

[On the following day I had a long conversation as to the power exercised by spirits on our earth, which was said to be great and wide-spread. I asked as to the power over individuals, and was pointed to cases where it was said absolute obsession was established. It was said that this power over men was being so wide-spread, it were wise to place it in the reach only of spirits of integrity and wisdom, and to give conditions for its exercise by them, and so to drive away obsessing and undeveloped spirits, or to materially reduce their sphere of action. It was insisted that spirit-action was universal, and that it was a question for man, to a great extent, whether that action was beneficent or not. I asked what character was most suitable for such influence.]

There are varieties of mediumship as you know, and there are divers modes in which spirit influence is exercised. Some are selected for the mere physical peculiarities which make them the ready vehicles of spirit power. Their bodily organisation is adapted for the purpose of manifesting external spiritual influence in its simplest form. They are not influenced mentally, and information given by the spirits who use them would be of a trifling or even foolish nature, and untrustworthy. They are used as the means of demonstrating spirit power, the external invisible agency capable of producing objective phenomenal results.

These are known to you as the instruments through whom the elementary phenomena are manifested. Their work is not less significant than that which is wrought through others. They are concerned with the foundation of belief.

And some are chosen because of their loving gentle nature. They are not the channels of physical phenomenal action, in many cases, not even of conscious communication with the spirit world; but they are the recipients of spirit guidance, and their pure and gentle souls are cultivated and improved by angel superintendence. By degrees they are prepared to be the conscious recipients of communications from the spheres; or they are permitted with clairvoyant eye to catch stray glimpses of their future home. A loving spirit friend is attracted to them, and they are impressionally taught and guided day by day. These are the loving souls who are surrounded by an atmosphere of peacefulness and purity of love. They live as bright examples in the world, and pass in ripe maturity to the spheres of rest and peace for which their earth life has fitted them.

Others, again, are intellectually trained and prepared to give to man extended knowledge and wider views of truth. Advanced spirits influence the thoughts, suggest ideas, furnish means of acquiring knowledge, and of communicating it to mankind. The ways by which spirits so influence men are manifold. They have means that you know not of by which events are so arranged as to work out the end they have in view. The most difficult task we have is to select a medium through whom the messages of the higher and more advanced spirits can be made known. It is necessary that the mind chosen should be of a receptive character, for we cannot put into a spirit more information than it can receive. Moreover, it must be free from foolish worldly prejudices. It must be a mind that has unlearned its youthful errors, and has proved itself receptive of truth, even though that truth be unpopular.

More still. It must be free from dogmatism. It must not be rooted and grounded in earth notions. It must be free from the dogmatism of theologies and sectarianism and rigid creed. It must not be bound down by the fallacies of half-knowledge which is ignorant of its own ignorance. It must be a free and inquiring soul. It must be a soul that loves progressive knowledge, and that has the perception of truth afar off. One that yearns for fuller light, for richer knowledge than it has yet received; one that knows no hope of cessation in drinking in the truth.

Again, our work must not be marred by the self-assertion of a positive antagonistic mind, nor by the proud obtruding of self and selfish ends and aims. With such we can do very little, and that little must all tend to the gradual obliteration of selfishness and dogmatism. We desire a capable, earnest, truth-seeking, unselfish, loving spirit for our work. Said we not well that such was difficult to find among men? Difficult indeed, well-nigh impossible. We select, then, such a soul as we can best find, and prepared by constant training for its appointed work. We inspire into it a spirit of love and tolerance for opinions that do not find favour with its own mental bias. This raises it above dogmatic prejudice, and paves the way for the discovery that truth is manifold, and not the property of any individual. Store of knowledge is given as the soul can receive it; and, the foundation of knowledge once laid, the superstructure may be safely raised. The opinions and tone of thought are moulded by slow degrees, so that they harmonise with the end we have in view.

Many and many fail here, and we abandon our work with them, finding that not in this world of yours can they receive the truth; that old earth-born prejudices are firm, dogmatic beliefs ineradicable, and so that they must be left to time, and are to us of no avail.

Moreover, a perfect truthfulness and absence of fearfulness and anxiety are the steady growth of our teaching. We lead the soul to rest in calm trust on God and His spirit teachers. We infuse a spirit of patient waiting for that which we are permitted to do and teach. This spirit is the very reverse of that fretful, restless querulousness which characterises many souls.

Here, too, many fall away. They are fearful and anxious, and beset with doubt. The old theology tells them of a God, who watches for their fall; and of a devil, who lays perpetual traps for them. They wonder at the novelty of our teaching; their friends are ready to point to so-called prophecies which tell of anti-Christ. The old foundations are shaken, and the new are not yet laid; and so the adversaries creep in and tempt the wavering soul, and it fears and falls away, and is useless to us.

Yet more, we must eradicate selfishness in all its many forms. There must be no obtruding of self, or we can do nothing. There is nothing so utterly fatal to spirit influence as self-seeking, self-pleasing, boastfulness, arrogance, or pride. The intelligence must be subordinated, or we cannot work upon it. If it be dogmatic, we cannot use it. If it be arrogant and selfish, we cannot come near it. Self-abnegation has been the virtue which has graced the wise and holy men of all time. The seers who bore of old the flag on which was inscribed for their generation the message of progressive truth were men who thought little of themselves, and much of their work. They who spoke to the Jews, whose messages you have in your sacred records, were men of self-denying purity and singleness of life. Jesus, when He lived amongst men, was a grand and magnificent instance of the highest self-abnegation and earnestness of purpose. He lived with you a life of pure self-denial and practical earnest work, and He died a death of self-sacrifice for truth. In Him you have the purest picture that history records of man's possible. They who since have purged the world from error, and have shed on it the beams of truth, have been one and all men of self-denial and earnest devotion to a work which they knew to be that for which they were set apart. Socrates and Plato, John and Paul, the pioneers of truth, the heralds of progress, all have been unselfish souls—souls who knew naught of self-seeking, of proud aggrandizement, of boastful arrogance. To them earnestness and singleness of purpose, devotion to their appointed work, forgetfulness of self and its interests were given in a high degree. Without that they could not have effected what they did. Selfishness would have eaten out the heart of their success. Humility, sincerity, and earnestness bore them on.

This is the character we seek. Loving and earnest, self-denying and receptive of truth; with single eye to God's work, and with forgetfulness of earthly aims. Rare it is, rare as it is beautiful. Seek, friend, the mind of the philosopher, calm, reliant, truthful, and earnest! Seek the spirit of the philanthropist, loving, tolerant, ready to help, quick to give the needed aid. Add the self-abnegation of the servant of God who does his work and seeks for no reward. For such a character work, high, holy, noble, is possible. Such we guard and watch with jealous care. On such the angels of the Father smile, and tend and protect them from injury.

But you have described a perfect character.

Ah no! You have now no conception of what the perfect spirit is. You cannot know; you cannot even picture it. Nor can you know how the faithful soul drinks in the spirit-teaching and grows liker and liker to its teacher. You see not as we see the gradual growth of the seed which it has cost us so much labour to plant and tend. You only know that the soul grows in kindly graces, and becomes more lovely and more loveable. The character we have faintly pictured in such terms as are intelligible to you is not perfect, nor aught but a vague and distant resemblance of that which it shall become. With you is no perfectness. Hereafter is progression and constant development and growth. What you call perfect, is blotted and blurred with faults to spirit vision.

Yes, surely. But very few such are to be found.

Few, few: and none save in the germ. There is the capability on which we work with thankfulness. We seek not for perfection: we do but desire sincerity and earnest desire for improvement: a mind free and receptive; a spirit pure and good. Wait in patience. Impatience is a dire fault. Avoid over-carefulness and anxiety as to causes which are beyond your control. Leave that to us. In patience and seclusion ponder what we say.

I suppose a secluded life is favourable for your influence, rather than the busy whirl of town.

[Here the writing suddenly changed from the minute and very clear writing of Doctor to a most peculiar archaic writing, almost indecipherable, and signed Prudens.]

The busy world is ever averse from the things of spirit life. Men become absorbed in the material, that which they can see, and grasp, and hoard up, and they forget that there is a future and spirit-life. They become so earthly that they are impervious to our influence; so material that we cannot come near them; so full of earthly interests that there is no room for that which shall endure when they have passed away. More than this, the constant pre-occupation leaves no time for contemplation, and the spirit is wasted for lack of sustenance. The spiritual state is weak: the body is worn and weary with weight of work and anxious care, and the spirit is well-nigh inaccessible. The whole air, moreover, is heavy with conflicting passions, with heart-burnings and jealousies, and contentions and all that is inimical to us. Round the busy city with its myriad haunts of vice, its detestable allurements, its votaries of folly and sin, hover the legions of the opposing spirits who watch for opportunity to lure the wavering to their ruin. They urge on many to their grief hereafter, and cause us many sorrows and much anxious care.

The life of contemplation is that which most suits communion with us. It is not indeed to supersede the life of action, but may be in some sort combined with it. It is most readily practised where distracting cares come not in, and where excessive toil weakens not the bodily powers. But the desire must be inherent in the soul; and where that is, neither distracting cares nor worldly allurements avail to prevent the recognition of a spirit world, and of communion with it. The heart must be prepared. But it is easier for us to make our presence felt when the surroundings are pure and peaceful.

SECTION VI.

[At this time I met Mr. Home. It chanced to be the Derby Day, and it was said through him that conditions were so interfered with that spirits could do nothing. On the next day (May 29) I had some conversation on the subject, in the course of which it was written,]—

Any such occasion disturbs the moral conditions, and renders it hard for us to reach you. The spirits who are antagonistic to us are massed together in great force whenever any occasion is offered for them to operate successfully on men who are gathered together for the purpose of gratifying their bodily passions. Yesterday there were vast masses whose passion of cupidity was excited to an enormous degree. They were the point of attack from similar spirits. Others there were whose bodies were wildly excited by intoxicating drinks; others who were feverish with expectation of coming gains; others again plunged into depths of despair by loss of all, the ready prey, these last, of the suggestions of tempting spirits; and even when these baser passions were not actively excited, the moral balance was upset; that calmness and equability which should regulate the temper, and which are as a shield against the foe, were absent, and so a chance of favourable assault was given. For, short of absolute evil, much ground for assault is given by an ill-regulated, disordered mind, by minds unhinged and ill-balanced. Avoid all such. They are frequently the ready agents of spirit influence, but of undeveloped and unwelcome guides. Beware of immoderate, unreasoning, excited frames of mind.

For these reasons the occasion to which you refer is one that would make largest demands on the efforts of the agents of good, lest the undeveloped, massed and disciplined for assault, succeed and draw down souls.

But what you say would apply to all national holidays?

Not necessarily so. So long as a holiday is associated with giving a loose rein to passion, with the immoderate use of fiery, intoxicating poison, with sensual gratifications, with the body and not with the spirit, it must needs be so. The body so situated places the spirit at the mercy of the adversaries. But the holiday that is associated with rest of body and refreshment of spirit is far from being such. When the bodily powers which have been drained by overtaxing work are recuperated by genial and moderate rest; when the mind, vexed and harassed by the worries and anxieties of daily toil, is refreshed by moderate amusement, and by being relaxed and plunged for awhile in oblivion of anxious care, the while it is braced and stimulated by pleasant change; when this is so, a gentle calm pervades the spirit, and renders it peculiarly open to the beneficent influences of the heavenly guardians. Thus the power of angel ministry is strengthened, and the plans of the most powerful adversaries are set at nought. You must progress far in knowledge of spirit guidance and of the duties you owe to yourselves before your national holidays become aught but opportunities for the degradation of your people. The holiday that is marked by riot and debauchery, by sensuality and gambling, and evil, angry passion and despair, this is no holy day to us, but one to be dreaded and watched and prayed over. God help and guard the blind souls in their insensate folly!

> [I find that our séance was disturbed at this time by some erratic manifestations, and an attempt to obtain photographs of some of the communicating spirits resulted in failure. Although the spirit whose figure was on the plate claimed the name of Rector, it was said by my friend that it was a spirit with whom they had no connection, a deceptive spirit, unknown to any of them. I sat down to obtain further information, but got nothing that was intelligible, and was obliged to cease.

> On the next day, when I had regained my usual passive state, the writing came unasked. Respecting the difficulties that had arisen in manifesting, I enquired if we could help in any way.]

Rector could not communicate with you on account of your disturbed condition, consequent on the sitting which had severely taxed you. The information given was quite unreliable. Your mind was violently positive. You had assumed the picture to be that of Rector, and he was not sufficiently acquainted with this kind of communication to know that your unhinged and feverish state, coupled with a positive and unimpressionable state of mind, made it impossible to convey any true information to you.

When you feel such conditions present, seek no communications on any subject. They will be unreliable or imperfect under such circumstances, and in many cases hurtful.

> [I was much annoyed, and complained that my scanty stock of faith would be drained by many such occurrences. It had never occurred before. It was replied]—

You have never placed yourself in communication save when I (Doctor) or some one who can warn and guard you has been present. You have done so when the spirits who control the physical elements in the circle have alone been present, and the results were violent and unmanageable. You were warned then: this is another warning. Your positive mind Rector could not influence: and your fevered state made it impossible to control you.

> [Since then I have been scrupulously careful never to attempt automatic writing when I am physically ill or in pain: mentally worried or anxious, or near any person so suffering, or in the midst of any influences that might be disturbing. To this precaution I attribute much of the regular and equable character of my communications. As a rule, they are curiously fluent; the books in which they are written show no erasure or alteration: and the tone of the messages is very level and sustained.]

Keep yourself as passive and quiet as you can. When overtired with work, or fretted with care, or exhausted, do not attempt to seek communion with us. Do not add to the circle any new elements which do but disturb and perplex conditions. Suffer us to perfect our experiments before you interfere to spoil them. We will advise you of any change we wish in the composition of our circle. Do not alter the room in which you meet: and strive in so far as may be, to meet with a passive mind and a healthy body.

Yes, working all day with body and brain does not improve conditions, I suppose. But Sunday is generally worse.

It is not a favourable day for us, because, when the strain is removed from mind and body, the reaction leaves the spirit disinclined for action and more apt for repose. We are fearful of cultivating new manifestations with you; we fear experimenting with physical manifestations lest they do harm. Moreover, they are not our object, only subsidiary to it. They are but the signs which witness to our mission; and we do not desire that you rest in them. There is also a special reason why we are unable to manifest on Sunday for you. You do not know the difficulty which changes in conditions make to us. You have heard before that sitting down immediately after a meal is not good. The bodily conditions which we seek for are passivity and quickness of receptivity: but not the passivity which comes from sluggishness and torpor. No worse condition can be than that state of somnolence and torpor which follows on a plentiful meal during which stimulating drink has been taken. Such stimulus may aid the physical manifestations in some cases, but it is a bar to us. It opens the door for the advent of the more material spirits, and stops our power. We have frequently found our plans frustrated by such means. You would do well to think of this and guard yourselves against excess in any way when you are about to seek communion with us. The body should not be heated nor torpid with food: nor the mind drowsy and inactive. Both conditions prevent us from operating freely.

They react on us, and sensibly mar our power. One such member in a circle, even as one ailing or suffering, will create conditions which we cannot overcome.

But a weak body and temper disturbed by want of food is bad surely?

We do but counsel moderation. The body should be strengthened with food, but you should not sit down until the food is assimilated. You require moderate stimulant to fit you for your daily work, but that should be guardedly taken, and you should see that you do not enter into communion with us save under such conditions as we have stated. When mind or body is predisposed to sleep or indisposed to sustained attention, or sick or suffering, it is better not to sit save under direction. Equally when the body is replete with food, the grosser spirits may be expected to be in the ascendant, and we are unable to operate. Even the physical phenomena are then of a ruder and more violent character, and not of the delicate and beautiful description, which they would assume under more favourable circumstances. We do not desire extremes. A body wasted by fasting is not in any way profitable: but neither is a body which is clogged and loaded by over-indulgence. Temperance and moderation are what help us. If you desire, friend, to facilitate our work, and to attain the best results, you should bring to the sitting a body healthy and sound, senses clear and watchful, and a mind passive and receptive. Then we can do for you more than you think. With a circle harmonious and properly constituted the manifestations would be more delicate, and the teaching given more refined and trustworthy. Even the light of which you spoke* under such conditions is pale, clear, and smokeless: under unfavourable conditions would be dull, dirty, and smoky in appearance.

---

* At this time we had a number of large phosphorescent lights at our ordinary sittings: clear and of a pale yellow under good conditions; red, and smoky when anything was wrong. These lights were similar to the lamp borne by the spirit John King, and attained a great size under favourable conditions. A full description will be found in my forthcoming volume of Personal Researches in the objective phenomena of Spiritualism.

It having been said that a friend and his wife who had frequently manifested were now removed to other spheres of work, I asked whether the marriage ties were perpetuated.

That depends entirely on similarity of taste and equality of development. In the case of this being attained, the spirits can progress side by side. In our state we know only of community of taste and of association between those who are on the same plane, and can be developed by mutual help. All things with us are subordinated in the education of the spirit which is perpetually being developed. There can be no community of interest save between congenial souls. Consequently no tie can be perpetuated which is not a help to progress. The uncongenial bonds which have embittered the soul's earth life, and marred its upward progress cease with the bodily existence. The union of soul with soul which in the body has been a source of support and assistance is developed and increased after the spirit is free. The loving bonds which encircle such souls are the greatest incentive to mutual development, and so the relations are perpetuated, not because they have once existed, but because in the eternal fitness of things they minister to the spirit's education. In such cases the marriage tie is perpetuated, but only in such sort as the bond of fellowship between friends endures, and is strengthened by mutual help and progress. All souls that are mutually helpful remain in loving intercourse so long as it is profitable for them. When the period arrives at which it is more profitable for them to separate they go their way without sorrow, for they can still commune and share each other's interests. The reverse of such law would only perpetuate misery, and eternally bar progress. Nothing is permitted to do this.

No. But some, I can conceive, may not be exactly on the same mental or moral plane, and yet be full of mutual love.

Spirits filled with mutual love can never be really separated. You are hampered in understanding our state by considerations of time and space. You cannot understand how souls can be far apart, as you count space, and yet be, as you would say, intimately united. We know no time, no space. We could not obtain really close union with any spirit unless the intelligence be absolutely on the same mental and progressive plane. Indeed, any such union would be impossible for us. Soul may be linked with soul in bonds of affection, without any intimate connection such as we mean by being on the same plane of development. Love unites spirits at whatever distance. You see that in your low state of existence. The brother loves the brother, though vast expanse of ocean separates their homes, the long years have rolled away since the eye looked on the form, and the ear listened to the words of the absent one. Their pursuits may be widely different: they may have no mutual idea, yet mutual love exists. The wife loves the degraded besotted ruffian who mutilates her body, and strives to crush her spirit.

The hour of dissolution will free her from slavery and pain. She will soar while he will sink; but the bond of love will not be snapped, though the spirits may no longer consort together. Even here space is annihilated; with us it does not exist. And so you may dimly understand that with us union means identity of development, community of interest, mutual and affectionate progression.. We know no such indissoluble ties as exist with you.

Then the Bible words are true, " They neither marry nor are given in marriage, but are as the angels of God."

It was truly said. We have before told you of the law of Progress, and of the law of Association. They are invariable. Much that now seems good to you, ye will throw aside with the body. Your state now colours your views. Much we are obliged to clothe in allegory, and to elucidate by borrowing your phraseology. So that you must not insist too strongly on literal meanings of words used by us to describe what exists only with us, which finds no counterpart in your world, and transcends your present knowledge, and which therefore can only be approximately described in language borrowed from earth. This is a necessary caution.

Yes. That would account for discrepancies in spirit communications in some cases.

Such differences arise in many cases from want of knowledge on the part of the spirits themselves; from their inability to get their ideas through the channel of communication: from imperfect conditions at the time of the communication and from other causes. Doubtless, one cause is, that curious and foolish questions bring foolish answers from spirits on the plane of the questioner.

But would not a high spirit endeavour to raise the questioner instead of " answering a fool according to his folly"?

Yes, were it possible; but the foolish frame of mind precludes too frequently such raising. Like attracts like, and the silly curious enquirers who ask from no desire for information, but only to gratify a whim or an idle curiosity, or to entangle us in our talk, is answered, if at all, by a spirit like to himself. Such is not the frame of mind in which to seek communion with us. A reverent, earnest mind gains for itself that information and instruction which it is capable of receiving. The self-conceited, flippant, ignorant, and curious receive only what they seek, and are sent away without reply, or with such as suits their query. Flee such. They are empty and foolish.

SECTION VII.

[Some communications respecting the Neo-Platonic philosophy followed. A spirit with whose features I was familiar, had been photographed, and his dress was something I was unused to. I enquired and was told that the conditions under which the partial materialisation necessary for photography are possible, differ from those in which the spirit presents himself to clairvoyant vision.

The account of the special phase of the Neo-Platonic teaching was most minute and entirely new to me. Souffism, the ecstatic meditation that endeavours by transport to throw off all that is not God, and to attain truth by transfusion into the Divine, was expounded at length, and illustrated in the person of one of its professors. I thus learned much that I have since been able to trace in operation, and especially in the teachings of the spirit in question, albeit toned down and modified by experience.

After this there was a short cessation; and another evidence of imposture at a circle which I attended caused me much questioning. I was urged to refrain from attending any circles at all so long as our own was held; and it was explained that it was of the greatest importance to avoid coming into contact with mediums, or strong magnetic influence of any kind. I should act as a disturbing element in other circles, and bring away disturbing influences to our own.

Some remarkable extracts from old poems, chiefly of Lydgate's, were now written by a spirit who seemed to delight in such work, who did nothing else, and who used a very marked handwriting.

Afterwards at a séance held, June 13th, 1873, many questions were put on points of theology, and a long trance-address was delivered, which was partially taken down at the time, but many points were necessarily omitted, or imperfectly recorded.

On the following day, without questioning, it was written by the same communicating spirit who had spoken on the previous evening]—

There was much in what was said last night that was imperfectly said, and hurriedly, and that was not accurately preserved in the record which was taken at the time. It is of the last importance that, on a subject so momentous, we should speak with care, and that you should understand exactly what we wish to convey. We therefore wish to state more clearly what we said imperfectly to the circle. The conditions of control do not always enable us to be so precise in speech as we are studious to be when communicating thus with you. Perfect isolation commands conditions suitable for precision and accuracy.

We were dealing with the Divine mission which we have in charge. Of the many difficulties which beset our path this is one of the most considerable, that those who are most congenial to our purpose, and whose co-operation we most desire, are usually so hampered by preconceived theological notions, or are so fearful of what seems to contradict some things which they have learned, that we are unable to influence them, and grieve sorrowfully to find that which is derived from God charged on the adversaries, and boldly attributed to an all-powerful and malignant Devil.

Of all classes of our opponents these are to us the most sad. The pseudo-scientific man, who will look at nothing save through his own medium, and on his own terms—who will deal with us only so that he may be allowed to prescribe means of demonstrating us to be deluders, liars, figments of a disordered brain—he is of little moment to us. His blinded eye cannot see, and his cloudy intelligence, befogged and cramped with life-long prejudice, can be of little service to us. He can at best penetrate but little into the mysteries of communion with the spheres, and the foundation of knowledge that he could acquire, though useful and valuable even, would be of little service to us in our special work. We deal with other issues than those which would principally engage the attention of those few men of science who deign to notice the phenomenal aspect of our work. The mind long trained in observation of the phenomena of physics, is best devoted to the elucidation of those facts which come within its province. Our sphere is different, connected rather with the influence of spirit upon spirit, and the knowledge of spirit-destiny that we can impart.

And the ignorant and uncultured mind which knows not of what we would tell, and cannot know until a long course of preliminary training has prepared the way—this class of mind, though hereafter it may attain to a plane of knowledge on which we can work, is of no service now.

To the proud, the arrogant, the wise in their own conceits, the children of routine and respectability, we can say very little. The more physical evidence is necessary to reach them. The story which we are charged with would be but an idle tale to them.

It is to the receptive souls who know of God and heaven, and love and charity, and who desire to know of the hereafter and of the haven to which they tend, that we turn with earnest longing. But, alas! too often we find the natural religious instincts, which are God-implanted and spirit-nurtured, choked or distorted by the cramping influence of a human theology, the imperceptible growth of long ages of ignorance and folly. They are armed at all points against the truth. Do we speak of a revelation of the Great Father?—they already have a revelation which they have decided to be complete. Do we tell them of its inconsistencies, and point out that it nowhere pretends to the finality and infallibility which they would assign to it?—they reply to us with stray words from the formularies of a Church, or by an opinion borrowed and adapted from some person whom they have chosen to consider infallibly inspired. They apply to us a test drawn from some one of the sacred records which was given at a special time for a special purpose, and which they imagine to be of universal application.

Do we point to our credentials, and to the miracles so-called, which attest the reality of our mission, even as they attested the mission of those whom we influenced of old?—they tell us that the age of such miracles is past, and that only the inspired of the Holy Ghost long centuries ago were permitted to work such wonders as evidence of Divine teaching. They tell us that the Devil, whom they have imaged for themselves, has power to counterfeit God's work, and they consign us and our mission to darkness and outer antagonism to God and goodness. They would be willing to help us; for, indeed, we say that which is probable, but that we are of the Devil. We must be, because in the Bible it is said that false and deceiving spirits will come; and so we must be the deceivers. It must be so, for did not a holy and elevated Teacher prophesy of those who should deny the Son of God? And do not we practically remove Him and His work from the place in which God has placed it and Him? It must be so; for do we not place human reason above faith? Do we not preach and teach a seductive Gospel of good works, and give credit to the doer of them? And is not all this the work of the arch-fiend transformed into an angel of light, and striving to win souls to ruin?

It is such arguments, honestly put forward by those whose respect we fain would win, that are to us a bitter sorrow. They are in many cases loving, earnest souls, who need but the progressive tendency to make them bright lights in the world's gloom. To them we fain would give our message; but before we can build on the sure foundation which they already have of knowledge of God and duty, we must perforce clear away the rubbish which renders further elevation unsafe.

Religion, to be worthy the name, must have its two sides —the one pointing to God, the other to man. What has the received faith, which is called orthodox by its professors, to say on these points; and wherein do we differ in our message; and how far is such difference on our part in accord with reason? For, at the very outset, we claim, as the only court to which we can as yet appeal, the Reason which is implanted in man. We claim it; for it was by Reason that the sages settled the list of the writings which they decided to be the exclusive and final revelation of God. To Reason they appealed for their decision. To Reason we appeal too Or do our friends claim that Divine guidance prescribed for them what should be for all time the body of revealed truth? We, too, are the messengers of the Most High, no less surely sent than the spirits who guided the Hebrew seers, and who ministered to those whose fiat settled the Divine word.

We are as they: our message as their message, only more advanced; our God their God, only more clearly revealed, less human, more Divine. Whether the appeal be to Divine inspiration or not, human Reason (guided doubtless by spirit agency, but still Reason) sways the final decision. And those who reject this appeal are out of their own mouths convicted of folly. Blind faith can be no substitute for reasoning trust. For the faith is faith that either has grounds for its trust or not. In the former case the ground is reasonable; in which case Reason again is the ultimate judge; or it is not, in which case it would commend itself to none. But if the faith rest on no ground at all, we need not further labour to show it baseless and untrustworthy.

To Reason, then, we turn. How far are we proved reasonably to be of the Devil? How far is our creed an evil one? In what respect are we chargeable with diabolic tendency? These are points on which we will instruct you.

SECTION VIII.

[After a long trance address on the subjects dealt with in the last communication, the writing was resumed on the following day, by the same spirit, Imperator using the ordinary amanuensis, who was known as Rector. After this was written, a séance was held in which some discussion took place on what had been said. Something further was added, and especially an attempt was made to refute the charges that I brought against the teaching given. From the standpoint that I then occupied it seemed to me that such teachings might be called by opponents atheistic or diabolic, I, at anyrate, should call them latitudinarian, and I maintained at some length, views more nearly approaching to orthodox teaching.

In order to follow the argument which I was now entering upon, it is necessary for the reader to remember that I was trained in strict accordance with Protestant Church principles: that I had spent much time in reading the theologies of the Greek and Roman Churches, and that I had accepted, as most nearly according with the views at which I had arrived, the tenets of that portion of the Church of England called Anglican. I had seen cause to revise some of my strong beliefs, but substantially I was what would be called a sound High Churchman.

From this time commences that state, to which I shall have often to refer, of great spiritual exaltation, during which I was profoundly conscious of the presence and influence of one commanding Intelligence, and of an action on my mind which eventuated in a development of thought amounting to nothing short of spiritual regeneration.]

You have objected to our teachings that they are not consistent with the received creed of orthodoxy. We have more to say on this subject.

Religion, the spirit's healthful life, has two aspects—the one pointing to God, the other to man. What says the spirit-creed of God?

In place of an angry jealous tyrant it reveals a loving Father who is not loving in name alone, but in very deed and truth; into whose dealings nought but love can enter; who is just and good and full of affection to the lowest of His creatures.

It does not recognise any need of propitiation towards this God. It rejects as false any notion of this Divine Being vindictively punishing a transgressor, or requiring a vicarious sacrifice for sin. Still less does it teach that this omnipotent Being is enthroned in a heaven where His pleasure consists in the homage of the elect, and in the view of the tortures of the lost, who are for ever excluded in quenchless misery from light and hope.

No such anthropomorphism finds any place in our creed. God, as we know Him in the operation of His laws is perfect, pure, loving, and holy, incapable of cruelty, tyranny, and other such human vices: viewing error with sorrow as knowing that sin contains its own sting, but eager to alleviate the smart by any means consistent with the immutable moral laws to which all alike are subject. God, the centre of light and love! God, operating in strict accordance with those laws which are a necessity of orderly existence! God, the grand object of our adoration, never of our dread!

We know of Him as ye cannot know, as you cannot even picture in imagination: yet none has seen Him: nor are we content with the metaphysical sophistries with which prying curiosity and over-subtle speculation have obscured the primary conception of God amongst men. We pry not. The first conception with you even, is grander, nobler, more sublime. We wait for higher knowledge. You must wait too.

On the relations between God and His creatures we speak at large. Yet here, too, we clear off many of the minute points of human invention which have been from age to age accumulated round and over the central truths. We know nothing of election of a favoured few. The elect are they who work out for themselves a salvation according to the laws which regulate their being.

We know nothing of the potency of blind faith or credulity. We know, indeed, the value of a trustful receptive spirit, free from the littleness of perpetual suspicion. Such is God-like, and draws down angel guidance. But we abjure, and denounce that most destructive doctrine that faith, belief, assent to dogmatic statements, have power to erase the traces of transgression; that an earth life-time of vice and sloth and sin can be wiped away, and the spirit stand purified by a blind acceptance of a belief, of an idea, of a fancy, of a creed. Such teaching has debased more souls than anything else to which we can point.

Nor do we teach that there is a special and potent efficacy in any one belief to the exclusion of others. We do not believe that truth is the perquisite of any creed. In all there is a germ of truth; in all an accretion of error. We know, as you know not, the circumstances which decide to what special form of faith a mortal shall give in his adherence, and we value it accordingly. We know exalted intelligences who stand high in spirit life, who were enabled to progress in spite of the creed which they professed on earth. We value only the earnest seeking after truth which may distinguish the professors of creeds, the most widely dissimilar. We care not for the minute discussions which men delight in. We shrink from those curious pryings into mysteries transcending knowledge which characterise your theologies. The theology of the spirit is simple and confined to knowledge. We value at nothing mere speculation. We care not for sectarianism, save that we know it to be a mischievous provoker of rancour, and spite, and malice, and ill-will.

We deal with religion as it affects us and you in simpler sort. Man—an immortal spirit, so we believe,—placed in earth-life as a school of training, has simple duties to perform, and in performing them is prepared for more advanced and progressive work. He is governed by immutable laws, which, if he transgresses them, work for him misery and loss; which, also, if respected, secure for him advancement and satisfaction.

He is the recipient of guidance from spirits who have trod the path before him, and who are commissioned to guide him if he will avail himself of their guidance. He has within him a standard of right which will direct him to the truth, if he will allow himself to be guided to keep it and protect it from injury. If he refuse these helps, he falls into transgression and deterioration. He is thrown back and finds misery in place of joy. His sins punish themselves. Of his duties he knows by the instinct of his spirit as well as by the teaching of his guardians. The performance of those duties brings progress and happiness. The spirit grows and gains newer and fuller views of that which makes for perfect, satisfying joy and peace.

This mortal existence is but a fragment of life. Its deeds and their results remain when the body is dead. The ramifications of wilful sin have to be followed out, and its results remedied in sorrow and shame.

The consequences of deeds of good are similarly permanent, and precede the pure soul and draw around it influences which welcome and aid it in the spheres.

Life, we teach you, is one and indivisible. One in its progressive development: and one in the effect on all alike of the eternal and immutable laws by which it is regulated. None are excused as favourites; none are punished mercilessly for error which they were unable to avoid. Eternal justice is the correlative of eternal love. Mercy is no divine attribute. It is needless; for mercy involves remission of a penalty inflicted, and no such remission can be made save where the results have been purged away. Pity is Godlike. Mercy is human.

We know nought of that sensational piety which is wholly wrapped up in contemplation to neglect of duty. We know that God is not so glorified. We preach the religion of work, of prayer, of adoration. We tell you of your duty to God, to your brother, and to yourself—soul and body alike. We leave to foolish men, groping blindly in the dark, their curious quibbles about theological figments. We deal with practical life; and our creed may be briefly written :—

Honour and love your Father, God.
(Worship) ... ...　　　Duty to God
Help your brother onward in the path
of progress. (Brotherly love) ...　　Duty to neighbour.
Tend and guard your own body. (Bodily
culture) ... ...
Cultivate every means of extending
knowledge. (Mental progress) ...
Seek for fuller views of progressive
truth. (Spiritual growth) ... ...　　Duty to self.
Do ever the right and good in accordance with your knowledge. (Integrity) ... ...
Cultivate communion with the spirit-land by prayer and frequent intercourse. (Spiritual nurture) ... ...

Within these rules are roughly indicated most that concerns you here. Yield no obedience to any sectarian dogmas. Give no blind adherence to any teaching that is not commended by reason. Put no unquestioning faith in communications which were made at a special time, and which are of private application. You will learn hereafter that the revelation of God is progressive, bounded by no time, confined to no people. It has never ceased. God reveals Himself as truly now as of old He was revealed on Sinai. God does not shut off the progressive revealing of Himself in measure as man can bear it.

You will learn also that all revelation is made through a human channel: and consequently cannot but be tinctured in some measure with human error. No revelation is of plenary inspiration. None can demand credence on any other than rational grounds. Therefore to say of a statement that it is not in accord with what was given through a human medium at any stated time, is no derogation necessarily from the truth of that statement. Both may in their kind be true; yet each of different application. Set up no human standard of judgment other than that of right reason. Weigh what is said. If it be commended by reason, receive it; if not, reject it. If what is put before you be prematurely said, and you are unable to accept it; then in the name of God put it aside, and cling to aught that satisfies your soul, and helps its onward progress. The time will come when what we lay before you of divine truth will be valued amongst men. We are content to wait, and our prayers shall join with yours to the supreme and all-wise God that He will guide the seekers after truth, wherever they may be, to higher and more progressive knowledge, to richer and fuller insight into truth. May His blessing rest on you!

SECTION IX.

[I objected to this statement, which did not by any means commend itself to me in my then state of opinion, that it was incompatible with the received teaching of Orthodox churches, and that, as a matter of fact, it traversed some cardinal dogmas of the Christian faith. I suggested that the message might have been adulterated in passage: and that much was omitted that I regarded as essential. If it were pretended that such a code was complete as a rule of life I was prepared to argue against it. It was said in reply]—

That which has been told to you in its outline is so far correct; but it does not pretend to be a perfect delineation of truth. It is but a faint outline, blurred and blotted in many ways, but substantially truthful. Doubtless it contravenes much which you have been taught to believe as necessary to salvation. No doubt it seems to the unprepared spirit to be new, and destructive of older forms of faith. But it is not so. In its broad outlines the spirit-creed would be accepted by all who have thought at all on theological subjects without trammel of preconceived ideas, and without fear of the consequences of seeking into the truth. It would be commendable to all who are not hampered by old prejudices. We said that we must clear away much rubbish; that the work of destruction must precede the work of construction; that the old and unserviceable must first give place; that, in short, we must clear before we can build.

Yes; but the rubbish which you seem to me to be clearing away is precisely what Christians have agreed in all ages to consider cardinal doctrines of the faith.

No, friend; not quite so. You exaggerate there. If you will read the records which so imperfectly record the earth life of Jesus, you will not find that He claimed for Himself any such position as the Christian Church has since forced upon Him. He was more such as we preach Him than such as the Church called by his name has made Him.

I cannot think so. And the Atonement: What do you make of that?

It is in some sense true. We do not deny it; we do but fight against that crude human view which renders God contemptible, and makes Him a cruel tyrant who needed to be propitiated by His Son's death. We do not detract from Jesus' work when we disavow the false and dishonouring fables which have gathered round His name, and have obscured the simple grandeur of His life, the moral purpose of His sacrifice. We shall have somewhat to say to you hereafter on the growth of dogma until an assumption becomes established as *de fide*, and its rejection or denial passes for mortal sin. Were God to leave man to his own ends it would be held to be a mortal heresy, deserving of eternal burnings, to deny that the Supreme has delegated to a man one of His own inalienable prerogatives. One great section of the Christian Church would claim infallible knowledge for its head, and persecute in life, and condemn in death, even to everlasting shame and torment, those who receive it not. This is a dogma of late growth in your very midst; but so all dogmas have grown up. So it has become difficult, nay impossible, for unaided human reason to distinguish God's truth from man's glosses upon it. So all who have had the boldness to clear away the rubbish have been held accursed. It has been the story of all time. And we are not justly chargeable with wrong-doing if from our superior stand-point of knowledge we point out to you human figments of error, and endeavour to sweep them away.

Yes; that may be. But the belief in the Divinity of Christ, and in His Atonement can scarcely be called dogmas which are of human growth. You always prefix to your name the sign of the Cross [+ IMPERATOR.] *I presume, therefore, that in your lifetime on earth you must have held these dogmas.* + RECTOR,—*another communicating spirit, who also uses the sign of the Cross, must almost if not altogether have died for them. Here then seems to me to be a contradiction. Suppose the dogmas to be unnecessary or mistaken truths—suppose them even to be false—what am I to conclude? Have you changed your opinions? Or were you a Christian while you lived on earth? or were you not? If not, why the Cross? If you were, why the change of sentiment? The whole question intimately concerns your identity. I cannot see how your teaching coincides with your belief when you lived on earth. It is pure and beautiful, but surely it is not Christian. Nor is it the teaching which one who uses the sign of the Cross would reasonably be expected to promulgate. So it seems to me. If I speak in ignorance, enlighten my ignorance. If I seem to be too curious, I must be excused, seeing that I have no means of judging you but by your words and deeds. So far as I am able to judge, your words and deeds are alike noble and elevated, pure and rational, but not Christian. I only desire such reasonable ground for forming an opinion as may satisfy my present doubts and difficulties.*

It shall be given in due course. Cease now.

[The writing, though I earnestly desired and strove to obtain it, did not come until June 20th. The previous message was written on the 16th.]

I salute you, good friend. We would now give you more information, touching points which have perplexed and distressed you. You would know how far the sign of the Cross may legitimately be associated with our teaching. We will show you of this.

Friend, the sign which is emblematic of the life and work of Jesus the Christ is one that cannot fairly be prefixed to much that now passes current for His teaching. The tendency of all classes of religionists has ever been to make much of the letter and to neglect the spirit: to dwell at large on expressions drawn from individual writers, and to neglect the general drift of teaching. Men have gone with preconceived notions to search for the truth, and have found that which they expected. Single words and expressions have been drawn out of their context by those who have professed to comment on the texts of your sacred books until they have been made to bear a meaning which their writers never intended. Others have gone to the authors solely to find words to prop up a theory without even the poor pretence of seeking after the truth; and they, too, have been able to dig out something which has served their purpose. And so, by slow degrees, the edifice has grown, built up laboriously by men who delight to dwell on peculiarities of language and expression, and by men who, having evolved for themselves an idea, strive only that it may be confirmed. Neither class has any idea beyond the text of the sacred records which lies before him.

We said before, that much of what we should have to say to you would turn on what you understand by Divine inspiration.

Those who are known to you as the orthodox defenders of the Christian creed tell you that a mysterious person—one of the three individual persons who compose the Undivided Trinity—took possession of the minds of certain men, and through their organisms gave to your world a body of truth, which was whole, complete, and of eternal force: a system of Divine philosophy from which nothing might be removed under the direst ban; to which nothing would ever be added; and which was the immediate word, the very utterance, the mind and will of God, containing within it the whole body of truth, actual and potential, contained in divinely worded phrases and expressions. Not only are the sentiments of David and Paul, Moses and John, consonant with the will of the Supreme, but they are the very thoughts of Deity. Not only are the words divinely approved, but they are the very diction of the Supreme. In short, the Bible is the very Word of God, both in matter and form: every word of it Divine, and fit to be studied and expounded as such, even in that version of it which is translated into your language by men who, to complete the marvel, are again supposed to be in their turn the recipients of Divine truth and guidance in their work of translation.

Hence, you will see, that doctrines the most tremendous, and conclusions the most far-reaching may be founded upon mere words and expressions, for is not every word and turn of phrase the revelation of God divinely preserved from admixture of human error? These are they who have grounded a number of dogmas on phrases picked out at their pleasure, neglecting and passing over all that pleases them not. To such the Bible is the direct utterance of the Supreme.

Those who have abandoned this view have entered upon a process of destructive handling of the Bible, the only termination of which is the view which we shall put for your acceptance. They revere the sacred records which compose your Bible as being the records of God's truth revealed to man from age to age, even as it is still being revealed. They study the records as showing man's progressive grasp of knowledge of God and of the destiny of the spirit. They watch the gradual unfolding of this revelation from times of ignorance and brutal barbarism when He was known as the friend of Abraham, who ate and conversed at the tent door, or the Judge who governed His people, or the King who fought at the head of the armies of Israel, or the Tyrant revealed through the medium of some seers, down to the time when He became known in His truer character of tenderness, and love, and fatherly kindness and compassion. In all this they see growth, and they will believe, if they pursue their investigations to the end, that such growth has never ceased; that such progressive revelation has never been closed; and that man's knowledge of his God is far from complete, though his capacity for receiving that knowledge is ever enlarging his means of satisfying the craving that is within him. And so the seeker after truth will be prepared to receive our teaching on this head at least. To such we address ourselves. To those who fondly fancy that they possess a perfect knowledge we say nothing. Before we can deal with them they must learn to know their ignorance of all that concerns God and Revelation. Anything that we could say would glide off the impenetrable defence of ignorance, self-conceit, and dogmatism in which they are encased. They must be left to unlearn hereafter in pain and sorrow that which has so retarded their spiritual growth, and will be so dire a barrier to future progress. If you have rightly understood what we have previously put before you, we may now proceed to add further some words on the nature of revelation, and the character of inspiration.

We say then, to you, that the sacred books which make up your Bible, together with many others which are not included in it, are the records of that gradual growth in knowledge of Himself which the great and good God has given to man. The principle which pervades all these utterances is one and the same: identical with that which governs our intercourse with you. So much of truth is given as man can grasp; no more under any circumstances, but just so much as he can grasp, so much as suffices for his present craving. That truth is revealed through the instrumentality of a man, and is always more or less mixed with the thoughts and opinions of the medium. Nay, the communicating spirits are perforce obliged to use the material which is found in the medium's mind, moulding and fashioning it for their purpose: erasing fallacies, inspiring new views of truth, but working on the material which is already gathered. The purity of the spirit message depends much on the passivity of the medium, and on the conditions under which the message is communicated. Hence, in your Bible there are traces here and there of the individuality of the medium; of errors caused by imperfect control; of the colour of his opinions; as well as of special peculiarities addressed to the special needs of the people to whom the message was first given, and for whose case it was primarily adapted.

You may see for yourself numerous cases of this. If Isaiah spoke to the people the words of the message with which he was charged, he impressed upon that message the individuality of his own mind, and adapted it to the peculiar needs of the people to whom he spoke. He told, indeed, of the one Supreme God, but he told of Him in strains of poesy and ecstatic imagery far different from the metaphorical and characteristic imagery of Ezekiel. Daniel had his visions of glory. Jeremiah, his burdens of the Lord who spoke through him. Hosea, his mystic symbolism: each in his individual fashion told of the same Jehovah, as he knew Him, but each told his message in his own style, as it had been revealed to him. Similarly, in later days, the characteristic nature of individual communications was preserved. If Paul and Peter found occasion to speak of the same truth, they almost necessarily viewed it from different sides. The truth was not less true because two men of varying minds viewed it from different points, and dealt with it in his own way. The individuality of the medium is palpable in the manner if not in the matter of the communication. The inspiration is Divine, but the medium is human.

Hence it is that man may find in the Bible the reflex of his own mind, whatever the tone of that mind may be. The knowledge of God is so small: that which man has grasped of His nature is so little, that each person who lives on past revelations, and cannot or will not extend them, must find in the Bible the reflex of his mind. He goes to find his own ideal, and lo! it is mirrored for him in the utterances of those who spoke for persons on his mental plane. If no one seer can satisfy his ideal, he selects from many the points which please him, rejects the remainder, and manufactures his own revelation piecemeal. So it is with all sects. Each frames its own ideal, and proves it by revelations taken from the Bible. None can accept the whole, because the whole is not homogeneous. But each picks out its suitable pieces, and from them frames its revelation. When they are brought face to face with others who have picked out other passages, then comes the twisting and distorting of words, the explanation (so they call it) and the commenting on texts: the darkening of plain meaning: the interpreting of sayings in a sense never meant either by the communicating spirit, or by the prophet or teacher. By this means inspiration becomes a vehicle for sectarian opinion; the Bible, an armoury from which each disputant may draw his favourite weapon; and theology, a matter of private notion, backed up by false and misleading interpretation.

With a theology so framed, we are accused of being at variance. It is true. We have no commerce with it. It is of the earth, earthy; base and low in its conception of God; degrading in its influence on the soul; insulting to the Deity whom it professes to reveal. We have no part in it. We do indeed contradict and disown it. It is our mission to reverse its teaching, to substitute for it truer and nobler views of God and of the Spirit.

Another reason why much that is false with respect to God is current among you, as derived from the Bible, is, that the assumption of infallible inspiration leads men not only to lay too much stress on words and phrases, but also to fall into the error of interpreting too literally that which was intended to be of spiritual and typical interpretation. In communicating to your mental plane ideas which are to you inconceivable, we are obliged to use expressions which are borrowed from your ways of thought. We ourselves are very frequently at fault in misusing such expressions; or they are themselves inadequate to convey our meaning. Almost all spirit utterances are typical. Especially when spirits have endeavoured to convey to men ideas of the great God of whom they themselves know so little, the language used is necessarily very imperfect, inadequate, and frequently ill chosen. But it is always typical, and must be so understood. To press to the end of *literal* accuracy any spirit-teaching about God is mere folly.

Moreover, the revelations of God have been made in language suited to the capacities of those to whom they were originally given, and are to be so interpreted. But they who have framed for themselves the idea of an infallible revelation applicable through all time, interpret every word literally, and so deduce erroneous conclusions. The hyperbole which was intelligible in the mouth of the impulsive seer who uttered it to an imaginative and enthusiastic Eastern hearer, becomes overstrained, untrue, and misguiding when coldly interpreted in the light of comment and verbal exactness to those whose habits of thought and language are widely different or even totally dissimilar

It is to this cause that we must attribute many views of the Supreme which are alike false and dishonouring to Him. The original language was inadequate enough; it has become coloured more or less by the medium through whom it has passed, and is then less adequate than before. But interpreted as we have pointed out, it becomes positively false; and is in no sense the revelation of God. Rather it is man's notion about a Deity whom he has framed for himself—framed as really as the image which the savage forms for his fetish.

With such views, again, we have no accord. Them, too, we denounce, and our mission is to substitute for them a truer and nobler knowledge. Moreover, in dealing with you, spirits always proceed in one uniform manner. They are sent to communicate through a human medium some portion of Divine truth. In the medium's mind they find a growth of opinions, some false, some partly true, some distorted and befogged by early prejudice and training. Are these to be eradicated before the truer ideas are suggested? Is the mind to be completely cleared of all preconceived ideas? By no means. It is not so we act. Were we to do so the work of eradication would be so tedious that we should risk leaving the mind bare of teaching altogether, and should have destroyed without being able to create. No; we take the opinions already existent, and mould them into closer semblance of truth. All have in some sort the germ of truth, or we destroy them. With such as contain truth, we strive to grapple, and to mould and form them to progress and advancement in knowledge. We know of how little worth are the theological notions to which men attach so much importance; and we are content to leave them to die in the brighter light to which we lead the soul, while we supply the needed information on important topics. Only we must eradicate dogmatism. That is all-important. Opinion, when harmless, we do not meddle with.

Hence it is that theological notions may remain very much what they were, only toned down and softened in their asperities. So men falsely say that spirits always teach that which a man has previously believed. It is far from being so. What we now teach you is sufficient proof of that. The spirit-guides do indeed work on that which they find already in the mind: but they mould and temper it, and imperceptibly change and adapt it to their ends. It is only when the views held are such as they cannot work upon, or of a positive and dogmatic type, that the change wrought becomes plain to your eyes. You find a man who has denied the existence of God and of spirit, who has believed only what he can see and feel and handle; such a materialist you see converted to a belief in God and a future existence, and you wonder at the change. But the spirit that has been tempered, and chastened and softened: that has been purified, and refined, and elevated: whose rude and rough beliefs have been toned and softened, of this change you make no note, because it is too gradual and subtle to be perceptible to your senses. Yet such are the glorious results of our daily work. The crude is softened; the hard, and cold, and cheerless are warmed into loving life; the pure is refined; the noble ennobled; the good made better; the yearning soul satisfied with richer views of its God and of its future happiness.

The opinions have not been suppressed, but they have been modified and changed. This is the real existent spirit influence all around of which ye know nothing as yet: the most real and blessed part of spirit ministry.

When, therefore, men say that spirits speak only the medium's preconceived opinions, they are partly right. The opinions, in so far as they are harmless, are the previous ones, only moulded in a way not perceptible to your gaze as yet. When the opinions are hurtful, they are eradicated and destroyed.

When we deal with special forms of theological creed, we strive, in so far as we can, to spiritualise previous opinion rather than to eradicate it. We know—as you cannot know—of how trifling moment are forms of faith, provided the faith be alive and spiritual: and we strive, therefore, to build on the foundation already laid. To this end, however, whilst the broad outlines, which are in themselves partially truthful, or which embody as much of truth as the intelligence can grasp, are preserved, much that is false and delusive must be cleared away. So the work of destruction precedes the work of construction. The soul is purged of gross error, and the truth is refined and purified as far as may be. Hence it is that we do usually teach a modification of the views of truth held by those to whom we speak.

And now, friend, you will see the bearing of this on your difficulty. We have endeavoured, not to uproot from your mind the views which you have entertained of theology, but to modify them. If you will recall the past, you will see how your creed has been gradually widened from a very narrow basis to a comprehensive and rational one. You have, under our guidance, been made acquainted with the theological tenets of many churches and sects. You have been led to see, in each, the germ of truth, more or less developed, but clouded with human error. You have studied, for yourself, the writings of the teachers of religion among the Christian world, and your own creed has been toned down and softened in its asperities by the divergent views of truth so let in upon it. The process has been long and gradual from the days when you were influenced to the study of ancient philosophies to later days, when systems of theology filtered through it, and left behind them that which you were able to assimilate.

The fixed and changeless creed of the Eastern branch of the Christian Church, with its crystallised dogmas no longer living and breathing truths; the destructive criticism of German scholars who have dealt a much-needed blow to blind belief in the verbal exactitude of human utterances; the speculations of advanced thought in your own country and Church; the ideas of those external to it, and even to the creed of Christendom—of all these have you learned, and have retained from the several systems that which was serviceable to you. It has been a long and very gradual work, and now we wish to carry you further, and to show you the ideal truth, spiritual, impalpable, but most real, which' underlies all with which you are familiar. We would strip off the earthly body, and show you the real, vital truth in its spiritual significance.

We would have you know that the spiritual ideal of Jesus

the Christ is no more like the human notion, with its accessories of atonement and redemption, as men have grasped them, than was the calf ignorantly carved by the ancient Hebrews like the God who strove to reveal Himself to them. We wish to show you, as you can grasp it, the spiritual truths which underlie the life of Him who is known to you as the Saviour, the Redeemer, the Son of God. We would tell you of the true significance of the life of the Christ, and show you, as we can, how low and mean are the views of Him which we are striving to do away with.

You ask how the sign of the Cross can be prefixed to such teaching. Friend, the spiritual truth of which that sign is typical is the very cardinal truth which it is our special mission to declare. The self-denying love which would benefit humanity even at the sacrifice of life and home and earthly happiness—the pure spirit of the Christ, this is what we would declare to you as the godlike spirit. This is the true salvation from meanness and self-aggrandisement, and self-pleasing and luxurious sloth, which can redeem humanity, and make of men the children of God. This self-abnegation and incarnate love is that which can atone for sin, and make man like to God. This is the true atonement! Not, indeed, a reconciliation of sin-stained humanity to an angry and holy God, purchased by the sacrifice of His sinless son, but a higher and truer atonement in the ennobling of the nature, the purifying of the spirit; the making of the human and the divine, ONE in aim and purpose:—the drawing of man's spirit, even whilst incarned, up nearer and nearer to the Divine.

This was the mission of the Christ. In this He was a manifestation of God: the son of God: the Saviour of man: the Reconciler: the Atoner: and herein we perpetuate His work, we carry on His mission, we work under His symbol, we fight against the enemies of His faith, against all who ignorantly or wilfully dishonour Him, even though it be under the banner of orthodoxy and under the protection of His Name.

Much that we teach must still be new and strange even to those who have progressed in knowledge; but the days shall come when men shall recognise the oneness of Christ's teaching on earth with ours; and the human garb, gross and material, in which it has been shrouded, shall be rent asunder, and men shall see the true grandeur of the life and teaching of Him whom they ignorantly worship. In those days they shall worship with no less reality, but with a more perfect knowledge; and they shall know that the sign under which we speak is the symbol of purity and self-sacrificing love to them and to their brethren for all time. This end it is our earnest endeavour to attain. Judge of our mission by this standard, and it is of God, godlike: noble as He is noble: pure as He is pure: truthgiving as He is true: elevating, and saving, and purifying the spirit from the grossness of earthly conceptions and raising it to the very atmosphere and neighbourhood of the spiritual and the divine.

Ponder our words: and seek for guidance, if not through us, then through Him who sent us, even as, in earlier days, He sent that exalted spirit of purity, charity and self-sacrifice, whom men called Jesus, and who was the Christ.

Him we adore even now. His Name we reverence.

His words we echo. His teaching lives again in ours.

He and we are of God: and in His Name we come.

+ IMPERATOR.

SECTION X.

[I was not content, and took time to consider what had been written. It was very contrary to any opinions I then held, but I was conscious of an extremely powerful and elevating influence during the time the writing was going on. I wished to get rid of the influence before I replied.
On the following day I had an opportunity of resuming my argument. I objected to what had been said, that such a creed would not be acknowledged as Christian by any member of a Christian Church that it was contradictory to the plain words of the Bible; and that such views appeared even to be the subject of special denunciation as those of Anti-Christ. Moreover, I suggested that such vaguely beautiful views, as I admitted them to be, had a tendency to take the backbone out of faith. It was replied]—

Friend, you have opened points on which we shall be glad to speak with you. As to our authority, we have touched on that point before. We claim it to be divine, and we await with confidence the acceptance of our mission when the times are ripe for our teaching. That time must come after much steady preparation, and we are quite prepared to find that none can yet accept in full the teaching which we promulgate, save the little band to whom it is given to precede in progressive knowledge the rest of their fellows. We say that this does not strike us with surprise. For, think! has it ever been that a fuller revelation has found acceptance among men at once? The ignorant cry has always been raised against progress in knowledge that the old is sufficient: that *it* has been proven and tried, whilst of the new, men say that they know nothing save that it *is* new and contradictory of the old. It was the self-same cry that assailed Jesus. Men who had laboriously elaborated the Mosaic theology, which had served its time, and was to give place to a higher and more Spiritual religion: men who had drawn out the minutiæ of this system until they had reduced it to an aimless mass of ritual, a body without a spirit, aye, a corpse without life: these cried out that this blasphemer (so they impiously called the Saviour of man's religion) would destroy the law and dishonour God. The Scribes and Pharisees, the guardians of orthodox religion, were unanimous in their disbelief of Him and of His pretensions. It was they who raised the howl which finally led the Great Teacher to the Cross. You know now that He did not dishonour God: and that He did but demolish man's glosses on God's revealed law in order that He might refine and spiritualise its commands, and raise it from the dead by infusing into it spiritual life and power, by breathing into it vitality and giving it renewed vigour.

In place of the cold and cheerless letter of the law which prescribed outward duty to a parent,—a duty discharged without heart of love, with scanty dole grudgingly offered,—he taught the spirit of filial affection springing from a loving heart, and offering the unbought and ungrudged tribute of affection to earthly parents and to the Great Father. The formalism of mere external conventionality he replaced by the free-will offering of the heart. Which was the truer, the nobler creed? Did the latter override the former, or did it not stand to it rather as the living man to the breathless corpse? Yet they who were content to buy off from filial duty at the poor cost of a few paltry coins scornfully given were they who finally crucified the Christ, as a man who taught a new religion blasphemously subversive of the old. The scene on Calvary was the fitting culmination to such a religion.

Again, when the followers of the crucified stood forth to declare their gospel to a world that cared not for it, and which was not prepared to receive it, the charge against them perpetually was that they taught new doctrine which was subversive of the old faith. Men taxed their ingenuity to discover horrible accusations which they might charge upon them. They found nothing too monstrous to be believed by those who were eager to credit any accusation of the new faith which "everywhere was spoken against." They were lawless; yet so rigidly respectful to the established faith, and to the "powers that be," that no cause of blame could be discovered. They were devourers of infants: they who were the followers of the loving and gentle Jesus. Nothing was too monstrous to be believed about them; even as men now *wish* to believe everything that can discredit us and our mission.

Has it not been so ever since? It is the story of all time that the new is spoken against and discredited in religion, in science, in all with which man's finite mind deals. It is an essential quality of his intelligence that such should be the case. The familiar commends itself: the new and strange is viewed with suspicion and mistrust.

Hence it is not any legitimate cause for surprise that when we teach a spiritualised Christianity we should at first be met with incredulity. The time will come when all men will admit, as you do, the beauty of the creed and recognise its divine origin.

It is not wonderful that our message should seem to contradict some human utterances. Nay, that it should really controvert some details of the teaching given through human minds more or less undeveloped in days long past is to be expected. We have no desire to hide the plain fact that there is much in some parts of the Bible which does not amalgamate with our teaching, being, indeed, the admixture of human error which came through the mind of the chosen medium. We need not repeat on this head our previous argument which is familiar to you.

Revelation, as contained in your Bible, includes many progressive developments of the knowledge of God which are in themselves irreconcileable in minute detail. And moreover, it contains much admixture of human error which has filtered in through the medium. You can only arrive at the truth by judging of the general drift. Private opinions selected without reference to the body of teaching are but the sentiments of the individual, valuable as showing his mind, but not in any way binding as of faith. To imagine that an opinion uttered many centuries ago is of binding force eternally is mere folly.

Indeed, all such opinions are contradictory in themselves, and are contradicted by other and opposite opinions contained within the same volume. No doubt it was a current belief, at the time when many of the writers of books in the Bible composed the treatises which you call inspired, that Jesus was God, and harsh denunciations are made against any who should deny the dogma. No doubt also that the same men believed also that he would, in mysterious manner, return in the clouds to judge the world, and that *before their generation should die*. They were mistaken in both beliefs, and over one at least more than 1800 years have rolled and still the return is unaccomplished. So we might push the argument were it necessary.

What we wish to impress on you is this You must judge the Revelations of God by the light which is given you: in the mass, not by the dicta of its preachers: by the spirit and general tendency, not by the strict literal phraseology. You must judge of us and our teaching, not by conformity to any statement made by any men at any special time; but by the the general fitness and adaptability of our creed to your wants, to your relations with God, and to the progress of your spirit.

What, then, is the outcome of our teaching? How far does it square with right reason? How does it teach you of God? How does it help your spirit?

You have been taught in the creeds of the orthodox churches to believe in a God who was propitiated by the sacrifice of his Son, so far as to allow a favoured few of His children to be admitted to an imagined heaven, where for ever and for ever more, with monotonous persistence, their occupation should be the singing His praise. The rest of the race, unable to gain admission to this heaven, were consigned to a hell of indescribable torment, perpetual, endless, and intolerable.

These miserable ones failed of bliss, some of them because they had not faith; and others, because they had evil surroundings by which they were degraded. And others fell, being assailed with fierce temptations, by which they were led away and seduced to sin. And others were incarned in debasing and sensual bodies, and were overcome of ungoverned passions. And others could not understand what was wanted from them, though they tried, and would fain have done what they could. And others had intellectual inabilility to accept certain dogmatic propositions which they had been taught to believe essential to their salvation. And others had not, when bodily existence ceased, assented to certain statements which were able to secure them the entry into the heaven we have described. And so they perished everlastingly; and on their endless torments, from a height serene and secure, the blessed who have gained their bliss through a faith in certain dogmatic assertions, though many of them had been men of grievous and degraded lives, look with the satisfaction of undisturbed and changeless repose.

A life of gross sensuality, or of sloth, or of offence against all law, you are taught is remediable by an act of faith. The grossest and most sensual ruffian may, by a cry on his death-bed, find himself instantaneously fitted for admission into the immediate presence of the God whom he has all his life blasphemed. He, the impure, base, degraded, earthy spirit admitted to association with the refined, the noble, the pure, the holy, in the immediate presence of the stainless perfection of the all-pure God!

And yet the half is not told, but enough by way of contrast. We tell you nothing of such a God—a God of whom reason cannot think without a shudder, and from whom the fatherly instinct must shrink in disgust. Of this God of love, who shows his love in such a fashion, we know nothing. He is of man's fashioning, unknown to us. We pause not to expose the miserable pretence that such a human idol can ever have been aught but the figment of a barbarous mind. We do but ask you to wonder with us at the presumptuous ignorance and folly which has dared to paint such a caricature of the pure and holy God. Surely, friend, man must have been in a degraded spiritual condition ere he could have pictured such a Deity. Surely, too, they who in this age have not shrunk from such a creation, must have sore need of a Gospel such as that we preach.

The God whom we know and whom we declare to you is in very truth a God of Love—a God whose acts do not belie His name, but whose love is boundless, and His pity unceasing to all. He knows no partiality for any, but deals out unwavering justice to all. Between him and you are ranks of minstering spirits, the bearers of His loving message, the revealers from time to time of His will to man. By His spirit messengers the train of ministering mercy is never suffered to fail. This is our God, manifested by His works, and operating through the agency of His ministering angels.

And you yourselves, what of you? Are ye immortal souls who, by a cry, a word, by an act of faith in an unintelligible and monstrous creed can purchase a heaven of inactivity, and avoid a hell of material torment? Verily, nay. Ye are spirits placed for a while in a garb of flesh to get training for an advanced spirit-life, where the seeds sown in the past bear their fruit, and the spirit reaps the crop which it has prepared. No fabled dreamy heaven of eternal inactivity awaits you, but a sphere of progressive usefulness and growth to higher perfection.

Immutable laws govern the results of deeds. Deeds of good advance the spirit, whilst deeds of evil degrade and retard it. Happiness is found in progress, and in gradual assimilation to the Godlike and the perfect. The spirit of divine love animates the acts, and in mutual blessing the spirits find their happiness. For them there is no craving for sluggish idleness; no cessation of desire for progressive advancement in knowledge. Human passions, and human needs and wishes are gone with the body, and the spirit lives a spirit life of purity, progress, and love. Such is its heaven.

We know of no hell save that within the soul: a hell which is fed by the flame of unpurified and untamed lust and passion, which is kept alive by remorse and agony of sorrow: which is fraught with the pangs that spring unbidden from the results of past misdeeds; and from which the only escape lies in retracing the steps, and in cultivating the qualities which shall bear fruit in love and knowledge of God.

Of punishment we know indeed, but it is not the vindictive

lash of an angry God, but the natural outcome of conscious sin, remediable by repentance and atonement and reparation personally wrought out in pain and shame, not by coward cries for mercy, and by feigned assent to statements which ought to create a shudder.

Happiness we know is in store for all who will strive for it by a consistent course of life and conduct commendable to reason and spiritual in practice. Happiness is the outcome of right reason, as surely as misery is the result of conscious violation of reasonable laws, whether corporeal or spiritual.

Of the distant ages of the hereafter we say nothing, for we know nothing. But of the present we say that life is governed, with you and with us equally, by laws which you may discover, and which, if you obey them, will lead to happiness and content, as surely as they will reduce you to misery and remorse if you wilfully violate them.

We need not specify at length now the creed we teach as it affects man in his relation to God, to his fellows, and to himself. You know its main features. One day you shall know it more fully. Sufficient has now been said to point the contrast, and to reply to our question: Whether such a view as this be not pure, divine, ennobling, the natural complement of that which Jesus himself preached?

Is it less definite, more vague than the orthodox? It may be less minute in details which are repulsive, but it breathes a nobler and purer atmosphere; it teaches a higher, holier religion; it preaches a diviner God. It is not vaguer, not less definite. But even were it so, it deals with subjects into which the reverent mind will not curiously pry. It throws a veil over the unknown, and refuses to substitute speculation for knowledge, or to apply the cruder human notions to the very nature and attributes of the Supreme.

If it be vagueness to vail the curious eye before the footstool of the divine and incomprehensible, then are we vague in our knowledge, and indistinct in our teaching. But if it be the part of the wise to dwell only on the known and the comprehensible; to act rather than to speculate; to do rather than to believe, then is our belief dictated by wisdom, comformable to right reason, and inspired by God himself.

It will bear the test of rational sifting and experiment. It will endure, and inspire the myriad souls in distant ages when those who cavil at its teachings and insult its authors shall be working out in sorrow and remorse the consequences of their folly and sin. It will have conducted countless myriads of pure spirits, who have progressed in its faith, to happiness and advancement, when that which it is destined to spiritualise shall have shared the fate of the mouldering body from which the spirit is withdrawn. It will live and bless its votaries in spite of the foolish ignorance which would charge its divine precepts on a devil, and anathematise its votaries as the children of darkness.

+ Imperator.

That seems to me rational and beautiful. And I think you meet the charge of vagueness. But I fancy most people would say that you do practically upset popular Christianity. I should like to have from you some ideas on the general outcome of Spiritualism, more especially as it affects the undeveloped, whether incarnated or not.

We will speak to you of this in due course. But not yet. Ponder what has been said before you seek for further messages. May the Supreme enable us to guide you aright!

+ Imperator.

SECTION XI.

[By this time the influence upon me had become so powerful as to shut out all other communications. On June 24, I attempted strongly to establish communication with the spirit who had usually written, but in vain. The influence was of a singularly elevating character, and dominated my mind. Though I did my daily work with punctuality, I devoted every minute that I could spare from it to pondering on this strange influence, and on the teaching which was so new to me. As I pondered, it seemed to grow into my mind, and to present itself with a force and orderly beauty that I had not recognised before. Though I had studied theologies long and deeply, I had not by any means studied the various systems with a view to pick holes in them. I had collated rather than criticised them. But now I was confronted with a totally new view, and one which seemed to me to strike at the root of much that I had previously accepted as *de fide*. On the 26th I recurred to what had been said by IMPERATOR, and put my case thus]:—

I have thought very much of what has been said by you and I have read some of it to a friend in whose judgment I rely. It is startling to find doctrines of Christianity, which we have been taught to consider as essential dogmas of the faith, denied under the symbol of the Cross. I cannot more strongly put my difficulty than by saying that though your statements command my assent intellectually, still the faith of Christendom which has lasted now 1800 years, and more, cannot lightly be upset by statements, however reasonable they may seem to me, which are not authenticated by any authority that I can test. Will you state clearly for me what position you assign to Jesus Christ? what authority you can show which gives you any power to reverse or develop teaching which bears his name, and to substitute a new gospel for the old one? Can you give me satisfactory evidence of your own identity and of the reality of the mission which you claim? Evidence that would be accepted by plain reasonable men. I cannot undertake to accept what seems to me so revolutionary a change as of Divine origin and binding force, on the unsupported word of any angel or man, whoever he may be. Nor ought I to be asked to do so. Though the change is very gradual, I think I discover a perceptible difference in your communications. And there seems to be a divergence in teaching between some spirits who have communicated through you: while the bond which can unite a number of opinions which profess to come from such discordant sources must be slight.

Friend, it is to us a source of pleasure that we have so far stirred your mind as to draw from you so earnest and rational a series of questions as these. Believe us, so far at least as this, that no frame of mind is more pleasing to the Supreme than that which seeks earnestly and intelligently for truth; refusing mere dogmatic statements from whatever source they come; weighing all in the balance of right reason, and prepared honestly to accept the result. Far from wishing to quarrel with such a temper, we hail it as the evidence of a receptive and honest mind, which will not resign a former belief without substantial reason, but which, yet, is willing to learn new views of truth so they be authenticated by reasonable internal and external evidence. Such doubts and difficulties are worth far more to us than the credulous frame of mind which gulps down indiscriminately all that comes under specious colour; far, far more than that stagnant temper which no storm can stir, whose glassy surface no breeze can ruffle, and on whose impassive, uninterested content no word of spirit warning can make any impression.

We hail your doubts as the best evidence of our successful dealing with you; we welcome your arguments as the intelligent proof that you have seen the full proportions of the claims we make as the messengers of the Most High. Your difficulties shall be answered so far as we have power to answer them. There is a point beyond which it is impossible for us to present evidence. Of that you are aware. We labour under one great disadvantage, as compared with human witnesses; we are not of your earth, and cannot produce for you the kind of evidence which would weigh in your courts of justice. We can but state for your acceptance the evidence on which we ground our claims to your hearing and acceptance, leaving to your own mind in fairness to decide upon the points which we cannot clear up by evidence.

For our own statements must to a very great extent be unsupported, save by statements of those who work with us. Many of us have told you of our earth identity, and have given to you proof that ought to be conclusive that we are fully acquainted with the earth lives of those whose names we bear, even in the minutest particulars. If that is not convincing to you: if you reply that such information might have been gained by false and deceiving spirits, who might have gathered the facts for the very purpose of deluding, we point to the tenor of our intercourse with you, and remind you of the standards of judgment set up by Jesus Himself, "By their fruits shall ye know them." "Men do not gather grapes of thorns, or figs of thistles." We fearlessly refer you to the whole tenor of our teaching for proof that it is Divine.

It would not consist with the dignity of our mission were we to dwell longer on this point. We are not surprised that you should have referred to it; but if our reply be not convincing to you, we have nothing further which we can add to it, and must await in patient prayer the time when the evidence will come home to you. We would not have you to accept our words before. We will patiently abide the issue.

With respect to the union of spirits who were in their earth-life divergent in their views of God and the hereafter; who dwelt in different climes, at different ages of the world's history, we could say much, and will at another season.

For the present we point to a misconception which is inseparable from the state in which you live. You cannot see, as we see, the almost utter worthlessness of what you call opinion. You cannot know while yet the eye is veiled, how the veil is rent by the dissolution of the spirit from the earth-body; how the speculations that have seemed so all-important are seen to be but idle, baseless fancies; while the germ of truth that has underlaid the theological creed is found to be very similar in essence, albeit of divers degrees of development.

Ah, friend! religion is not so abstruse a problem as man has made it. It is comprised within narrow limits for the intelligence that is domiciled on earth. And the theological speculations, the dogmatic definitions with which man has overlaid the revelation of God, serve but to perplex and bewilder, and to involve the spirit struggling up to light in the mists and fogs of ignorance and superstition. The groping after truth which has been characteristic of the progressive spirit in every age has been but the same story, different, indeed, in detail, but identical in issue. As with the blinded eye of sense, so with the spirit that gropes blindly to the light. The mazes of superstition bewilder it; the mists of human ignorance close around it. It staggers and wanders on its devious way, now here, now there, now cast down to earth and trodden under foot by the adversaries, but rising anon, and with outstretched arms struggling onwards still. Those wanderings seem to you similar, and when confined within the limits of a single sect they are indeed alike, but to spirit gaze they have very many points of difference. The struggling spirits who in all ages have been groping their way through the maze of human opinion to the fount of light have pushed their way through tortuous paths which bear only a superficial similarity. To us the theological opinions which have characterised certain sets of men called churches are not so identical as you think. We see the inner points of divergence; and we know that to no two spirits yet created were precisely identical views of the unknown ever presented. They have framed for themselves ideas more or less like those of other spirits, but never identical with them. It is only when the veil is removed that the fog lifts; the speculations die with the body of earth, the opinions shift aside, and the purged eye sees what it has dimly pictured, and corrects by the quickened senses the impressions of earth. Then it sees how the germ of truth is at the base, helped in some to progress by a receptive mind and a clearer spiritual vision; hampered and clogged in others by a cramped intelligence, and a debased earth-body. But in all cases of yearning souls thirsting for true knowledge of God and of their destiny, the opinions of earth rapidly fade, and the spirit sees how baseless and unreal they were. It is only when there is no desire for truth that error is permanent.

So you see, friend, that truth is the exclusive heritage of no man, of no sect. It may and does underlie the philosophy of Athenodorus, as he yearned after the refining of the spirit, and the subjection of the flesh in ancient Rome. It was as really existent in the groping after union with his Master which enabled Hippolytus to endure the loss of earthly existence in sure anticipation of a real life, even though he only dimly saw its characteristics. The self-same seeking after truth elevated and ennobled Plotinus, and raised him, even in earth-life, above and beyond the earth-sphere. It dwelt in the breast of Algazzali, in spite of the errors by which it was dimmed. It—the same blessed germ of Divine truth—lightened the speculations of Alessandro Achillini, and gave force and reality to the burning words which fell from his lips. The same pure jewel shines now in one and all of them. It is the common heritage which enables them to be banded together in a common work and for a common end—the purifying of that desposit of the truth which man has from his God—and the ennobling and elevating of man's destiny by the outpouring of more spiritual views of God and of the destiny of spirit. To them their earth-opinions are of little moment now. They have vanished long ago, and have left behind them no trace of the prejudice which clouded the soul on earth and hampered its progress. They have died and are buried, and over their grave no tear of sorrow is dropped. No resurrection awaits them: they are for ever done with: but the jewel which they once enshrined shines with ever-increas-

THE UNITY OF THE TEACHING.

ing lustre, and is imperishable and eternal. In its illuminating influences, in the aspirations which its presence inspires, lies the mysterious bond of sympathy which is powerful to unite in one work spirits who, in earth-life, were so apparently divergent in opinion.

This may serve to suggest for your consideration reasons why it may not be so strange as it now seems to you, that we should be now banded together for a common object, consecrated to a common work by one earnest desire to spread abroad the knowledge of a higher and purer religion, through an instrument chosen by us for special indications of fitness, of which we are the best judges.

We are confident that continued thought will lead you to recognise the reasonableness of what we say. For definite proof you must be content to wait until you, too, have rent the veil, and stand with unclouded eye in our company. The most we hope for now is the gradual establishment of conviction. We desire that you should apply to us the same law by which the Master judged—the Divine law of judging others as you would yourself be judged.

You err in supposing that there has ever been any discrepancy in our teaching to you. Arguments have been variously put, and different points have been taken by different intelligences who have communicated with you. We do not deny that we have gradually led you up to the general idea which we have wished to convey, and we have, in so doing, avoided points of indifferent opinion which were not essential to our message, as well as points on which we know full well that your previous notions were rooted firm, and would clash with our knowledge. We have sought rather to develop the germs of truth which we discovered than to come into contact with the singularities of opinion which exist. To this end we have seized upon points of contact, and have made much of them; while we have not dwelt on disputed and unimportant points, and have avoided discussing matters that do not lie in our path. Hereafter many points that at present are slurred over, or avoided, will be taken up. But when you have sought information on points whereon we knew your opinion to be erroneous and untenable for long, we have not scrupled to enlighten you. We can see well when the drift of thought is carrying you away from old mooring-places which no longer afford safe anchorage for your spirit; and, seeing this, we have preferred to pilot you rather than to allow you to drop down the stream at the mercy of wind and current, and at risk of shipwreck. We have loosened the ropes, one by one, gently and gradually, and we have charged ourselves with the mission of landing you in safer and surer harbourage. Had we tightened the moorings, the old ropes would have broken, and your spirit would have been tossed helpless on a stormy sea of doubt and difficulty, with no pilot at the helm, and no port in view, at the mercy of wind and wave, and with scant prospect of rescue. Do not blame us that we have chosen to anticipate the inevitable, and to smooth the rough passage. We could not prevent; we may and can assist. We would not, if we could, have added to the chains which would bind your spirit to the dead past. We will, if you co-operate with us, enable it to rise superior to the storm, and to emerge with a new and living faith, on a calmer and more open sea, ready to cross what yet remains between the probation of earth and the haven of peace.

In this endeavour we have studiously guarded ourselves from inflicting on you any rude shocks. We have not misled you on any point. We have never deceived you in aught. Scrupulous exactness has characterised all our statements to you. But we have preferred to take the ideas which we found in your mind, and to enlarge and develop them. We have fostered, directed, instilled newer and truer views, but we have in no point falsified, distorted, or misled.

Nor is there actually any divergence in the teachings of those who have spoken to you. Any apparent discrepancy is referable to difficulties of communication, to the varying influence of your own mind, to the state of your bodily health; to the novelty of the work to some; and especially to your own circumscribed views. We cannot teach what you cannot receive. We can only dimly symbolise truths which one day your unclouded eye will see in their full splendour. We cannot speak with clearness when the spirit of our medium is troubled, when his body is racked with pain, or his mental state vitiated by disease. Nay, even a lowering atmosphere, or electric disturbance, or the neighbourhood of unsympathetic and unfavourable human influences, may colour a communication, or prevent it from being clear and complete. Hence the various discrepancies which your minute gaze has detected. They are small enough and few enough, and they will all vanish when the difficulties are removed. Then will you recognise the superior insight which has guided you in a time of no ordinary difficulty and peril.

You complain that there is little chance of the acceptance of such views as we have put forward. Of this you can know very little. The time is far nearer than you think when the old faith which has worn so long, and which man has patched so clumsily, will be replaced by a higher and nobler one—one not antagonistic, but supplementary—and the pure Gospel which Jesus preached shall find its counterpart again on an advanced plane of knowledge. For know, good friend, that no effort which, as this, is the plan of the Supreme, is entered on untimely, or with disregard of the correlation between God's Gospel and man's wants. What comes to you from us is coming to others too. This is but one among many branches of one great plan. It will go on gradually and spread steadily among the children of faith who are fitted to receive it. The Master has so willed it. His time is not yours, nor is our vision circumscribed as yours. In due time the knowledge which we come to spread will be known among men. Meantime, progressive souls are being educated; precious seed is being sown, and the reaping and garnering shall come in their course. For that you and we alike must wait.

If you will now think carefully over what has been said, you will see that the nature of the case precludes more than presumptive proof being given of the validity of our claims. We say again, that God forces blessings on none. He offers: the responsibility of acceptance or refusal rests with you. The internal evidence will be admitted by you and by all to whom we are now concerned to address ourselves. None but those who are hopelessly involved in the meshes of the shallowest bigotry, who are bound by the fetters of a conventional theology, and shackled by an iron dogmatism, will refuse to acknowledge the internal evidence of a Divine origin in the creed which we put forward. With such as we have enumerated, the dogmatist, the bigot, the narrow-minded, the wise in their own conceit, we have no dealings. Nay, we do not even speak to those who find in the faith which has become ingrained in their very souls a sure and sufficient guide. In God's name let them cling to it. Hereafter their time of progress will come. It is not yet. To you, and to those who have advanced far enough to think with you, we need not further prove that we are not of diabolic origin or intent.

If you will further consider the views which we have put forward with respect to inspiration, you will see that we claim for our teaching that it is just one of those rungs in the ladder of progressive knowledge of God, which mankind has been gradually mounting from the time when man framed for himself a god like himself to the present, when you are slowly learning that to attribute human infirmities and passions to the Supreme is not to do Him honour. Our revelation is in no respect different from that which has preceded, save that it is a step in advance, even as each development of human knowledge has been. Our knowledge flows from the same source, and is made known through similar channels. They are now, as then, human, fallible, and at times wrong. It must be so, as long as God reveals Himself through human agencies.

If you will further recollect the standpoint we have selected, you will see that in place of blind faith, which accepts traditional teaching—the old, merely because it *is* old—we appeal to your reason : and in place of credulity we demand rational, intelligent investigation, and acceptance grounded on conviction. So far from desiring you to accept what we tell you simply because we are spirit-messengers—the new merely because it *is* new—we ask you to weigh in the scales of reason, to ponder in the light of intellect, to reject if you be not satisfied, in no case to assent or to act until conviction has been thoroughly established.

So that not only is the matter of the spirit-creed eminently conformable to right reason, but the grounds on which we ask you to accept it are those which a rational and logical mind will be most disposed to accept. God forbid that we should even seem to hurry any man into antagonism, real or fancied, with a creed which has for eighteen hundred years and more been adorned by the lives of many myriads of earnest and progressive, as well as earnest though mistaken souls. The fact that it has long endured entitles it to the reverence due to antiquity, though with our extended view we can see that it also makes it needful that some of its provisions, admirably suited as they were for a less advanced generation, should now fitly be enlarged and spiritualised. At any rate, we would not disturb its reign with violent revolution. We would refine and infuse new life; we would not dethrone and humble in the dust. As the Saviour told, in the accents of a life of loving and self-sacrificing purity, the story of a nobler faith than that which Sinai had revealed in accents of thunder, so we take up the Divine story at a later day, and proclaim for a world's acceptance a creed more fitted to its advanced capacities, more suited to its later wants.

"*It will reject it!*" Well, then, we at least have offered it, and to those who will surely grasp at it, its blessed influence shall seem the brighter from the contrast. It is long frequently between the first promulgation of a truth and its final acceptance. The seed-time must precede the crop, and the rain and the frost and the cheerless wintertide may seem to be long drawn out, but the sun bursts forth at length, and the crop springs up, and the glad summer comes with the reaping and housing of the fruit. The day of preparation may be long, the night during which the sower waits may be weary, but the harvest surely comes. You cannot retard it; you may aid in reaping it; you may even assist in sowing the seed; but in spite of man's opposition, whether he aids or not, God's work will be done. It is to the individual alone that acceptance or rejection of the Divine message matters materially. A soul is advanced or retarded in the life of progress; and the angels rejoice or mourn over the issue. That is all.

You inquire from us what position we assign to Jesus the Christ. We are not careful to enter into curious comparisons between different teachers who, in different ages, have been sent from God. The time is not yet come for that; but this we know, that no spirit more pure, more godlike, more noble, more blessing and more blessed, ever descended to find a home on your earth. None more worthily earned by a life of self-sacrificing love the adoring reverence and devotion of mankind. None bestowed more blessings on humanity; none wrought a greater work for God. It is not necessary that we should enter into curious comparisons between God's great teachers. Rather would we give to all the meed of praise that is their due, and hold up the example of self-denial, self-sacrifice, and love to the imitation of a generation which sadly needs such a pattern. Had men devoted their energies to the imitation of the simplicity and sincerity, the loving toil and earnest purpose, the self-sacrifice and purity of thought and life which elevated and distinguished the Christ, they had wrangled less of His nature, and had wasted fewer words upon useless metaphysical sophistries. Those of your theologians who dwelt in the days of darkness, and who have left to you an accursed heritage in their idle and foolish speculations, would have turned their minds into a more useful channel, and have been a blessing instead of a curse to mankind. Men would not have derogated from the honour due to the great God alone, but would have accepted, as Jesus intended, the simple Gospel that He preached. But instead of this they have elaborated an anthropomorphic theology which has led them to wander further and further from the simplicity of His teaching; which has turned His name and creed into a battle-ground of sects; and has resulted in a parody on his teachings—a sight on which His pure spirit looks with sorrow and pity.

Friend, you must discriminate between God's truth and man's glosses. We do not dishonour the Lord Jesus—before whose exalted majesty we bow—by refusing to acquiesce in a fiction, which He would disown, and which man has forced upon His name. No, assuredly: but they who from a strict adherence to the literal text of Scripture—a text which they have not understood, and the Spirit of which they have never grasped —have dishonoured the Great Father of Him, and of all alike, and have impiously, albeit ignorantly, derogated from the honour due to the Supreme alone. Not we, but they dishonour God! Not we, but they, though they have the prescription of long usage, though their words be coloured by extracts from writings which they have decided to be Divine: and though in those writings there be found words which pronounce a curse on any who may disagree with what is stated there. We do not regard such curses save with pity. We do not labour to upset belief when it is a harmless error, but we can lend no countenance to views that dishonour God, and retard a soul's progress. The attributing to a man of Divine honour, to the exclusion in very many cases of personal honour and love for the Great Father, is a mischievous error which derogates from the duty of man to his God. The holding of a narrow, cold, dogmatic creed, in all its rigid, lifeless literalism, cramps the soul, dwarfs its spirituality, clogs its progress, and stunts its growth. "The letter," says your Scripture, " the letter killeth, but the spirit giveth life." Hence we denounce such views of God as are contained in the fable of a material hell; and we proclaim to you purer and more rational ideas than are contained in the orthodox notions of Atonement and vicarious sacrifice. We proclaim to you a spiritualised religion. We call you from the dead formalism, the lifeless, loveless literalism of the past, to a religion of spiritualised truth, to the lovely symbolism of angel teaching, to the higher planes of spirit, where the material finds no place, and the formal dogmatism of the past is for ever gone.

We have spoken to you with care, and with a due sense of the importance of what we say. Dwell on it with care. Ponder it with single desire for truth, and seek the Divine aid ministered to all who pray for it.

✠ Imperator.

SECTION XII.

{I am reluctant to publish what is so private in its nature and bearings: but I am constrained to do so, and my justification is that what was the experience of one may be the experience of many, and the history of my mental and spiritual struggles may be helpful to others who are passing through a similar phase. After an interval of some days, during which I received no communication on the subject of the religious teaching of spirits, I requested permission to state further objections which pressed strongly on my mind. As I recall my state, I was perplexed and startled by what had been said. I was unable to accept what was so new; and the great point that weighed with me was that of "Spirit Identity." It seemed in my then state that I must have complete proof of the earth identity of the communicating spirit before I could accept the statements made. I believed such direct demonstration to be procurable; and I was distressed that it was not given. I did not then know (July, 1873) as I do now that the evidence of conviction is what alone is to be had; and that no cut-and-dried plan such as I propounded would really have carried with it the conviction I imagined. Moreover, I was distressed by the feeling that much that passed current for spirit communication was silly and frivolous, if not mischievous. I compared the teaching of the Christian moralists with spirit teaching very much to the disadvantage of the latter. I also considered that there was very wide divergence between teachings given by spirits, and that all sorts of opinions were professed. Most of these I disliked personally, and I did not believe that they benefited the people who received them. I fancied that many such were enthusiasts and fanatics, and was repelled by the idea. Neither from internal nor external evidence was I greatly attracted, and the objections that I put at that time were directed to the points above noticed. They related principally to evidence about identity, to what I thought would be the probable dealings of God with mankind, and to the general character and outcome of Spiritualism. The next answer made to me was as follows] :—

Friend, we are pleased to converse with you again; and if it be impossible for us to answer all your queries, and to solve all your problems, we can at least rectify some errors into which you have fallen as to the dealings of God with man, and the tendency of the mission which we have in charge.

The root of your error seems to lie in a false conception of God and of His dealings with mankind. Surely the page of human history bears upon it the story of one uniformly progressive revelation of One and the same God. The attempts of men to realise and picture to themselves the God whom they ignorantly worship have led to the strangest and most fallacious notions as to His nature and operations.

In the early days of man's history the crude notion of a God inherent in his spiritual nature took shape as a fetish, which was alternately prayed to with reverence or cast aside with contumely, in proportion as the prayer was granted or delayed. Men knew not that the block before which they bowed was powerless, and that round them hovered ever the bands of spirit ministers who were ready to succour and defend them, and to bear to them answers to their reasonable prayers. They could grasp no more of God than that. The tangible, palpable image was to them the embodiment of their idea. Mark this! of *their idea of God*, not of God Himself, but of the crude conception which was the best idea they could frame. Drawing their information from their own dealings, they imagined for themselves certain rules of conduct by which they proceeded to judge the God whom they had created. They feigned for Him human passions such as they found worthy of respect in their fellows. They credited Him with some failings which were inseparable from humanity as they knew it. He was jealous of His honour; long-suffering and of tender pity; according as they who spoke of Him imagined that He ought to be. He was, in short, a glorified man—a man endued with omnipotence, omniscience, and omnipresence. They feigned Him such and made Him act accordingly. Consequently all the revelation of God is characteristic of the age in which it is given. It grows with human development, and is progressively proportioned to the development of human intellect and refinement, simply because the human medium becomes capable of being impressed with more accurate views of the Deity in proportion as he has shaken himself free from his former fetters of ignorance, and has himself progressed towards light and knowledge.

We have frequently said that God reveals Himself as man can bear it. It must needs be so. He is revealed through a human medium, and can only be made known in such measure as the medium can receive the communication. It is impossible that knowledge of God should outstrip man's capacity. Were we now to tell you—if we could—of our more perfect theology it would seem to you strange and unintelligible. We shall, by slow degrees, instil into your mind so much of truth as you can receive, and then you will see your present errors. But that is not yet. Indeed, since the conception which each frames for himself is to him his God, it cannot be that revelation can be in advance of capacity. It is in the nature of things impossible.

Hence you see that when you credit God with motives and say "This cannot be. God is acting here contrary to His nature. He cannot so act now, because He did not so act then," you are simply saying, "My idea of God is so and so, and I cannot at present get another one. According to what I believe, my God would not do so." And that is precisely what we say. You have made your God, and you have made Him act as you see fit. By and bye, as your mind expands—either in your present state of being or in another—you will get fresh light, and then you will say, "Now I see that I was wrong. God is not what I fancied at all. How could I ever have entertained such notions!"

This is very much the case with all progressive minds. To some the time of development comes not in this life. They must wait for a newer light in a newer life. But to some there comes a flood of knowledge even in their present place of existence. The old grows flat and profitless. The soul craves for a newer and truer revelation; for something which shall be as the spirit among the dry bones, and shall give them a resurrection unto life.

Well, you have had, or you are having, your revelation. Your mind, as some would say, has widened, and has pictured a God more in accordance with its advanced capacities.

You have received from an external source—the same whence all other Divine knowledge flows down to man—a newer and richer revealing of the Supreme, others may say.

Call it what you will. The two operations of revelation and comprehension, of knowledge and capacity, must be correlative. The knowledge does not come until there is capacity to receive it. Neither does the mind get higher revelation until it has so far advanced as to feel the want of it; and that for the simple reason that it is itself the agent through which comes the revelation of which it is the recipient.

All your fancied theories about God have filtered down to you through human channels; the embodiments of human cravings after knowledge of Him; the creation of minds that were undeveloped, whose wants were not your wants, whose God, or rather whose notions about God are not yours. You try hard to make the ideas fit in, but they will not fit, because they are the produce of divers intelligences in divers degrees of development.

Think! You say to us that we are not of God, because our ideas of Him made known to you are not compatible with some notions which you have derived from certain of the books in your sacred records. Tell us which is the God with whom we are at variance in our ideal. Is it the God who walked in human form with Adam, and is fabled to have wreaked direful vengeance on the ignorant creatures who are said to have committed what you now see to be a very venial fault? Or, is it the God who commanded his faithful friend to sacrifice to Him the only child of His love as an acceptable offering? Or is it the God who reigned over Israel as an earthly monarch, and whose care was feigned to be devoted to the enunciation of sanitary laws, or to the construction of a tabernacle, who went forth with the armies of Israel to battle, and issued bloodthirsty laws and regulations for the extirpation of innocent and unoffending peoples? Or is it, perchance, the God who enabled his servant Joshua to arrest the course of the universe and to paralyse the solar system, in order that the Israelites might revel a few hours more in gore and carnage? Or is it rather with the God who was feigned to be so angry with His chosen people because they wished for a visible monarch, that He visited upon them an elaborate revenge extending over many hundred of years? Or with which of the Gods of the prophets are we at variance? with Isaiah's God, or with Ezekiel's? or with the lugubrious Deity that Jeremiah's morbid mind imagined? or with David's Divinity; half father, half tyrant, cruel and yielding by turns, always inconsistent and irrational? or with Joel's? or with John's? or with Paul's calvinistic conception, imagined and painted with horrid phantasies of predestination, and hell, and election, and a dreamy listless heaven? Are we at variance with Paul, or John, or Jesus?

But there is no need to press the fact that Revelation has always been proportioned to man's capacity, and coloured by man's mind. The idea of God has been throughout the ages the conception, more or less vivid, of those who have been the media of revelation. The implanted idea has taken form and shape from the mental surroundings of the medium through whom it was given. Such portion of truth as the teachers have been able to impart has been moulded by the spirit of the medium into an individual shape. To none has complete truth been given, only so much of truth, such aspect of truth as was necessary for a particular age and people. Hence it is that the conceptions of God, such as those we have now alluded to, are various and divergent. Of course we and our God are not Joshua and his God: neither are we Paul and his God: though we challenge comparison between the God we know and reveal, and that God who was dimly shadowed forth to a people that knew Him not, by Him who knew Him best, and lived nearest to Him, the man Christ Jesus. He had received conceptions of Deity far clearer than any which His followers have grasped; His religion was simple, plain, and earnest. His theology was equally plain. The cry to "Our Father who art in Heaven," how widely does it differ from the elaborate dissertations on theology in which the Supreme is first informed of the character which man has assigned to Him, and then is requested to act up to it with especial reference to the wants or fancied wants which the ignorant worshipper puts forward!

God! Ye know Him not! One day, when the Spirit stands within the veil which shrouds the spirit world from mortal gaze, you shall wonder at your ignorance of Him whom you have so foolishly imagined! He is far other than you have pictured Him. Were He such as you have pictured Him, were He such as you think, He would avenge on presumptuous man the insults which he puts on his Creator. But He is other, far other than man's poor grovelling mind can grasp, and He pities and forgives the ignorance of the blind mortal who paints Him after a self-imagined pattern. He blames not the ignorance. That is no shame, so it be not wilful. But He blames the folly which hugs a low conception of Him, and will have no light let in on the dark and musty temple in which that idol is enshrined. He blames the lovers of darkness, the haters of light, who cling to the undeveloped fancies of the past, and can see no beauty in the simple moral grandeur of the God whom Christ revealed, but must needs graft on to that noble conception the anthropomorphic fancies of previous unenlightened ages. Of such there are not a few who cannot receive higher teachings yet. But of such are not you! When you rashly complain of us that our teaching to you controverts that of the Old Testament, we can but answer that it does indeed controvert that old and repulsive view of the good God which made Him an angry, jealous, human tyrant: but that it is in fullest accord

8

with that divinely-inspired revelation of Himself which He gave through Jesus Christ—a revelation which man has done so much to debase, and from which the best of the followers of Christ have so grievously fallen away.

If there be nought in what we say of God and of man's after-life that commends itself to you, it must be that your mind has ceased to love the grander and simpler conceptions which it had once learned to drink in. It must be that the machinations of the adversaries have availed to reach your spirit, and that the dark edge of that cloud which they have interposed between your world and its God, is resting with baleful influence upon you. We pray that we may be permitted to raise it, and to pour into your soul once more the beams of enlightenment and peace. We do not fear that any permanent harm will rest with you. Nor do we regret that you should try the foundations on which your knowledge rests. It will not be wasted time to do so.

Cease to be anxious about the minute questions which are of minor moment. Dwell much on the great, the overwhelming necessity for a clearer revealing of the Supreme: on the blank and cheerless ignorance of God and of us which has crept over the world: on the noble creed we teach, on the bright future we reveal. Cease to be perplexed by thoughts of an imagined Devil. For the honest, pure, and truthful soul there is no Devil nor Prince of Evil such as theology has feigned.

Evil comes not nigh him; the adversaries flee from his presence, and the powers of evil are powerless before him. He is guarded around by angel guards, ministered to by bright spirits, who watch over him and direct his footsteps. For him there waits a career of progressive increase in knowledge, and in all that elevates and ennobles the intelligence. He need fear no Devil, unless he creates one for himself. His affinity for good draws around him influences for good. He is fenced around by guardians; nor can he, save by voluntary surrender, fall a final victim to the foe. His is no exemption from temptation, from the snares of the destroyer, or from the atmosphere which during his probation time he must breathe. The clouds of sorrow and anguish of soul may gather round him, and his spirit may be saddened with the burden of sin— weighed down with consciousness of surrounding misery and guilt, but no fabled Devil can gain dominion over him, or prevail to drag down his soul to hell. All the sadness of spirit, the acquaintance with grief, the intermingling with guilt, is part of the experience, in virtue of which his soul shall rise hereafter. The guardians are training and fitting it by those means to progress, and jealously protect it from the dominion of the foe.

It is only they who, by a fondness for evil, by a lack of spiritual and excess of corporeal development, attract to themselves the congenial spirits of the undeveloped who have left the body, but have not forgotten its desires. These alone risk incursion of evil. These by proclivity attract evil, and it dwells with them at their invitation. They attract the lower spirits who hover nearest Earth, and who are but too ready to rush in and mar our plans, and ruin our work for souls. These are they of whom you speak when you say in haste, that the result of Spiritualism is not for good. You err, friend. Blame not us that the lower spirits manifest for those who bid them welcome. Blame man's insensate folly, which will choose the low and grovelling rather than the pure and elevated. Blame his foolish laws, which daily hurry into a life for which they are unprepared, thousands of spirits, hampered and dragged down by a life of folly and sin, which has been fostered by custom and fashion. Blame the ginshops, and the madhouses, and the prisons, and the encouraged lusts and fiendish selfishness of man. This it is which damns legions of spirits—not, as ye fancy, in a sea of material fire, but in the flames of perpetuated lust, condemned to burn itself out in hopeless longing till the purged soul rises through the fire and surmounts its dead passions. Yes, blame these and kindred causes, if there be around undeveloped intelligences who shock you by their deception, and annoy you by frivolity and falsehood.

More of this hereafter. Already we have said more than we had intended. And for myself, I hear the call which summons me to the adoration of the Supreme, when my prayer shall rise to the throne of Divine pity that a rill of that consoling grace may trickle down to your vexed spirit, and may shed on it healing and peace—the peace of God, the quietness of assurance and peace.

✝ IMPERATOR.

SECTION XIII.

[On reading over consecutively this series of communications which I had received, I was more than ever struck by their beauty, both of form and matter. When I considered that they were written with vast rapidity, without conscious thought on my part, that they were free from blot or blemish of grammatical construction, and that there was no interlineation or correction throughout their whole course, I could not but wonder at their form. As regards the subject-matter, I was still in difficulty. There was much in them with which I sympathised; but at the same time I could not get rid of the idea that the faith of Christendom was practically upset by their issue. I believed that, however it might be disguised, such would be their outcome in the end. No man, I reasoned, could accept such teaching, in its spirit as well as in its letter, without being led to throw aside very much that the Christian world had agreed to receive as *de fide*. The central dogmas seemed especially attacked: and it was this that startled me. A very extended acquaintance with the writings of theologians—Greek, Roman, Anglican, and Protestant, especially those of the modern German school of thought—had prepared me to make little of divergence of opinion on minor matters. I knew that such divergences were inseparable from the subject. I also knew that individual opinion on abstruse mysteries of revelation is of little worth. I should have even been prepared for startling statements on such matters. But here was a very different matter. The points impugned seemed to me to be of the very essence of the Christian religion. To "spiritualise," or, as I preferred to call it, to explain away these, seemed to me absolutely fatal to my belief in any revelation whatsoever. After long and patient thought, I could come to no other conclusion; and I shrank from accepting such momentous issues on the *ipse dixit* of an intelligence of whom I knew, and could know, so little. I felt that I must have more time for thought: and that I, at any rate, was not ripe for the acceptance of a creed, however beautiful, which was not better attested, and less iconoclastic. These objections I stated. In answer it was written] :—

You have said wisely. Time is requisite that you may ponder deeply that which is indeed of vital import. We leave you to think over what we have advanced with a full conviction that you will, in time, assimilate the teaching, and appreciate its importance. Should you desire enlightenment from us on any points, it shall be given; but we will not force upon you other communications until time has done for you what you require. Let patience and earnest prayerfulness have full sway.

You know not in your cold earth atmosphere, so chilling, so repellent to spirit life, how the magnetic rapport between your spirit and the guides who wait to bear its petition upwards is fostered by frequent prayer. It is as though the bond were tightened by frequent use; as though the intimacy ripened by mutual association. You would pray more did you know how rich a spiritual blessing prayer brings. Your learned sages have discussed much of the value of prayer, and have wandered in a maze of opinion, befogged and ignorant of the real issue. They do not know—how should they?—of the angel messengers who hover round ready to help the spirit that cries to its God. They know not of the existence of such, for they cannot test their presence by human science in its present state; and so, with crude effort, they would reduce the results of prayer to line and measure. They try to gauge its results, and to estimate its effect by the compilation of statistics. And still they find themselves in difficulty, for though they grasp the shell, the spirit eludes their ken. Such results are not to be so measured, for they are imperceptible by man's science. They are spiritual, varying in various cases: different as are the agencies at work.

Frequently it is the unspoken petition which is not granted that is the cause of richest blessing to the praying soul. The very cry of the burdened spirit shot forth into the void,—a cry wrung out by bitter sorrow—is an unknown relief. The spirit is lightened, though the prayer is not granted in the terms of its petition. You know not why: but could you see, as we see, the guardians labouring to pour into the sorrow-laden soul the balm of sympathy and consolation, you would know whence comes that strange peace which steals over the spirit, and assures it of a sympathising and consoling God. The prayer has done its work, for it has drawn down an angel friend: and the bursting heart, crushed with its load of care and sorrow, is comforted by angel sympathy.

This, the magnetic sympathy which we can shed around those with whom we are in close communion, is one of the blessed effects which can be wrought by the cry of a human soul reaching upward to its God. And under no other conditions can the full blessedness of spirit intercourse be realised It is the spirit that is most spiritualised that alone can enter into the secret chambers where the angels dwell. It is to the soul that lives in frequent communion with us that we are best able to come nigh. This, friend, is invariable: another part of that unchangeable law which governs all our intercourse with your world. To the spiritual soul come, in richest measure, spiritual gifts.

Nor is it always the answer which man in his ignorance expects, that is the truest response to his petition. Many times to grant his request would be to do him grievous harm. He has asked ignorantly, petulantly, foolishly: and his prayer is unheeded in its request: but it has availed to place his spirit in communion with an intelligence which is waiting an opportunity of approach, and which can minister to him strength and consolation in his necessity.

'Twere well if men would more strive to live a life of prayer. Not the morbid life of devotion falsely so-called, which consists in neglecting duty and in spending the precious hours of the probation life in morbid self-anatomy: in developing unhealthy self-scrutiny: in idle dreamy contemplation, or in forced and unreal supplication. The life of prayer is far other, as we advise it. Prayer to be real must be the heart-cry, spontaneous and impulsive, to friends who hover near. The fancy of a prayer to the ear of an ever-present God who is willing to alter unalterable laws in response to a capricious request, has done much to discredit the idea of prayer altogether. Believe it not! Prayer—the spontaneous cry of the soul to its God through the friends who, it knows, are near, and are ever ready to catch up the unuttered petition and bear it upwards and ever upwards till it reach a power that can respond—this is no matter of formal preparation. It consists not in any act of outward show. It is not necessarily syllabled in utterance: far less is it trammelled by conventional form, or bound up in stereotyped phraseology. True prayer is the ready voice of spirit communing with spirit: the cry of the soul to invisible friends with whom it is used to speak: the flashing along the magnetic line a message of request which brings, swift as thought, its ready answer back.

It is the placing of a suffering soul in union with a ministering spirit who can soothe and heal. It needs no words, no attitude, no form. It is truest when these are absent, or at least unstudied. It needs but a recognition of a near guardian, and an impulse to communion. To this end it must be habitual: else, like the limb long disused the impulse is paralysed. Hence, it is those of you who live most in the spirit who penetrate deepest into the hidden mysteries. We can come nearest to them. We can touch hidden chords in their nature which vibrate only to our touch, and are never stirred by your world's influences. 'Tis they who reach highest in their earth-life, for they have learned already to commune with spirit, and are fed with spiritual food. For them are opened mysteries closed to more material natures: and their perpetual prayer has wrought for them this at least, that they live above the sufferings and sorrows from which it cannot exempt them, seeing that such are necessary to their development.

Alas! alas! we speak of that which is little known. Were this grand truth better realised, man would live in the atmosphere of the pure and elevated spirits. His spiritual attitude would drive from him the base and baleful influences which too often beset those who pry unbidden into mysteries that are too high for them, and which, alas! beset and annoy even the best at times. If it prevailed not to obtain exemption it would provide protection, and do more to strengthen us than all else that man could do. It would avail more to sanctify the acts, to purify the motives, and to keep alive the reality of spirit communion than anything which we know of.

Pray then; but see that you pray not with formality, heartlessly, and with unreal supplication. Commune with us in communion of the spirit. Keep a single eye to the issues of such communion as respect your own spirit. The rest will follow in due course. Leave abstruse and perplexing questions of man's theological controversy, and keep close to the central truths which so intimately affect the well-being of your spirit. The vain bewilderments which man has cast around the simplicity of truth are manifold. Nor is it for you to disentangle them, nor to decide what is or is not essential in that which has hitherto been revealed. You will learn hereafter to view much that you now regard as vitally essential truth, rather as a passing phase of teaching which was necessary for those to whom it was given. It is human weakness that impels you to rush to the end. You must tarry, friend, tarry long yet in the early searchings before you reach the goal. You have much to unlearn before you can penetrate all mysteries.

We have more to say to you on this. But for the present enough has been written. May the Supreme keep us and you, and enable us so to lead and guide you that in the end truth may shine on your darkened soul, and peace may dwell within your spirit.

+ IMPERATOR.

[I made no rejoinder to what was last said, but I thought over it, and was preparing to say somewhat, when I was imperiously stopped. The hand dashed off with violent speed, and the communication following was written without pause in an incredibly short space of time. So vehement was the effort that I was in a state of semi-trance until it was complete.]

Stay! stay! stay! Attempt not now to argue, but learn yet again of the truth. You are impatient, and it is in your mind to say foolish things. What matters it to you if what we say contradicts that which others have believed? Why shrink back at that? Does not all faith firmly grasped contradict some other faith? Nay, does not each faith contain within itself elements of contradiction? If you know not so much as that, then are you not fit to go forward. From those old creeds and faiths, venerable in their antiquity, but crude too frequently in development, men have derived comfort. They have found their utterances convenient and suitable for them. They have derived from them a satisfaction which they do not bring to you. Why? Because your spirit has outgrown those old, and to you lifeless, utterances. They benefit you not. They are powerless to stir your soul. They have no voice for your spirit: no remedy for your wants. They are but faint and far-off echoes of what to some was a living voice, but which to you is cold and meaningless.

Why, then, perplex yourself at that? Why linger, striving in vain to extract a meaning from that which to you has none? Why turn a deaf ear to the living voice which cries to your soul from the land beyond in accents which are living, burning, true? Why refuse to listen when the voice speaks of the true, the spiritual, the noble, of all that is real and actual in place of the dying or the dead? Why, for a fancy—from reverence for a lifeless past—cut yourself off from the living present, from the communion of spirits, from the society of those who can tell you noble truths of God and of your destiny?

Surely this is but madness, only the influence of spirits who would gladly hold back the soul, and drag it down to earth. Were our revelation a blank contradiction of the old, what is that to you? Ours speaks in living accents to your spirit; you know it; you drink it in, and find it to be a blessed influence. The old is dead to you. Why linger round the lifeless form? Why embrace the mouldering corpse which was once a living being instinct with Divine truth?

Your sacred records tell you how, at the sepulchre of Jesus, the angel message to the sorrowing friends was one of aspiration. "Why seek ye the living among the dead? He is not here, He is risen." So, friend, we say to you. Why linger in the dead past, the sepulchre of buried truth, seeking, in fruitless sorrow, for that which is no longer there? It is not there, it is risen. It has left the body of dogmatic teaching which once for a restless age enshrined Divine truth. There remains but the dead casket. The jewel is gone. The spirit has risen, and lo! we proclaim to you sublime truth, a nobler creed, and a Diviner God.

The voice which in ages past has sounded in the ears of those to whom has been entrusted the Divine mission on their earth and to their generation, reaches even to this age and to you. It has ever been so. God deals now in no other sort than he has ever dealt with men. He calls them up to fuller light, to higher truth. It is theirs to accept or to reject the heavenly message. Probably it has been to each aspiring soul a difficulty that the past, the familiar, the venerable faith, has charms from which it is hard to sever. In the first blush of perplexity it seems to the bewildered spirit that all must go that is old and cherished, and the new and untried must be accepted. It seems to be a death; and man shrinks from death. Yes; but it is a death unto life. It is a passage through the tomb to a land of life and hope. Even as the spirit soars in freedom from the body of death from which it has been emancipated, so does the enfranchised spirit, set free from the trammels of the past, soar aloft in liberty, the liberty of the truth which, Jesus said, alone can make man free. You know it not now; but you shall know it hereafter.

This, then, is our cry to you. Why turn your face to the dead past, when the living present and the bright future attract, and promise rich store of blessing? Were we in our mission the absolute contradiction of the old, what is that to you? The old words are spiritless, and you cannot infuse into them again the spirit that is gone. Leave them to those for whom they still have a voice and a meaning, and follow with unfaltering step the impulses of the Divine Spirit which lures you on to higher views of truth. Quit the dead past, though it be to journey through a new present to an unknown future.

But, friend, it is not so. The past casts a glamour over you, and you share the common idea that the new must utterly destroy the old. Did Jesus so say? Did He counsel the abolition of the Mosaic teaching? Yet, as we have before said, our teaching is no more startling development as compared with His than was His as compared with Moses'. That which we present for your acceptance is the complement rather than the contradiction of the old; the growth to a fuller stature; the development of a wider knowledge.

If you meditate deeply on the state of the world when Jesus proclaimed to it His reformed faith, you will see many points of similarity to that which now obtains among men. It is not, we reiterate, more startling to read the gospel which we preach alongside of that which passes current among men for religion, than it was to put the gospel of Jesus in juxtaposition to the ritual of Pharisaism, or the sceptical indifferentism of Sadducee. The world then needed a new revelation, even as it does now; and that which it received was not less startling than is this to those who love the old, and desire not to be stirred from the paths to which they are accustomed.

In those days, even as now, the revelation of God, which had been adapted to the special wants of a special people, had been overlaid with rubbish, until it had become a mass of ritual without a meaning and without life. For many long years the voice of God had not been heard, and man had begun to crave, as he craves now, for a renewal of the Divine message. The old had become dead, and he sought for a new and living voice. It came to him—this Divine utterance—in the voice of Jesus; from a source the most unlikely, as men think; from a quarter least calculated to command the respect of the educated Pharisee, or to carry conviction to the scoffing Sadducee. Yet that voice prevailed, and for 1800 years has animated the religious life of Christendom. The creed so originated has become debased, but the spirit of the Crucified is in it even now; and it needs but the vivifying touch to call it forth into new life. The old rags with which man has thought to clothe it may readily be thrown aside, and the truth shine all the brighter for their loss.

The source from which our revelation comes is not more strange than was the source of that power wielded by Him who was to His generation the despised carpenter of Nazareth. Men sneered at Him in the plenitude of their scorn; even as they have sneered at everything new; even as they sneer at us. They were ready to stare at His marvels; they would follow Him in hosts to marvel at the physical miracles which were wrought through Him; but they were not sufficiently spiritual to drink in His teachings. They are ready now to wonder at us and our mighty works, even as they wondered then. Even as then they sought for yet further and further tests—"Come down from the cross, and we will believe on thee"—so now there is even one more test which is necessary to ensure complete conviction. They called Him a deceiver, even as they cry out now. They hooted Him out of their society; they drove Him out of their midst, and they strove by their laws and by their influence to crush out the new doctrine from their land. New it was indeed, but the truth that it enshrined was old, old as the God who gave it, only new in form. Ours is new now, but the time shall come when men shall see that it is but the risen truth of ages past, rejuvenescent and eternal.

The Divine truth which we proclaim is not more strange to you than was the message of Jesus to His age—the age that sneeringly asked whether any educated person of position and respectability—"any of the Pharisees or the rulers"—had believed on him. Both were progressive developments of the same continuous stream of truth, suited to the wants and cravings of those to whom they were vouchsafed. Meditate on the mental condition of Nicodemus, and contrast it with that of many such in your own day. And be assured that the same power which availed to stir the dead faith of the Jew, and to reveal his God more clearly, is still able to infuse new life into the well-nigh lifeless body of Christian faith, and to restore it to energy and vitality.

May the All-wise guide, bless, and keep you.

+ Imperator.

SECTION XIV.

[THE communication last recorded produced considerable effect on me, and it was some days before I replied. When I did so, I objected thus]:—

The parallel between the days of Christ and the present days is comprehensible. I can quite imagine an educated Sadducee looking on the pretensions of Christ with scorn; and he would have been wrong, as we now know; but, as I think, very excusably wrong. Judged by the mere light of reason, they would seem monstrous. And a Sadducee of that day, whose tone of mind was set against the supernatural, would excusably refuse to credit what must seem to him a lie, or a delusion. For myself, I do not see how he could do anything else. Yet he had a concrete man before him—one whom he could see, and whose words he could hear; one whose life he could test as to whether it was in accord with the holy teaching which fell from His lips. I am so far worse off that I have only an impersonal influence to deal with, only utterances which may conceivably be the voice of my spirit questioning with itself. I have nothing to lay hold of. All around me I see Spiritualism vague, and frequently contemptible in its utterance. Its revelations are shadowy where they are not silly; and frequently one is shocked by that which passes current under its name. I cannot see my way. As to you, I know nothing of you, even if you be an entity at all. I do not see any way of satisfying myself about you; nor would it help me very much if you were to assume shape as a previous dweller on this earth. Had you ever a personality, or are you merely an influence? It would help me somewhat if I could picture you as a definite individuality. But, on the whole, I wish you would leave me alone.

[I had in fact become wearied out with this strenuous conflict between my own strongly-conceived opinions and those of an Intelligence so powerful in statement and so coherent in argument. I was torn by conflicting emotions, and undergoing, no doubt, a state of preparation necessary for what was to follow. The answer came thus]:—

Friend, we sympathise with your questionings, and will try to aid you. You say that the sceptical Sadducee was better off in that he had the definite personal Jesus before him. Doubtless he had; but, so far from that being a help to him, it would be an additional cause of perplexity. He would find it far harder to associate the son of the carpenter of Nazareth with God's new revelation, of which he recognised the want, than you do to associate us with the Supreme. "Is not this the carpenter?" would be to him a far more serious difficulty than your query, "Is this an individuality?" For he would see all around him the tangible and palpable difficulties which he could not surmount. The lowly origin, the humble friends, the world's scorn, the rejection of the mission by all on whose opinion he had been accustomed to rely, all this would form a real and very insuperable difficulty; one which, if your words are to be taken literally, you would yourself hold him justified in considering final. And, assuredly, if in the end he failed to grasp the message and to accept the Messenger, he would, if honest, be guilty of no sin. He would but have lost an opportunity of progress which would recur when he was more fitted to avail himself of it.

With you the case is otherwise. You have to deal with no external difficulties. You have simply to battle with intellectual doubt. You know and acknowledge that the words which have been spoken to you are such as you might reasonably expect from a teacher sent from God. They are fraught with a message the need of which you feel, the beauty of which you admit, and the moral grandeur of which commends itself to all who are fitted to receive it. You know full well that it originates in some source external to yourself. You must know that no unconscious effort of your own mind could produce that which contradicts the outcome of your own thoughts. Were the thoughts we utter those which would naturally spring from your own mind, you might have room for hesitation. But it is not so. And no theory of self-questioning, however ingenious, will satisfy your mind. You know that it is not so; and the phase of doubt through which you now pass, and which is so evanescent, can exercise no permanent influence upon you. When it is gone, you will wonder how you can ever have imagined that I am not an entity as real as yourself, as real as any embodied intelligence whom you call "man."

Yes, friend, time is all that you require; time for patient thought; time to weigh issues, to estimate evidence, and to tabulate results. The words which have stirred you so deeply —you know not how deeply—are the words of one who sees your thoughts, who sympathises with your difficulties, and not least with those very doubts and questionings which now perplex you. During my earth life I was a prominent actor in scenes of difficulty not unlike those which preceded the life of the Christ, and which are now recurring. It has been so in all cycles where the revolving course of time brings round a similar condition of things. Man in all ages has been constituted mentally the same. He is developed: he progresses; he thinks more deeply; he knows more. But sure as in your world night succeeds to day, so surely there comes a time when his conceptions of the Deity become faint and unreal; when the spark of Divinity within him craves for a fuller knowledge, and cries to heaven for a message from its God. A new revelation is needed. The craving spirit of man yearns for it. The old has done its work, and from its ashes rises the new, which is to the receptive soul the voice from on high that speaks words of consolation and comfort. It has ever been so. You know it. You can trace it all through the history of God's dealings with mankind. And why should it cease to be so now? Why now, when man most needs it, should the voice be dumb, and the ear of the Supreme be deaf?

You say that you know nothing of me. Why will you confuse the messenger with his message, why will you insist

·on associating with that which is Divine the vehicle through whom it is conveyed?

[The result of the argument was that, in reference to my weak-kneed faith, I got what I obstinately fought for. And when I had so far prevailed, I saw how hollow was the boon for which I had contended. I began to grasp, as I had been unable to grasp before, the tendency of the teaching, and to separate it from the individuality of the messenger. I went back over the time during which this argument—portions of which only I think it well to print—had been in process, and I grasped as I could not grasp before what was to me, in very truth, a new Revelation. The messenger became lost in the importance to me of his message: and the desire to probe and prove minute points of detail was lost in the full blaze of conviction that then first burst upon me.

This state, however, was evanescent. I was too wedded to old habits of analysis to let impulse and enthusiasm take the place of logical conviction. Moreover, early religious training asserted itself, and I recurred to my old theological objections. The first effect passed, and after an interval of two days I resumed my objections. During that time I had carefully read over and over again all that has been printed here, and much that is too personal for publication. I had estimated the experience of a year, during which I could discover no departure from strict truth. And I came clearly to the conclusion that the Power which was in action was—(1) External to myself; (2) Truthful and consistent in its statements; (3) Pure and elevated in the religious teaching which it conveyed. This seemed clear to me: and I turned to consider the question of identity, and the claims put forward. As to other matters, I felt that they might wait. The points which had settled themselves in my mind raised a strong presumption that the truthful intelligence of the past was truthful still. But then came the doubt as to how far all might be the work of "Satan transformed into an angel of light," labouring for the subversion of the faith. My exact objection was put thus]:—

May it not be said with some pretence of fair criticism that your teaching tends to what men call Deism, Pantheism, or (wrongly, I know) even to Atheism? Does it not degrade God to the level of a Force, and tend to breed in man a doubt as to the absolute truth of anything? God, one begins to think, is only a name for the influence which permeates the universe, pictured differently by different peoples in different ages. The revelation of Him comes ab intrà, *imagined in the mind, not revealed to it. Christianity is one of many forms of faith, all more or less mistaken. Man gropes on more or less blindly, evolving for himself, from time to time, ideas more or less erroneous. Since God exists only in the conceptions, each man has his God peculiar to himself. Absolute truth out of mathematics does not exist. And so man, at his best, becomes a solitary unit, alone with his own spirit, replying to its questionings, evolving views which satisfy for a moment, only to be succeeded by others, which in their turn give way to newer ideas; unless, indeed, intellect becomes fossilised, and the old views are permanent because they have ceased to live.*

This colourless idea is to supplant a Gospel which bears the Divine imprimatur : *whose precepts are precise, whose morality is as elevated as most men can grasp, and which is enforced by a system of definite reward and punishment such as experience has always found necessary in dealing with men. This Gospel, so backed, has not been, as you say, successful in raising men to a very high pitch of moral perfection. How, then, am I to expect that a philosophy such as yours, which has a shadow of good, indeed, but a shadow only, dim, vague, and impalpable, which is destructive of the past, without the power to construct for the future; how can I believe that this can hold in hand rebellious minds which have chafed under a religion so precise in its moral* dicta, *so forcible in its appeals to human interests, so commended by its Divine origin and by the halo* shed around it from the saintliest life ever held up for human imitation? It seems to me most unlikely. I do not now repeat what I have said about the hazy source from which this teaching comes: nor do I insist upon the dangers which I foresee from its general adoption. That danger is too remote to need enlarging on. At the same time it is an important factor in the argument, that your teaching would, as it seems to me, relax many of the wholesome bonds which have been valuable morally, socially, and religiously to mankind. And were that which we know as Spiritualism to flood the community, I sadly fear that it would leave men enthusiasts and fanatics; and that the world, so far from having gained ground, would have relapsed into the blindest superstition, and the shallowest credulity. I may be utterly wrong; but so it strikes me. I cannot see that your teaching is any substitute for what men have believed. Even if it be what it pretends to be, surely man is no more fit to be governed according to such notions than he is to live on angels' food. Even in its highest form it is of doubtful practical utility, while, in many of its more vulgar shapes, it seems simply pernicious and demoralising.

In the name of the Supreme, we greet you. It is not in our power to help you now. What we say seems to you other than it is. The upheaval which has so disturbed your mind, has left it in a condition little fit to weigh niceties. For that you must bide your time as patiently as may be; meantime the training is valuable to you. You will know the why as you knew it not before; and impulse and enthusiasm will yield to experimental knowledge and calm conviction. The venerable belief which has been assented to rather than accepted, will pale before the knowledge of truth which is born of investigation and logical analysis. What we have said merits the deepest study. We would have you take every opportunity of reading over consecutively what has been written; and of thinking deeply on the whole tenor of our intercourse with you. We claim to be judged by our whole communion with you, by words and deeds alike; by the moral effect of our teaching, no less than by its relation to previous creeds; by the spiritual atmosphere which we bring with us, no less than by the imperfect utterances in which logical subtlety may readily find a flaw.

For the present it is enough that we solemnly reiterate our claim to be the bearers of a Divine message. The words we speak are the words of God. You know it; and no additional argument can add any weight to our claim on this head. You are no more the sport of evil, than you are deluded by phantasies of a diseased brain. Evil does not tell of God, as we tell. Nor can any brain tell you what we have told, and give you evidence such as we have given. When you are more calm you will see this. Were you in other state now, we should have somewhat to say concerning the sin of curiously seeking out indication of evil which may be fastened on that which is holy and divine, even as when the holy Jesus walked your earth 'mid its corruptions and its curses, the devils whom He ejected turned on Him through the mouths of the orthodox religionists, and charged Him with association with Beelzebub. We do not care to answer such objections. They bear on their face their own sufficient refutation. When you have had time to think calmly, we will make such answer to your objections as may be requisite. For the present it is better that you give yourself to meditation and prayer. Pray, friend, with zeal and earnestness, that you may be guided into all truth.

That prayer at least you cannot refuse to put up, even though it be dictated by the very Tempter. Pray, in company with us, for enlightenment and patience; for power to see, and for grace to follow the truth. Pray that you may be released from the fetters of dogmatism which would bind your aspiring soul; and that being released you may be guided in your upward progress, lest you soar and fall. Pray that the influence of others may be separated from your own soul's wants; that you may have grace to choose the right, and to leave others to select what they find suitable for them. Pray that you

SILENT GROWTH.

may realise clearly the responsibility of choice or rejection, and that you may be saved, on the one hand, from obstinate prejudice, and on the other, from hasty acceptance. And, above all, pray for honesty, sincerity, and humility, that you may not mar God's work by pride, by obstinacy, or by unworthiness.

And our prayers shall join with yours to draw down an answering message of love and consolation from those who watch on high, in anxious expectation of the spread of Divine Truth. We have answered so much of your objection as relates to the general outcome of the movement at large. We have shown you that deep down below the surface there is a something which does not meet the eye. As in the days of the development of the knowledge of God, in whatever age it may occur, there are many silent devotees of whom the world knows little, who grow steadily up to more and more perfect knowledge, so we have told you it is now. Many there are, very many, who deplore the unlicensed vagaries which shock and distress them, but which have no power to alter or diminish the faith which is founded on experience.

We would further point out to you that all our intercourse with the material plane is governed by laws which your science has not yet defined. Neither we nor you know as yet many of the causes which interfere with our power. We are not able to lay down laws for your guidance, scarce even for our own. With you the vast importance of the subject is little appreciated even by those who interest themselves in our work. In many cases sentiments of mere curiosity predominate. With some, even lower motives obtain. No proper care is taken of our mediums. The instrument is out of tune, unstrung, or overworked. The atmospheric conditions vary. We know not always how to meet the various effects so caused. Circles are not properly composed; and many things combine to make it impossible that phenomena should always be similar in their nature, or be evoked with precise regularity.

This will account for much of the erratic character of the phenomena, as well as for the influence which is exercised over the curious who obtrude themselves perpetually into communion with the spheres, and attract spirits congenial to themselves. Much might fitly be said on this topic, but other matters press. What has been hinted may suggest to you another reason for dealing mercifully in your estimate of the vagaries of some circles. Nothing now is said of those into which deceit is admitted. There none but the most undeveloped spirits enter, and all is untrustworthy and repellent.

You can do much to aid us. You may help us to crush out idle curiosity and deceit. You know well how, in our own circle, the manifestations have gradually developed as you have followed our advice. You may say to others that they should use the same means. The cloud will in time be blown away. Meantime, the causes which produce it are at least as much in your hands as in ours.

✝ IMPERATOR.

SECTION XV.

[The argument was continued, almost without a break, and with much energy and under powerful influence. I cannot hope to convey any idea of the influence that possessed me, and seemed to inspire my thoughts.]

RELIGIOUS TEACHING OF SPIRITUALISM.

You question whether the tendency of our teaching be not Deism, or pure Theism, or even Atheism. It is indicative of the ignorance which obtains among you, that one usually accurate in thought and well-informed should class Theism with Atheism. We know nothing of that cheerless, futile nonsense which denies the existence of a God whose acts are palpable to all, even to the meanest comprehension amongst the most debased of His creatures. Were it not that we know how man can blind himself, we should refuse to believe that any one could so blunt his senses.

Doubtless we teach that there is one Supreme Being over all: one who is not manifested as man has fancied, but who has always announced to His creatures from time to time such facts about Himself as they are able to comprehend; or, more strictly, has enabled them to develop in their minds truer views of Himself and of His dealings. We tell you, as Jesus told His followers, of a loving, holy, pure God, who guides and governs the universe; who is no impersonal conception of the human mind, but a real spiritual Father; who is no embodiment or personification of a force, but a really-existent Being, albeit known to you only by His operations, and through your conceptions of His nature and attributes. This is what we have spoken to you, eradicating, so far as we have been able, that which in your mind seemed to us to be dishonouring to the All-Wise Father, but leaving undisturbed other theological fancies which are not of special import.

If you say that our teaching tends to show that there is no such thing as absolute truth in such matters, we can but express our thankfulness that we have so far made ourselves intelligible. No doubt there is for you, in your present imperfect state, no such thing as absolute truth, as there is no such thing as absolute perfection. You surely do not expect that your eye can gaze undimmed into mysteries which dazzle the vision of the highest intelligences. Surely you do not hope that your circumscribed mind can grasp the Infinite and Incomprehensible; that which to us in remotest cycles shall still remain a subject of adoring wonder. The suggestion can but be born of ignorance caused by the imperfect state of development in which you now live. For you truth must be variable, not to be grasped in its entirety, not to be viewed in minute detail, but seen only in shadowy outline through an encircling veil. We do not even pretend that we reveal to you absolute truth, seeing that we ourselves are yet ignorant, longing to dive deeper into much that is still mysterious. We do but give you such aid as we are permitted in shadowing forth for yourself conceptions of the Supreme, which are less widely removed from truth than those which have passed current among you as the immediate revelation of the Most High.

We have succeeded in evolving a system of theology which you admit to be coherent, beautiful, and elevated, and which is acceptable to your mind. We have not ventured to do more. We have shown you a God who commands your adoration and respect. We have displayed to you a rational and comprehensible view of your duty to Him, to mankind, and to your own self; and we have established our moral code not by the persuasive inducements of a heaven and hell such as you are wont to hear of, but by arguments not less persuasive, by inducements which do not come home less forcibly to the mind.

To say that we teach a motiveless religion is surely the strangest misconception. What! is it nothing that we teach you that each act in this, the seed-time of your life, will bear its own fruit; that the results of conscious and deliberate sin must be remedied in sorrow and shame at the cost of painful toil in far distant ages; that the erring spirit must gather up the tangled thread and unravel the evil of which it was long ages ago the perpetrator?

Is it nothing that we tell you that words and deeds are as the pebble thrown into the stream which causes an ever-widening ripple, ceaselessly enlarging in its effects; and that fo such influence you are accountable; that every word, every act, is of incalculable import in its results and influence; that the good which your influence produces is to you a source of gratification hereafter, while of the ill you must view the baleful effects in agony and remorse?

Is it nothing that we tell you that reward and punishment are not delayed till a far-off day faintly imagined, after a period of torpor, almost of death, but are instant, immediate, supervening upon sin by the action of an invariable law, and acting ceaselessly until the cause which produced it is removed?

Is this no incentive to a life of sanctity and holiness? Which, say you, is the most potent incentive to a holy life of progress: that creed which we have indicated? or that which teaches that a man may live as seems to him good, may wrong his neighbours, insult his God, and debase his own spirit, may break all laws divine and human, may be loathsome in his moral nature, a blot on the name of man, and then, by a fanatical cry, by a fancied faith, by a momentary operation of the mind, may be fitted to enter into a dreamy heaven, where his sole joy is to be that which his nature would view with distaste, but which, now that the magic change has been effected, is to become the congenial occupation of eternity? Which faith will move the degraded most? To tell him that for each sin, discovered or undiscovered by his fellow, he will have to repent; that each must be remedied, not by another, but by himself; and that no happiness is possible for him till he grows a purer, better, truer *man?* or, to tell him that, do what he will, heaven is open to the vilest reprobate, and that a dying cry when fainting nature is wrung with agony, can magically change his spirit, and send it, after a distant judgment, pure and good, in the immediate presence of his God, in a heaven where his unvarying occupation will be that which he would now regard as most insipid and undesirable?

We know and *you* know which faith is most likely to appeal to a man's reason and judgment; which would be the strongest deterrent from sin; which would keep a wanderer in the paths of rectitude most surely. And yet you say that we preach a vague religion in place of a definite; a colourless gospel in place of one backed by a definite system of reward and punishment. Nay, nay. *We* are they who preach a definite, intelligible, clear system of reward and punishment, but in doing so we do not feign a fabled heaven, a brutal hell, and a human God. You are they who relegate to a far off speck the day of retribution, and encourage the vilest to believe that he may enter into the very presence of the Most High sometime, somewhere, somehow, if he will only assent to statements which he does not understand, which he does not believe, and in the truth of which he feels no sort of real interest.

We boldly assert that we teach a faith which is more calculated to deter from open sin than any yet propounded for man's acceptance; one that holds out to him more rational hopes for his hereafter, one that is to him more real, more comprehensible than any which has yet been put before him. That faith, we say again, is Divine. It comes to you as the revelation of God. We do not expect or wish that it should become current among men until they are fitted to receive it. For that time we wait in patient prayer. When it does spread among men and they can yield its precepts an intelligent obedience, we do not hesitate to say that man will sin less in hope of a cheap salvation; that he will be guided by a more intelligent and intelligible future; that he will need fewer coercive regulations, fewer punishments by human law, and that the motive-spring within him will be found to be not less forcible and enduring than the debased system of heavenly inducements and hellish deterrents which can stand no serious probing, and which, when once rationally examined, ceases to allure or to deter, and crumbles into dust, baseless, irrational, and absurd.

[In answer to my objection that the outcome of Spiritualism was bad in the mass, or, at anyrate, of mixed benefit, it was written, July 10th, 1873]:—

We would speak to you on this point, and endeavour to show you the errors into which you have fallen. You fall, first of all, into a mistake almost inseparable from your circumscribed vision. You mistake the results which obtrude themselves on your notice for the total outcome of the movement. You are as they who are bewildered by the din and outcry of a small sect of enthusiasts, and who mistake them and their vociferations for a mighty power, for the voice of a representative body of opinion; and lo! they heed not the silent power which works deep down below, which is seen only in its results, and is not heard by its much crying. You hear much of a noisy, undisciplined mass, not numerous, indeed, but obtrusive; and you say well that it is not such cries that can regenerate the world. You shrink intellectually from their utterances, and are inclined to question whether this, that is so forbidding, can indeed be of God, and for good. A part only is visible to you, and that part but dimly. Of the hidden silent votaries of a faith which comes to them from the God who is revealing Himself to them in ways which come home to their several necessities, you hear and know nothing. Such are outside of your ken; though they may and do exist all around you, the faithful communers with the spheres, who know in what they have believed, and who drink in, hour by hour, fresh store of grace and knowledge, waiting for the time when they, too, shall be emancipated from the prison-house of the body, and rise to take their part in the glorious work.

And so it chances that, both from the obtrusive crying of the one and from the silence of the other, both from the limited nature of your faculties and from the still more limited opportunities for observation, you take a narrow view, and substitute a part for the whole, representing the great body by that limb which is least fairly a specimen of it. We are disposed to question your conclusion as to any phase of Spiritualism being bad or mischievous in its outcome, while we deny altogether your ability to pronounce any opinion upon the broad question in its ultimate issues.

For what is the real truth? The operations of the Supreme are uniform in this as in all things else. The evil and the good are mingled. He does not use great messengers for that work which can be accomplished by more ordinary spirits. He does not send the high and exalted ones to minister conviction to an undeveloped and earth-bound spirit. Far otherwise: He proportions his causes to the effects which they are intended to produce. In the operation of the ordinary processes of nature, He does not produce insignificant results from gigantic causes. So in this domain of spirit agency. They who are crude in intellect, and undeveloped in aspiration, whose souls do not soar to heights of moral and intellectual grandeur, such are the charge of spirits who know best how to reach and touch them; who proportion their means to the end in view; and who most frequently use material means for operating on an undeveloped intelligence. To the uneducated in mind and soul, the spiritually or intellectually unprogressed, they speak in the language most intelligible to their wants. The physical operation of force that can be gauged by external sense is necessary to assure some—nay, very many, of existence beyond the grave.

Such receive their demonstration, not from the inspiring voices of angels, such as those who in every age have spoken to the inner souls of the man who formed and guided that age, but from spirits like unto themselves, who know their wants, their mental habits and altitudes, and who can supply that proof which will come home to and be acceptable by those to whom they minister. And you require to remember, good friend, that extreme intellectual may co-exist with scarce any spiritual development; even as a progressive spirit may be hampered by the body in which it is confined, or bound down by imperfect mental culture. Not to every soul is the spirit voice audible. Not to every spirit is the same proof made clear. And it is very frequently the case that souls which have been so hampered by superabundance of corporeal or deficiency of mental development, find their spiritual progress in a sphere where those faults are remedied.

For nature is not changed all at once as by a magic wand. Idiosyncrasy is gradually modified and elevated by slow degrees. Hence, to one who has been born with mental faculties in a high state of development, and who has improved them by perpetual culture, the means employed to reach the uneducated and unrefined must needs seem coarse and rude, even as the issues must seem rough and undesirable. The voice is harsh, and the zeal evoked is not according to discretion. The nature is being gradually changed from a blank and cheerless materialism, or a still more hopeless indifferentism, and there springs within them an enthusiasm at the new life which they feel swelling in their souls. They give vent to the joy they feel in tones not cultured but not less real, not pleasing, perhaps, to your critical ear, but not less grateful to the ear of the Good Father than the cry of the returning son who has wandered from his home and disowned his kindred. The voice is real, and that is what He and we regard. We are not scrupulously nice to mark the exact accents in which the cry is syllabled.

So to the spiritually undeveloped the means used to insure conviction are not the voices of the Angels who minister between God and man, for they would cry in vain. Means are used which may lead the spirit to ponder on spiritual things, and guide it to discern them spiritually. Through the agency of material operations the spirit is led up to the spiritual. Such operations you are familiar with, and the time will never come when they will be unnecessary. To some it will always be requisite that such training should be the commencement of their spiritual life. And none can deny the wisdom of adapting means to ends, but those who are unwise and narrow in the view they take. The only danger is in substituting the physical for the spiritual, and resting in it. It is but a means, a valuable and indispensable means to some, which is intended to eventuate in spiritual development.

So, then, to confine ourselves to the more conspicuous example which offends you—the rude, uncultured, undeveloped spirit. Is the voice which cries to Him in tones which sound so harsh, and which produces such results, the voice of evil as you seem to fancy?

With the question of evil we have dealt before and shall deal again; but here we fearlessly say that, save in cases readily discernible, and which bear on their face the marks of their origin, it is not as you fancy.

Evil there is enough, alas! nor will it cease till the adversaries be overthrown, and the victory be complete. We are far from denying or making light of the danger which encompasses us and you; but it is not such as you imagine. Not everything ill-regulated, uncultured, or rude is necessarily bad. Far from it! There is little, very little there that is bad; while evil may lurk where you least suspect it. Those struggling souls, so young in their spiritual life, are learning to know that an existence of infinite progression is before them, and that their progress then depends on their mental, bodily, and spiritual development now. So they try to care for their bodies. In place of grovelling drunkards they become enthusiastic abstainers from intoxicating drinks; and in their zeal they would force the habit upon all. They cannot discern nice shades of difference. And frequently their zeal outruns their discretion. But is the rabid enthusiast, with all his illogical reasonings and his exaggerated utterances offensive to cultured taste, is he a worse man spiritually than was the loutish, loafing sot, whose mind was paralysed with fiery drink, whose body was defiled with sensuality, and whose moral and spiritual progress was utterly checked by habitual intoxication? You know that he is not; that he is alive and awake to what he believes to be his duty; that he is not the hopeless, aimless creature that he was; that he has risen from the dead, a resurrection which causes joy and thankfulness amongst the angels of God. What if his cries lack in logic what they gain in zeal and energy! They are the voice of conviction, the cry of a spirit awaking from the lethargy of death. There is more value, friend, to us and to our God in the one earnest, honest voice of a spirit struggling to make its new-found convictions heard, more to gladden us in our mission, and to cheer us on to renewed exertion than in the conventional, dreamy *dilettante* respectability which will only utter its half convictions in the monotonous drawl of decorous fashion, and will, moreover, be studious to avoid even a whisper that may chance to be unpopular.

You say that popular or vulgar Spiritualism is undesirable; that its utterances are rude, and its tone repellent. We tell you nay. Those who thus forcibly state their convictions in terms not very exact and polished come home to the masses far more than any others could with polite and polished utterance. The rough jagged stone shot from their sling with all the rude energy of assured conviction, is more forcible than the calculated utterance of the most cultured and refined mind, whose words are measured by custom, and toned down to the line of respectable moderation. Because they are rough, they are serviceable; and because they deal with actual physical facts they come home to minds which are incapable of discerning metaphysical distinctions.

In the army of the spirit messengers there are ministers suited to every want. There is for the hard materialist who knows of nought but matter, the spirit that can show him of an invisible force superior to material laws. To the shrinking, timid soul which cares not for great issues, so it can be assured of the welfare of its own loved ones and of reunion with them, there comes the voice of the departed, breathing in recognisable accents, the test needed for conviction, or conveying assurance of reunion and of affectionate intercourse in the hereafter. To the spirit that is best approached through the avenues of the mind by processes of logical argument, there comes the voice that demonstrates external agency, evolves orderly and sequential proof, and builds up by slow degrees an edifice of conviction founded on indisputable fact. Aye, and above all, to those who have passed beyond the alphabet of spiritual agency, and who long to progress further and further into the mysteries which are not penetrable by the eye of sense, to such come teachers who can tell of the deep things of God, and reveal to the aspiring soul richer views of Him and of its destiny. To each there is the suitable-messenger and the appropriate message, even as God has ever adapted his means to the end in view.

Yet once again. Remember that Spiritualism is not, as was the Gospel message of old, a professedly external revelation, coming from the spiritual hierarchy to mankind: proclaimed as a revelation, as a religion, as a means of salvation. It is all this: but it is also other than this. To you, and to such as approach it from your point of view, it is this: but to the lowly and suffering, the sorrow-laden and ignorant, it is other far. It is the assurance of personal expectation of reunion; an individual consolation, of private application first of all. It is, in effect, the bridging over, for divers purposes, of the gulf which separates the world of sense from the world of spirit. With the disembodied as with the incarned, degrees of development differ: and to the undeveloped man comes most readily the spirit who is on his own mental plane. Hence it is that manifestations vary in kind and in degree; and that frequently enough the scum rises to the surface, and prevents you from seeing what is going on beneath.

Could you see, as you now see, the signs which have attended and followed similar movements in other ages of the world, you would not fall into the error of supposing that these signs are exclusively confined to our mission. They are inherent in your human nature, inseparable from anything which deeply stirs the heart of man. They attended the mission of Moses to the Israelites of old, of the Hebrew Prophets, as well as of the Christ. They have appeared at every fresh epoch in the history of man, and they attend the present development of divine knowledge. They are no more a sample of our work than in your political history are the ravings of the excited demagogue evidence of real and influential political opinion.

You must distinguish: and to one who lives in the midst of a great movement, it is not always easy to do so. It will be easier when, in the time to come, you look back upon the struggle which is now seething around you.

We shall have more to say in answer to you.

For the present—Farewell.

+ Imperator.

SECTION XVI.

[As I attempted to put other objections, many of which occurred to me, I was stopped.]

We have something to say by way of summing up what has already been spoken. You do not sufficiently grasp the fact that religion has a very scanty hold on the mass of mankind; nor do you understand the adaptability of what we say to the needs and aspirations of mankind. Or perhaps it is necessary that you be reminded of what you cannot see clearly in your present state, and in the midst of your present associations. You cannot see as we see the carelessness that has crept over men as to the future state. Those who have thought about their future condition have come to know that they can find out nothing about it except that the prevalent notions are vague, foolish, contradictory, and unsatisfying. Their reasoning faculties convince them that the Revelation of God which they are taught to believe to be of plenary inspiration, contains plain marks of human adulteration; that it will not stand the test of sifting such as is applied to works professedly of human origin; and that the priestly fiction that reason is no measure of revelation, that it must be left behind upon the threshold of inquiry, and give place to faith, is a cunningly-planned means of preventing man from discovering the errors and contradictions which throng the pages of that infallible guide which is forced upon him. Those who use the touchstone of reason discover them readily enough: those who do not, betake themselves to the refuge of faith, and become blind devotees, fanatical, bigoted, and irrational; conformed to a groove in which they have been educated, and from which they have not broken loose simply because they have not dared to think.

It would be hard for man to devise a means of cramping the mind and dwarfing the spirit more complete than this persuading a man that he must not think about matters of religion. It is one which paralyses all freedom of thought, and renders it almost impossible for the soul to rise. The spirit is condemned to a hereditary religion, whether suited or not to its wants. It is absolutely without choice as to that which is the food of its real life. That which may have suited a far-off ancestor may be quite unsuited to a struggling spirit that lives in other times from those in which such ideas had force and vitality. And so the spirit's vital nourishment is made a question of birth and locality. It is a matter over which they can exercise no personal control, whether they are to be Christian, Mahommedan, or, as you say, heathen; whether their God is to be the Great Spirit of the Red Indian, or the fetish of the savage; whether his prophet be Christ, or Mahomet, or Confucius; in short, whether their notion of religion be that prevalent in east, west, north, or south; for in all quarters they have evolved for themselves a theology which they teach their children as of binding force, as supremely necessary for salvation.

It is important that you ponder well this matter. The assumption that any one religion, which may commend itself to any one race, in any portion of your globe, has a monopoly of Divine Truth, is a human fiction, born of man's vanity and pride. There is no such monopoly of truth in any system of theology which flourishes or has flourished among men. Each is, in its degree, imperfect; each has its points of truth adapted to the wants of those to whom it was given, or by whom it was evolved. Each has its errors: and none can be commended to those whose habits of thought and whose spiritual necessities are different, as being *the* spiritual food which God has given to man. It is but human frailty to fancy such a thing. Man likes to believe that he is the exclusive possessor of some germ of truth. We smile as we see him hugging himself in the delusion, congratulating himself on the fancied possession, and persuading himself that it is necessary for him to send missionaries far and wide, to bear his nostrum to other lands and other peoples, who do but laugh at his pretensions and deride his claims.

It is, indeed, supremely marvellous to us that your wise men have been and are unable to see that the ray of truth which has shone even unto them, and which they have done their best to obscure, is but one out of many which have been shed by the Sun of Truth on your world. Divine Truth is too clear a light to be tolerated by human eyes. It must be tempered by an earthly medium, conveyed through a human vehicle, and darkened somewhat lest it blind the unaccustomed eye. Only when the body of earth is cast aside, and the spirit soars to higher planes, can it afford to dispense with the interposing medium which has dulled the brightness of the heavenly light.

All races of men have had a beam of this light amongst them. They have received it as best they might, have fostered it or dimmed it according to their development, and have in the end adapted to their different wants that which they were able to receive. None has reason to vaunt itself in exclusive possession, or to make futile efforts to force on others its own view of truth. So long as your world has endured, so long has it been true that the Brahmin, the Mahommedan, the Jew, and the Christian, has had his peculiar light, which he has considered to be his special heritage from heaven. And, as if to make the fallacy more conspicuous, that Church which claims to itself an exclusive possession of Divine Truth, and deems it right to carry the lamp throughout all lands, is most conspicuous for its own manifold divisions. Christendom's divisions, the incoherent fragments into which the Church of Christ is rent, the frenzied bitterness with which each assails other for the pure love of God; these are the best answers to the foolish pretension that Christianity possesses a monopoly of Divine Truth.

But the days are approaching when a new ray of light shall be shed on this mist of human ignorance. This geographical sectarianism shall give place before the enlightenment caused by the spread of the New Revelation, for which mankind is riper than you think. They shall be made to see that each system of religion is a ray of truth from the Central Sun, dimmed, indeed, by man's ignorance, but having within it a a germ of vital truth. Each must see the truth in his neighbour's belief, and learn that best of lessons, to dwell on the good rather than on the evil; to recognise the Divine even through human error, and to acknowledge the godlike even in that which has not commended itself to his own wants hitherto. The time draws nigh when the sublime truths which we are commissioned to proclaim, rational and noble as they are, when viewed from the standpoint of reason, shall wipe away from the face of God's earth the sectarian jealousy and theological bitterness, the anger and ill-will, the rancour and Pharisaic pride which have disgraced the name of religion, and have rendered theology a byeword amongst men. Alas! alas! that that divine science which should tell man of the nature of his God, and in telling should breathe into his soul somewhat of that divine love which emanates from Deity; alas! that it should have become the battle-ground for sects and parties, the arid plain where the pettiest prejudices and the meanest passions may be aired, the barren, cheerless waste, where man may most surely demonstrate his own ignorance of his God, about whose nature and operations he so bitterly disputes!

Theology! it is a bye-word even amongst you. You know how, in the ponderous volumes which contain the records of man's ignorance about his God, may be found the bitterest invective, the most unchristian bitterness, the most unblushing misrepresentation. Theology! it has been the excuse for quenching every holiest instinct, for turning the hand of the foeman against kindred and friends, for burning and torturing and rending the bodies of the saintliest of mankind, for exiling and ostracising those whom the world should have delighted to honour, for subverting man's best instincts and quenching his most natural affections. Aye, and it is still the arena in which man's basest passions vaunt themselves, stalking with head erect and brazen front over all that dares to separate itself from the stereotyped rule. "Avaunt! there is no room for reason where theology holds sway." It is still the cause for most that may make true men to blush, for in its stifling atmosphere free thought gasps, and man becomes an unreasoning puppet.

To such base ends has man degraded the science which should teach him of his God.

We tell you, friend, that the end draws nigh. It shall not be always so. As it was in the days which preceded the coming of the Son of Man, as it has been in the midnight hours which precede every day-dawn from on high, so it is now. The night of ignorance is fast passing away. The shackles which priestcraft has hung around struggling souls shall be knocked off; and in place of fanatical folly, and ignorant Pharisaism, and misty speculation, you shall have a reasonable religion and a Divine Faith. You shall have richer views of God, truer notions of your duty and destiny; you shall know that they whom you call dead are alive amongst you; living, as they lived on earth, only more really; ministering to you with undiminished love; animated in their unwearying intercourse with the same affection which they bore to you whilst they were yet incarned.

It was said of the Christ that he brought life and immortality to light. It is true in a wider sense than the writer meant. The outcome of the Revelation of Christ, which is only now beginning to be seen amongst men, is in its truest sense the abolition of death, the demonstration of immortality. In that great truth—man never dies, cannot die, *however he may wish it*—in that great truth rests the key to the future. The immortality of man, held not as an article of faith, a clause in a creed, but as a piece of personal knowledge and individual experience, this is the key-note of the religion of the future. In its trail come all the grand truths we teach, all the noblest conceptions of duty, the grandest views of destiny, the truest realisations of life.

You cannot grasp them now. They daze and bewilder your spirit, unaccustomed to such a glare. But, mark well, friend brief space shall pass before you recognise in our words the lineaments of truth, the aspect of the divine.

+ IMPERATOR.

SECTION XVII.

[I THINK that all my friends were satisfied that I was too persistent in my objections. I, however, felt that I had no conscientious course open but to do my best to probe to the very depths this strange message that stirred me so violently. I could not satisfy myself: nor could I rest unsatisfied. I recurred to the strife. IMPERATOR'S argument being concluded, I pondered it carefully, and two days after (July 14th, 1873) made a rejoinder on the points which still seemed difficult to me. These referred to—1, Identity; 2, The nature and work of Jesus Christ; 3, External evidence confirmatory of the claims made.—I requested that independent communications should be made through another medium, and expressed my intention of seeking out some medium with a view to getting such authentication. I also traversed the views put forward respecting the teachings in many ways which it is not now important to particularise. My answer expressed fairly my convictions at that time; but I see now that my rejoinders were based upon insufficient knowledge, and they have since been met in many ways; sufficiently, at any rate, to assure me that what remains unanswered will in due time receive its reply. But, at the time, I was very far from being satisfied, and expressed my dissent emphatically. In reply it was written as follows]:—

Friend, your statement has the merit of candour and perspicuity, which you allege that ours lacks. We have no difficulty in seeing your difficulty, though we find it impossible to supply it; and undesirable even if it were possible. If we fail at once to comply with all the conditions which you prescribe, we say again that it is from no lack of desire to afford you every satisfaction. We desire earnestly to bear conviction in upon your mind; but in so doing we must use our own means at our own time. It would be to us most sad, most deplorable, that our work should be marred or delayed by the failure of part of our plans. If it were so we should regret it both on your account and on our own; but we are unable to change the result. We are not omnipotent; and we cannot influence you save by the ordinary processes of argument and evidence which do not now reach your mind. That being so, we recognise the fact that you are not yet prepared to receive our words, and we wait in patience for the time when they shall find an entrance into your mind.

Into most of the questions which you have raised we do not follow you. They have been answered before, so far as it is now desirable to answer them. Nothing that we could now say would add any force to the replies which have been already given. Into matters of opinion it is idle for us to enter. Whether what we say seems to you consistent with what we do or have previously done, is a very small matter. You are not now in the best condition to judge dispassionately on such a matter. Whether the eventual outcome of what you call Spiritualism is what we say, or what you think, is equally beside the point. We view the question from a more extended standpoint, one to which you are not yet able to mount. Your vision is circumscribed, and we see with clearer eye than yours. Whether you consider our teaching to be a legitimate development of Christianity is also of small moment. You admit its moral grandeur, and we need not discuss the meaning of development. Whether you believe it or not, it is teaching of which the world stands in sore need; teaching which it will sooner or later receive with thankfulness, whether you accept it or not; whether or not you receive us, and are prepared to aid us in disseminating it. We had hoped that we had found an instrument suited to our wants. We hope so still; for we know that the phase through which you are now passing is but a transient one, soon to give place to that assured conviction which is born of doubt. But even if it were not so, we must bow to the Almighty fiat, and seek anew for means of carrying on the work which we have in charge. No instrument is necessary to our end; though a good one is desirable. We should deplore greatly that you should put aside what is to you a means of enlightenment and progress. But over the issue we have no power. Should you, in the freedom of your will, decide to do so, we shall bow to the decision, and regret that your mind is not sufficiently developed to accept what we have presented to it.

Any attempt to prove identity by such imposed tests as you have put upon us would be worse than useless.

It would probably end in failure; and would certainly fail to ensure conviction. It may be possible for us to give collateral proofs from time to time. If it be so, we shall gladly avail ourselves of the opportunity; and if your connection with us is prolonged, you will find hereafter that many such proofs are accumulated. But the validity of our claims must rest on some more solid foundation than that. The evidence is not to be built on so shadowy a foundation. It would not stand the test of time. It is on moral grounds that we must appeal to you; and you yourself, we trust, will one day see that the physical is transient and unsatisfactory. For the present your mind is not sufficiently calm to weigh judicially the moral evidence. We are either of God or of the devil. If of God, as our words argue, then we shall not be likely to fabricate a story which, as you say, the world would receive with derision. But if we are, as you incline to think, of evil, then it rests with you to account for a story, which bears on its face the marks of a Divine origin, coming from an evil source. We do not trouble ourselves much on this score. We have no fear that what we have said will, in the end when fairly weighed, be held to be attributable to an evil source. It is to the matter of the message rather than to the character of the messenger that we direct attention.

For ourselves it is a small matter. For God's work and God's truth it is serious. For you and for your future it is of most vital moment. It may be well that you should have time for thought and reflection. The growth of the revelation which has centred round you has been rapid and dazzling. It may be well that you should have time for serious and sober thought before we say more. We think that we may well withdraw for a time, and allow you to be at peace with your thoughts. We do not leave you alone; but rather with guardians more vigilant, and with guides more experienced. It is better, too, for us; for time may decide whether it be possible for us to continue the work begun; or whether precious time has been wasted, and the work must be begun anew. It must in any case be a grievous disappointment that the fruit of so many labours, of so many prayers, should drop untimely to the ground. But we and you must act according to that light which is in us as the guide of our actions. We are responsible in the sight of God for so much as that; and we must see to it that we weigh the issues aright. Our prayers shall be not less frequent nor less earnest than heretofore. We trust that they may be more effectual.

Farewell: and may the Great God guide and direct you.

+ IMPERATOR.

[After this I made several attempts at communication. I also went, as I had intimated, to a medium to whom I was not known. I tried to the best of my power to elicit some information as to my guides, and especially as to the identity of Imperator. The effort was vain. All I got was that the spirit with me was Zoud, a Russian historian. I inquired as soon as I got home by writing, and was told that the statement was false. It was said]:—

We are not able to advise you to place reliance on the statements made. They are not trustworthy. If, contrary to our advice, you place yourself in communication with strange spirits who do not know you, and who are not in harmony with us, you will receive communications which are perplexing and unreliable.

[I remonstrated energetically, and said that it would have been so easy to satisfy my reasonable desire.]

No. We wish to give you every satisfaction; but the chief ordered us not to attend, and we were unable to prevent you from going. You get more harm than you can know from

such experiments in your present state. We urge you very
earnestly to refrain from such sittings in your present state,
lest evil ensue. You require only patience. Impatient
attempts to force matters on do but cause annoyance and distress to all of us. Far better that you rest in peace, and await
the issue. The chief will do what is right, and any premature
steps are mistaken.

*But (I remonstrated) you all seem leagued to bewilder us.
Can you do nothing that I ask?*

Friend, you cannot have the mathematical proof that you
crave. Nor can we give you proof exactly when you wish
for it. Nor would it be good for you if we were able. All
is arranged wisely and well.

> [The spirit who communicated thus is the same who
> gave the earlier messages. I was fain to stop, for
> I could get no satisfaction. On July 24th, some
> questions were put on theological questions, one
> touching the passage, " I and my Father are one "
> (John x. 30). I had insisted, in the course of conversation, that they were incompatible with Imperator's statements. A question was accordingly
> asked, and the explanation given was as follows]:—

The words which you have quoted must be taken in their
context. Jesus was at Jerusalem at the Feast of the Dedication, and the old question was put by the Jews—" If thou be
the Christ, tell us plainly?" They wished for a sign as you
wish for some resolution of your doubts. He referred them,
as we have referred you, to the works and tenor of his teaching, as evidences of its Divine origin. Those, he said, who
were prepared—his "Father's sheep"—heard and answered his
voice. They accepted his mission. The questioners could not
accept, because they could not understand, and were not prepared to believe. The prepared ones heard and followed Jesus
to eternal life, to progress and happiness. Such was the Father's
will, and no man had power to hinder it. They were kept in
the Father's hand, and in the mission which was to regenerate

them and mankind at large, the Father and the Teacher were One—" I and my Father are One."

Such were the claims put forward. The Jews understood them as an assumption of Divine honour, and stoned him. But he justified himself. How? By admitting his Divinity, and defending the claim—I am the Son of God, and I prove it? Nay, verily. But he, the pure, truthful Spirit, over whose transparent sincerity no shadow of duplicity ever passed, he asked, in amazement, for which of his miracles they were about to stone him. For none, his accusers said, but for blasphemously claiming union with the undivided Godhead. Thus challenged, he distinctly put aside the claim. Why, he says, in your own sacred records, the term is applied to many on whom the Spirit was outpoured, "Ye are gods." How then can it be blasphemy to say of Him whom the Father himself hath sanctified and separated for so special a work, He is the Son of God? If you doubt, regard the works I do. There is no claim of Divinity there, but the reverse.

[On July 25th, we had a sitting at which Imperator controlled, and some information was given; but nothing that touched my mental condition. The other members of the circle were not in sympathy with my difficulties, and during the control their questions were answered, and their difficulties solved. My spirit being in abeyance did not affect the conditions. Then a friend of mine, lately passed from earth, was brought, and strong proof of identity, by means of reference to events known only to me and him, was given. Though impressed, I was not satisfied. Then came the vacation, and I left London for Ireland. Then I had curious communications respecting a friend who lay sick in London, but nothing that bore upon the question now at issue. I then went on to Wales, and received on August 24th another message from Imperator, which it is necessary to transcribe. I had endeavoured to elicit answers, and was warned that it was not well for me to do so. My bodily condition was below par, and my mental state was disturbed. I was advised to review the past rather than to attempt to look further into the future.]

Employ yourself in meditating on the past. Think carefully over that which we have been permitted to do for you. Weigh again and again the total outcome of what is before you. Estimate its value, and watch the moral tendency of our words. We do not blame you for doubts which have been the natural outcome of your peculiar frame of mind. It is inevitable that you should weigh and test everything, and your impetuous nature hurries you along too fast, while a mind naturally inclined to doubt conflicts with the two eager impetuosity. Hence your distracted state of mind. Hence the difficulties in your way. We do not blame: we do but point out that such a frame of mind is not that which is best fitted for impartial judgment. It needs that you should curb your impetuous mind, and resist the tendency to form hasty conclusions on the one hand, while you put aside carping criticism, and allow weight to that which we may call the constructive side of our teaching. At present, you dwell too exclusively on the destructive.

And remember, friend, that your doubts and difficulties must, until they are removed, operate as a barrier to our further progress. They have already hindered us much, and caused us to withhold much. This is unavoidable. We urge you, then, to clear your mind once and for ever, by stern exercise of will, of all the mists which now becloud your judgment. This is what we hope for as the result of rest and isolation. It is all important that the circle to whom we communicate should be in perfect harmony. Rising doubts are to us as the fogs of earth which bewilder the traveller, and hinder him on his way. We cannot work in the midst of them. They must be removed. And we do not doubt that an honest and unprejudiced survey of the past will clear them away: as the sun of truth rises on your horizon, they will disperse, and you will be astonished at the prospect that shall dawn upon you.

Be not too eager. If anything seems new and strange to

you, do not therefore reject it. Estimate it according to your light, and, if need be, put it aside to wait for further enlightenment. To the honest and true heart all else will come in God's time. In the end you will arrive at a plane of knowledge, when much that now seems so new and strange will be revealed and explained. Only keep before you the fact that there is much that is new and true of which you now know nothing; many fresh truths to be learned; many old errors to be dissipated. Wait and pray.

✢ IMPERATOR.

SECTION XVIII.

[On Aug. 26, 1873, I had been reading over previous communications, and had thought much about the symbolic nature of spirit utterances. I had wondered whether we erred in being too literal in their interpretation. I put the question, and was told that I was in no fit state for communing. This is one instance out of many where the difficulty of communication was apparent. I was told to refresh myself. The day was rainy, dreary, and comfortless. I was below par, and in a strange place, being from home on a visit. I did as I was bid, and then it was written, at first with pain and slowly, then more easily] :—

The conditions, though still unfavourable, are better. You would be well advised to prepare yourself always, both mentally and bodily, for communion. As we have before said that we cannot operate when the body is overloaded with food, so now we say, that a system depressed and weak is not favourable for our purposes. We do not advocate the depression of the vital powers by neglect of due food any more than we countenance gluttony and drunkenness. We preach the mean in all things where it is knowable. Asceticism and self-indulgence are the extremes which are evil in their results. That is the mean for each which leaves the bodily powers in perfect play whilst it leaves the mental faculties unclouded and unexcited. A clear, active, undepressed yet unexcited mind we ask for, and a body whose powers are vigorous and neither in excess nor defect of their capacity. Each man might do much by the exercise of a judicious self-control, to render himself better fitted both for his work on earth, and also for receiving instruction from those who are sent to minister to him. The habits of daily life are frequently unwise, and lead to a diseased state of body and mind. We lay down no rule beyond the general one of care and moderation. We can only tell what suits individual wants by being brought into personal contact. Each must learn to settle for himself what is best for him.

It is part of our mission to teach the religion of the body as well as of the soul. We proclaim to you, and to all, that the due care of the body is an essential prerequisite to the progress of the soul. So long as spirit is prisoned in the earth body through the avenues of which it finds its expression on the plane of matter, it is essential that you care intelligently for that body, lest it react on the spirit and affect it injuriously. Yet it is only in rare cases that intelligent discrimination is exercised with regard to food and clothing, and the habits of life which have so great an effect on spirit. The artificial state of existence which prevails, the ignorance with respect to all or nearly all that influences health, the vicious habits of excess that are so nearly universal, these are all bars and hindrances to true spiritual life.

Touching the matters on which you question, we remind you that we have many times said that we take the knowledge already existing in the mind, refine and spiritualise it, and build upon it as a foundation, only rejecting that which is noxious and untrue. We deal with old opinions as Jesus dealt with the Jewish law. He apparently abrogated the letter while He gave to the spirit a newer and nobler meaning. We do the same with the opinions and dogmas of modern Christianity as He did with the dicta of the Mosaic law, and the glosses of Pharisaical and Rabbinical orthodoxy. Even as He proclaimed the truth, true for all ages, that the letter might well be dispensed with, so that the spirit were retained; so do we, in words drawn from your own teachings, say to you that the letter kills, but the spirit gives life. Rigid adherence to the strict letter of the law is quite compatible with—nay, usually leads to—neglect of the true spirit. The man who begins by observing scrupulously the minutiæ of the ritual law ends by becoming the proud, arrogant, unlovely Pharisee, whose religion is swallowed up by his theology, and who yet can thank God that he is not like other men.

It is against this insidious form of religion that we wage determined war. Better for each struggling spirit that it should grope unaided after its God, trusting in the end to find Him, though after many wanderings, than that it should be cramped and confined by the trammels of an earth-born orthodoxy, which prescribes the God, as well as the way to reach Him—that way being through a wicket of which it holds the only key—which cramps all natural aspirations, drowns all soaring thoughts, and condemns the free spirit to mere mechanical action without a particle of true spiritual religion in it. Better, we say, anything than this parody on spiritual religion.

Some there are, and they not the noblest of your race, for whom it is essential that deep subjects of religion should be thought out ready to their hand. For them free spiritual thought would mean doubt, indecision, despair, death. They cannot climb the giddy heights where man must gaze into hidden mysteries, and face the unclouded radiance of the Sun of Truth. Not for them the pinnacles which overhang precipices deep down in which lie hid the Eternal Verities. They cannot gaze lest they fall: they cannot endure the ordeal: they must fall back on safer and more beaten paths, where others have walked before, even though the way be tortuous and uncertain. They must be hemmed in between high walls over which they dare not look. They must walk warily, picking their way step by step, and avoiding all inequalities, lest they stumble and fall. And so they fall back on the prescribed dogmas of unyielding orthodoxy. So it has been decided by the wisdom of the Church is the answer of their priests. Doubt is ruin; thought only ends in bewilderment; faith is the only safety. Believe and be saved. Believe not, and be damned. They are not able to receive these things. How should they? They have not yet grasped the fragments of truth that lie on the very threshold of knowledge. How, then, should they enter in and dwell in the penetralia where truth is enshrined in fulness?

Some there are who are not merely unable, but unwilling, to receive or entertain anything which militates against that ancient and received theology which they have learned to consider as the embodiment of Divine truth.

It has sufficed the needs of the saints of Christendom. It has cheered the martyr at the stake, and consoled the dying saint in ages long gone by even as now. It was their fathers' creed. It was the gospel of salvation which they learned from a mother's lips. It is that which they have received as the deposit of the truth, and which they are determined to teach their children, that they in turn may hand on the truth whole and undefiled. And so a feeling of heroic determination comes over them that they will not even touch that which seems to contravene this faith of theirs, consecrated to them by so many associations, and endeared by so many memories. They are, as they fancy, defenders of the faith: and all a martyr's zeal burns within them. They cannot be reached by any influence that we can bring to bear. Nor would we willingly interfere with so comfortable a faith. Were we to make the attempt, we should need to upset from the very foundations the edifice they have reared. We should need to make war on this faith which they love so well, and hew it down with merciless axe. Their Immutable God and their stereotyped religion, changeless and unchangeable, we should need to attack, and show that though God changes not, yet the mind of man does, and that what was sufficient for the past may be, and often is, quite inadequate for the future. We must show them—what they could never see—the progressive march of revelation, the gradual enlightenment of man in proportion to the freedom of his thought and the enormous mass of purely human fiction which they have dignified by the title of Divine Revelation. The task would be vain: and we are not so foolish as to attempt it. They must gain their knowledge in another sphere of being.

Some, again, have never thought about the matter at all. They have a sort of conventional idea about the external profession of religion, because they cannot get on well socially without it. But it is of the slenderest make, and will go into very small compass when not in use. It is indeed but the outside covering, which is not intended for anything but show. So long as it looks well from a distance, it serves the purpose for which they use it. These and such as these are our bitterest opponents. To force them to think about religion is most irksome and annoying to them. The subject is distasteful, tolerated only in its lightest form from sheer necessity. It is the business of priests to settle what is right, they take as much as is necessary on trust. To force them not only to see the flaws in the old faith, but to admire the excellencies in the new, is a double aggravation, involving double trouble. They will have none of it. They cling to the past, and live in it. They are well as they are. Progress they hate. Freedom they know nothing of save in that conventional sense in which it approaches very near to slavery. Free thought to them means scepticism, doubt, atheism, and these all are not respectable. They are social blunders. Progress means something which politically and religiously is horrible to them. They not only shrink from it, but they view it with loathing and contempt. The good old times enshrine their ideal; and in the good old times such things were never heard of. Hence they are manifestly wicked, and to be avoided.

It is, no doubt, plain to you that we have no dealings with these three classes, and with the myriads who lie in between them, enclosed within the poles of inability and unwillingness, or positive aversion. Hereafter you will learn that it does not rest with us to choose in the matter. We cannot reach them even if we would.

We strive to inculcate on all that the way to know God is open and free, and that the man who prefers stagnation to progress is violating one of the first conditions of his being. We say that man has no right to close the road to God, and to lock up the wicket, compelling all to pass through his door. We say again that rigid orthodoxy, dogmatic faith prescribed in human words, inflexible lines within which he who walks not is therefore lost—these are human figments, bonds of man's making to tie down aspiring souls, and pin them to earth. Better, we reiterate, for each struggling spirit to wander forth with no guide but its appointed angel, to pray for itself, to think for itself, to work for itself till the day-dawn of truth rise upon it, than that it should surrender its freedom and accept its religion at the dictation of any. Far, far better that the wanderings should be tortuous and long drawn out, and the creed scant and little satisfying; better that the cold winds should brace it, and the storms of heaven beat upon it, than that it should be cramped within the narrow, choking, airless avenue of human dogmatism, gasping for breath, crying for bread, and fed only with the stones of an ancient creed, the fossilised imaginings of human ignorance. Better, far better, that the shallowest and crudest notions of the Great Father should come to His child direct from spirit to spirit, the Divine inbreathing of Divine truth, than that he should consent to receive the most elaborate theology which fits and suits him not, and dream on in drowsy carelessness through the probation life, only to awake to a bitter consciousness of the falsity of that which he has so heedlessly accepted. Honesty and fearlessness are the search after the first pre-requisites for finding truth. Without these no spirit soars. With these none fail of progress.

We have yet to show you more of this as exemplified in the Life and Example of the Lord Jesus.

We have shown you what to the enlightened mind is the true attitude of the spirit. This fearless thinking out of the way to God by those who are enabled to attempt it, will infallibly lead to what we unceasingly proclaim, a spiritual, refined, and elevated religion, in place of a literal, dogmatic interpretation of the words of your sacred records. For all utterances of spirits through man have a spiritual interpretation as well as a material one which meets the eye. And it is this spiritual interpretation which is entirely missed by a materialistic age. Man has gradually built around the teachings of Jesus a wall of deduction, and speculation, and material comment, similar to that with which the Pharisee had surrounded the Mosaic law. The tendency has increasingly been to do this in proportion as man has lost sight of the spiritual world. And so it has come to pass that we find hard, cold materialism deduced from teachings which were intended to breathe spirituality, and to do away with sensuous ritual.

It is our task to do for Christianity what Jesus did for Judaism. We would take the old forms and spiritualise their meaning, and infuse into them new life. Resurrection rather than abolition is what we desire. We say again, that we do not abolish one jot or one tittle of the teaching which the Christ gave to the world. We do but wipe away man's material glosses, and show you the hidden spiritual meaning which he has missed. We strive to raise you in your daily life more and more from the dominion of the body, and to show you more and more of the mystic symbolism with which spirit life is permeated. They take but a shallow view of our teaching who pin themselves to the letter. We would raise you from the life of the body to that which shall be to you the fit approach to the state disembodied. There is but a glimpse possible as yet; but the time will come when you will be able to see, as we cannot explain to you in your present state, the true dignity of man's higher life even on the earth sphere, and the hidden mysteries with which that life is teeming.

Before you can reach so far you must be content to learn that there is a spiritual meaning underlying everything; that your Bible is full of it; man's interpretations, and definitions, and glosses being but the material husk which enshrines the kernel of divine truth. Were we to throw away this husk the tender kernel would wither and die. So we content ourselves with pointing out, as you can bear and understand, the living verity which underlies the external fact with which you are familiar.

This was the mission of the Christ. He claimed for Himself that fulfilment of the law, not its abolition or abrogation, was His intent. He pointed out the truth which was at the root of the Mosaic commandment. He stripped off the rags of Pharisaical ritual, the glosses of Rabbinical speculation, and laid bare the divine truth that was beneath all, the grand principles divinely inspired which man had well-nigh buried. He was not only a religious but a social reformer; and the grand business of His life was to elevate the people, spirit and body, to expose pretenders, and to strip off the mask of hypocrisy; to take the foot of the despot from the neck of the struggling slave, and to make man free by virtue of that truth which He came from God to declare. "Ye shall know the truth," He told His followers, "and the truth shall make you free: and ye shall be free indeed."

He reasoned of life and death and eternity; of the true nobility and dignity of man's nature; of the way to progressive knowledge of God. He came as the Great Fulfiller of the law; the man who showed, as never man showed before, the end for which the law was given—the amelioration of humanity. He taught men to look into the depths of their hearts, to test their lives, to try their motives, and to weigh all they did by the one ascertained balance—the fruits of life as the test of religion. He told men to be humble, merciful, truthful, pure, self-denying, honest in heart and intent; and He set before them a living example of the life which He preached.

He was the great social reformer, whose object was at least as much to benefit man corporeally, and to reveal to him a salvation from bigotry and selfishness, and narrow-mindedness in this life, as it was to reveal glimpses of a better life in the hereafter. He preached the religion of daily life, the moral progress of the spirit in the path of daily duty forward to a higher knowledge. Repentance for the past, amendment and progress in the future, summed up most of his teaching. He found a world buried in ignorance, at the mercy of an unscrupulous priesthood in matters religious; under the absolute sway of a tyrant in matters political. He taught liberty in both; but liberty without license; the liberty of a responsible spirit with duties to God and to itself; of a spirit corporeally enshrined with a corresponding duty to its brethren in the flesh. He laboured to show the true dignity of man. He would elevate him to the dignity of the truth, the truth which should make him free. He was no respecter of persons. He chose His associates and His apostles from the mean and poor. He lived amongst the common people; of them, with them, in their homes; teaching them simple lessons of truth which they needed and which they could receive. He went but little among those whose eyes were blinded by the mists' of orthodoxy, respectability, or so-called human wisdom. He fired the hearts of His listeners with a yearning for something nobler, better, higher than they yet possessed; and He told them how to get it.

The gospel of humanity is the gospel of Jesus Christ. It is the only gospel that man needs; the only one that can reach his wants and minister to his necessities.

We continue to preach that same evangel. By commission from the same God, by authority and inspiration from the same source, do we come now as apostles of this heaven-sent gospel. We declare truths the same as Jesus taught. We preach His gospel, purified from the glosses and misinterpretations which man has gathered around it. We would spiritualise that which man has hidden under the heap of materialism.

We would bring forth the spirit truth from the grave in which man has buried it, and would tell to the listening souls of men that it lives still; the simple yet grand truth of man's progressive destiny, of God's unceasing care, of Spirit's unslumbering watch over incarnated souls.

The burdens that a dogmatic priesthood has bound upon men's backs, we fling them to the winds; the dogmas which have hampered the soul, and dragged down its aspirations, we tear them asunder, and bid the soul go free. Our mission is the continuation of that old teaching which man has so strangely altered; its source identical; its course parallel; its end the same.

[I inquired whether I rightly understood that the work of teaching, a section of which is under the direction of Imperator, derived its mission from Christ.]

You understand aright. I have before said that I derive my mission, and am influenced in my work, by a spirit who has passed beyond the spheres of work into the higher heaven of contemplation. * * * Jesus Christ is now arranging His plans for the gathering in of His people, for the further revelation of the truth, as well as for the purging away of the erroneous beliefs which have accumulated in the past.

I have heard something of this from other sources. Is this then the return of Christ?

It is the spiritual return. There will be no such physical return as man has dreamed of. This will be the return to His people, by the voice of His Messengers speaking to those whose ears are open; even as He himself said, "He that hath ears to hear, let him hear; he that is able to receive it, let him receive it."

Is this message coming to many?

Yes, to many it is being made known that God is now specially influencing man at this epoch. We may not say more. May the blessing of the Supreme rest on you.

+ IMPERATOR.

SECTION XIX.

[Some reiterated objections of mine, which have been stated before, were finally answered thus (Aug. 31, 1873)]:—

We propose to speak to you on a subject of which we have before treated, but not at large. You have alleged, and it has frequently been said, that the creed we profess and the system of religion which we teach, are vague, shadowy, and impalpable. It has been said that the effect of our teaching is to unsettle men's minds as to the old faith, without providing a new and rational form of belief. Many of these objections we have dealt with separately, but we have not yet attempted to set before you an exhaustive outline of the religion which we desire to see rooted among men. This we propose to do now, so far as it is possible.

We commence with God, the Supreme, All-Wise Ruler of the universe, who is enthroned over all in eternal calm, the Director and Judge of the totality of creation. Before His Majesty we bow in solemn adoration. We have not seen Him, nor do we hope yet to approach His presence. Millions of ages, as you count time, must run their course, and be succeeded by yet again myriads upon myriads ere the perfected spirit—perfected through suffering and experience—can enter into the inner sanctuary to dwell in the presence of the All-pure, All-holy, All-perfect God.

But though we have not seen Him, we know yet more and more of the fathomless perfection of His nature, through a more intimate acquaintance with His works. We know, as you cannot, the power and wisdom, the tenderness and love of the Supreme. We trace it in a thousand ways which you cannot see. We feel it in a thousand forms which never reach your lower earth. And while you, poor mortals, dogmatise as to His essential attributes, and ignorantly frame for yourselves a being like unto yourselves, we are content to feel and to know His power as the operation of a Wise and Loving and All-pervading Intelligence. His government of the universe reveals Him to us as potent, wise, and good. His dealings with ourselves we know to be tender and loving.

The past has been fruitful of mercy and loving-kindness; the present has been instinct with love and tender considerations; into the future we do not pry. We are content to trust it in the hands of One whose power and love we have experienced. And we do not, as curious mortals please themselves with imagining, picture a future which has its origin in our own intelligence, and is disproved by each advancement in knowledge. We trust Him too really to care to speculate. We live for Him and to Him. We strive to learn and do His will, sure that in so doing we shall benefit ourselves and all created beings whom we tend; the while we pay to Him the honour which is His due, and the only homage which His Majesty can accept. We love Him; we worship Him; we adore Him; we obey Him; but we do not question His plans, or pry into His mysteries.

Of man we know more than we are permitted to tell, as yet. We are not charged to gratify curiosity, nor to open out to you views and speculations which would but bewilder your mind. Of the origin of man you may be content to know that the day will come when we shall be able to tell you more certainly of the spiritual nature, its origin and destiny; whence it came and whither it is going. For the present you may know that the theological story of a fall from a state of purity to a state of sin, as usually detailed and accepted, is misleading. Few, perhaps, even of those among you who have pondered on the subject, have not given up all attempts to reconcile with reason so distorted a legend. You may better direct your attention for the present to man's condition as an incarnated spirit, and seek to learn how progressive development, in obedience to the laws which govern him, leads to happiness in the present and advancement in the immediate future. The far off spheres, into which only the refined and purified can enter, you may leave in their seclusion. It is not for mortal eye to gaze into their secrets. Sufficient that you know that they unfold their portals only to the blessed ones, and that you and all may be ranked within them after due preparation and development.

It is more important that we speak of man's duty and work in the earth-life. Man, as you know, is a spirit temporarily enshrined in a body of flesh; a spirit with a spiritual body which is to survive its severance from the earth body, as one of your teachers has inculcated rightly, though he erred in minor particulars. This spiritual body it is the object of your training in this sphere of probation to develop and fit for its life in the sphere of spirit. That life, so far as it concerns you to know, is endless. You cannot grasp what eternity means. Sufficient now that we demonstrate to you enduring existence, and intelligence existing after the death of the physical body.

This Being, temporarily enshrined in the body of earth, we regard as a conscious, responsible intelligence, with duties to perform, with responsibilities, with capacities, with accountability, and with power of progress or retrogression. The incarnated spirit has its conscience, rude frequently and undeveloped, of inherent right and wrong. It has its opportunities of development, its degrees of probation, its phases of training, and its helps in progression if it will use them. Of these we have spoken before, and shall say more hereafter. For the present we tell you of man's duty in the sphere of probation.

Man, as a responsible spiritual being, has duties which concern himself, his fellow-man, and his God.

Your teachers have sufficiently outlined the moral code which affects man's spirit, so far as their knowledge has extended, and has been communicable to you. But beside and beyond what they have taught you lies a wide domain. The influence of spirit upon spirit is only now beginning to be recognised among men; yet therein lie some of the mightiest helps and bars to human progress. Of this, too, you will learn more hereafter; but for the present we may sum up man's highest duty as a spiritual entity in the word PROGRESS —in knowledge of himself, and of all that makes for spiritual development. The duty of man considered as an intellectual being, possessed of mind and intelligence, is summed up in the word CULTURE in all its infinite ramifications; not in one direction only, but in all; not for earthly aims alone, but for the grand purpose of developing the faculties which are to be perpetuated in endless development. Man's duty to himself as a spirit incarnated in a body of flesh is PURITY in thought, word, and act. In these three words, Progress, Culture, Purity, we roughly sum up man's duty to himself as a spiritual, an intellectual, and a corporeal being.

Respecting the duty which man owes to the race of which he is a unit, to the community of which he is a member, we strive again to crystallise into one word the central idea which should animate him. That word is CHARITY. Tolerance for divergence of opinion; charitable construction of doubtful words and deeds; kindliness in intercourse; readiness to help, without desire for recompense; courtesy and gentleness of demeanour; patience under misrepresentation; honesty and integrity of purpose, tempered by loving-kindness and forbearance; sympathy with sorrow; mercy, pity, and tenderness of heart; respect for authority in its sphere, and respect for the rights of the weak and frail: these and kindred qualities, which are the very essence of the Christ-like character, we sum up in the one word Charity, or Active Love.

As to the relation between man and his God, it should be that which befits the approach of a being in one of the lowest stages of existence to the Fountain of Uncreated Light, to the great Author and Father of all. The befitting attitude of spirit before God is typified for you in the language of your sacred records when it is said that the exalted ones veil their faces with their wings as they bow before His throne. This in a figure symbolises the REVERENCE and ADORATION which best become the spirit of man. Reverence and awe, not slavish fear. Adoring worship, not cowering, prostrate dread. Mindful of the vast distance that must separate God from man, and of the intermediary agencies which minister between the Most High and His children, man should not seek to intrude himself into the presence of the Supreme, least of all should he obtrude his curiosity, and seek to pry into mysteries which are too deep for angel-minds to grasp. REVERENCE, ADORATION, LOVE; these are the qualities that adorn a spirit in its relation to its God.

Such, in vaguest outline, are the duties which man owes to himself, to his fellow, and to his God. They may be filled in by future knowledge; but you will find that they include within them those qualities which fit a man for progress in knowledge, and render him a good citizen, and a model for imitation in all the walks of life. If there be nothing said of that external and formal duty which is made so much of by the Pharisaic mind, both now and heretofore, it is not that we do not recognise the importance of external acts. So long as man is a physical being, physical acts will be of importance. It is because we have no fear that sufficient importance will not be attached to them that we have not dwelt on this side of the question. We are concerned rather with spirit, and with the hidden spring, by which, if it be working aright, the external acts will be duly done. We carry throughout the principle on which we have always dealt with you, of referring you back to that which is your true self, and of urging you to consider all you do as the outcome and external manifestation of an internal spirit, which, when you leave this sphere, will determine your future condition of existence. This is the true wisdom; and in so far as you recognise the spirit that animates everything, that is the soul of all, the life and reality which underlies Nature and Humanity, in all their several manifestations, are you actuated by true wisdom. This being the duty of man in such sort as we are now able to put it before you, we have now to deal with the results of the discharge of that duty, or its neglect. He who fulfils it according to his ability, with honesty and sincerity of purpose, and with a single desire to discharge it aright, earns his legitimate reward in happiness and progress. We say progress, because man is apt to lose sight of this enduring fact, that in progress man's spirit finds its truest happiness. Content is, in the pure soul, only retrospective. It cannot rest in that which is past; at best it views the achievements of the bygone days only as incentives to further progress. Its attitude to the past is one of content, to the future, of hope and expectation of further development. That soul which shall slumber in satisfaction, and fancy that it has achieved its goal, is deluded, and in peril of retrogression. The true attitude of the spirit is one of striving earnestly in the hope of reaching a higher position than that which it has attained. In perpetually progressing it finds its truest happiness. There is no finality; none, none, none!

And this applies not only to the fragment of existence which you call life, but to the totality of being. Yea; even the deeds done in the body have their issue in the life disembodied. Their outcome is not bounded by the barrier which you call death. Far otherwise; for the condition of the spirit at its inception of its real life is determined by the outcome of its bodily acts. The spirit which has been slothful or impure gravitates necessarily to its congenial sphere, and commences there a period of probation which has for its object the purification of the spirit from the accumulated habits of its earth-life; the remedying in remorse and shame of the evil done; and the gradual rising of itself to a higher state to that which each process of purification has been a step. This is the punishment of transgression, not an arbitrary doom inflicted to all eternity by an angry God, but the inevitable doom of remorse and repentance and retribution, which results invariably from conscious sin. This is the lash of punishment, but it is not laid on by a vengeful Deity; a loving Father leads his child to see and remedy his fault.

Similarly, reward is no sensuous ease in a heaven of eternal rest; no fabled psalm-singing around the great white throne, whereon sits the GOD; no listless, dreamy idleness, cheaply gained by cries for pity, or by fancied faith; none of these, but the consciousness of duty done, of progress made, and of capacity for progress increased; of love to God and man fostered, and the jewel of truth and honesty preserved. This is the spirit's reward, and it must be gained before it can be enjoyed. It comes as the rest after toil, as the food to the hungry, as the draught to the parched, as the pulsation of delight when the wanderer sights his home. But it is only the toil-worn, the travel-stained, the hungry, the parched traveller who can enter into the full zest. And it is not with us the reward of indolent, sensuous content. It is the gratification which has been earned, and which is but an additional spur to future progress.

In all this you will see that we have dealt with man as a living intelligence, alone in his responsibilities, and alone in his struggles. We have not thought it necessary here to touch upon the aid ministered by guardian spirits, nor upon the impulses and impressions which flow in upon the receptive soul. We are concerned now with that phase of man's existence which is open to your inspection, and which is manifested to your eye. Neither have we made any mention of a boundless store of merit laid up for him by the death of the sinless Son of God, or of the Co-equal Partner of the Throne of Deity —a store on which he may draw at will to make up for his own shortcomings. We have not spoken of such an atonement of magical potency and universal application in answer to a cry of faith. Nor have we told you that a death-bed repentance has power to obtain for man—base, evil, grovelling animal as he may be—an entrance into the very society of God and the blessed ones, by the charm of imputed righteousness bought by vicarious suffering. We have not pointed to any such conception of a debased and foolish imagination. Man has helps, powerful, near, always available. But he has no reserve fund of merit on which he can draw at large at the close of a lifetime of debauchery, sensuality, and crime, when he has drunk to the very dregs the cup of physical enjoyment, and so go straight to the holy of holies and the sanctuary of God. He has no vicarious sacrifice on whom he can call to suffer in his stead when his coward heart is wrung with fear at the prospect of dissolution, and his base spirit trembles at the prospect which remorse conjures up. Not for such base uses would any of the messengers come; not to such would the ministers bring consolation. They would let the coward feel his danger, if perchance he may see and repent him of his sin. They would let the lash be laid on, knowing that so only can the hard heart be made to feel. Yet for such, your teachers tell you, the Son of God came down, and died! Such are the choicest recipients of mercy! the most appropriate subjects for divine compassion!

No such fable finds a place in our knowledge. We know of no store of merit save that which man lays up for himself by slow and laborious processes. We know of no entrance to the spheres of bliss save by the path which the blessed themselves have trod; no magical incantation by which the sinner may be transformed into the saint, and the hardened reprobate, the debased sensualist, the purely physical animal become spiritualised, refined, glorified, and fitted for what you call heaven. Far from us such blasphemous imaginations.

And while man feigns for himself such ignorant and impossible fancies, he neglects or ignores those helps and protections which encircle him all around. We have no power, indeed, to work out for man the salvation which he must work out for himself; but we are able to aid, to comfort, and to support. Appointed by a loving God to minister, each in our several spheres, to those who need it, we find our power curtailed, and our efforts mocked at by those who have become too gross to recognise spirit-power, and too earthy to aspire to spiritual things. These helps man has ever round about him; helps which he may draw to himself by the mighty engine of prayer, and knit to him by frequent communion with them.

Ah! you little know what power you neglect when you omit to foster, by perpetual prayer, communion with the spirits, holy, pure, and good, who are ready to stand by and assist you. Praise, which attunes the soul to God, and prayer, which moves the spirit agencies—these are engines ever ready to man's service. And yet he passes them idly by, and makes his hopes of future bliss rest on a faith, on a creed, on an assent, on a vicarious store of merit, on any shadowy, baseless figment rather than on fact.

We attach little importance to individual belief: *that* is altered soon enough by extended knowledge. The creed which has been fought over with angry vehemence during the years of an earth lifetime is surrendered by the enfranchised spirit without a murmur. The fancies of a lifetime on earth are dissipated like a cloud by the sunlight of the spheres. We care little for a creed, so it be honestly held and humbly professed; but we care much for acts. We ask not what has such an one *believed*, but what has he *done?* For we know that by deeds, habits, tempers, characters are formed, and the condition of spirit is decided. Those characters and habits, too, we know are only to be changed after long and laborious processes; and so it is to acts rather than words, to deeds rather than professions, that we look.

The religion which we teach is one of acts and habits, not of words and fitful faith. We teach religion of body and religion of soul; a religion pure, progressive, and true; one that aims at no finality, but leads its votary higher and higher through the ages, until the dross of earth is purged away, the spiritual nature is refined and sublimated, and the perfected spirit—perfected through suffering, and toil and experience—is presented in glorified purity before the very footstool of its God. In this religion you will find no place for sloth and carelessness. The note of spirit-teaching is earnestness and zeal. In it you will find no shirking of the consequences of acts. Such shirking is impossible. Sin carries with it its own punishment. Nor will you find a convenient substitute on whose shoulders you may bind the burdens which you have prepared. Your own back must bear them, and your own spirit groan under their weight. Neither will you find encouragement to live a life of animal sensuality and brutish selfishness, in the hope that an orthodox belief will hide your debased life, and that faith will throw a veil over impurity. You will find the creed taught by us is that acts and habits are of more moment than creeds and faith; and you will discover that that flimsy veil is rent aside with stern hand, leaving the foul life laid bare, and the poor spirit naked and open to the eye of all who gaze upon it. Nor will you find any hope that after all you may get a cheap reprieve—that God is merciful, and will not be severe to mark your sins. Those human imaginings pale in the light of truth. You will gain mercy when you have deserved it; or rather repentance and amendment, purity and sincerity, truth and progress will bring their own reward. You will not then require either mercy or pity.

This is the religion of body and spirit which we proclaim. It is of God, and the days draw nigh when man shall know it.

✝ IMPERATOR.

SECTION XX.

[At this time many communications were made to me from various sources with the avowed purpose of accumulating evidence and producing conviction in my mind. One of these was a well-known person with whom I had been acquainted. I asked permission to bring the fact of his communicating under the notice of his relatives. It was replied]:—

It is impossible and unwise to attempt it. They know not of the truth of spirit communion, nor could we manifest to them. Were you to tell them, they would receive your word as the idle tale of a madman. You would not be able to reach them. This is one of the sore trials of those who endeavour to communicate with the world which they have lately quitted. Usually they cannot reach personal friends. The very anxiety with which they strive, prevents the realisation of their wishes. It seems to them so important, so desirable, that personal evidence should be given to their friends, that their very eagerness, coupled with the sorrowing tearfulness of their friends, places an impassable barrier between them. It is not till the eagerness is past, and they have soared above the atmosphere of personal feeling, that they are able to reach your sphere. You will know more of this hereafter.

Our friend who now communicates is shut off from those who were united to him by ties of kindred. Any attempt to force on them knowledge for which they are unprepared, would be mischievous and fruitless. This is one of the unalterable laws with which we have no power to interfere, we can no more force on men a knowledge for which they are unfit than you can explain to a child the deep mysteries of science into which your sages gaze with wonder. Nay, less, the child would not understand, indeed, but he would not be injured. We, on the contrary, should retard, by unconscious forcing, the end we have in view, and should injure those whom we would benefit. No such attempt is made by the wise. They see, as you cannot, that if they were able to force on the unprepared advanced knowledge, and to anticipate the orderly working of Divine laws, your world would cease to be a sphere of probation. It would become merely a field for the experiments of any spirits who desired to try their power, and there would be an end to law and order. No such reversal of law would be permitted. Rest assured of that.

. .

[About this same time, my perplexity as to the question of Identity was much increased by the fact that a spirit who had written his name "direct," *i.e.*, without the intervention of any human agency, had spelt it wrongly. Here, apparently, the fault could not be charged on the medium: and I put it strongly that I could not be expected to believe in the identity of a spirit that gave a well-known name which it could not even spell. IMPERATOR replied]:—

We do not desire to argue out the question of identity, but the incident to which you refer is susceptible of a ready explanation. The identity of the spirit was avouched by me, and you have at least found my words to be accurate. The error was committed by the manifesting spirit who wrote. The intelligences who are able to compass the particular manifestation which you call direct writing, and for which you had on this particular occasion expressed a strong wish, are few. Most frequently the actual writing is done by one who is accustomed to manifest in that way, and who acts, as it were, as the amanuensis of the spirits who wish to communicate. In many cases several spirits are concerned. The error which arose in this way through inadvertence, was during the séance corrected in a communication given through the table; but it would seem to have escaped you. It is well that you inquire patiently into seeming errors and contradictions. Many, so inquired into, would be found susceptible of explanation, even as this.

[The disturbed state of my mind now caused our sittings to be disturbed. Phenomena were evolved in a very erratic fashion, violently at times, and with great irregularity. It was said that "the instrument being out of tune, the notes extracted from it were jarring and discordant." Sometimes a sitting would soothe me, but sometimes it would work me up to a pitch of nervous tension, which was extremely painful. It was written on Sept. 30, 1873]:—

Sometimes we are able to quiet and soothe, but not when every nerve is quivering, and the over-wrought system is strained to an extremity of tension. We have little power then, and at best can only save you from the risk you run of being seized upon by undeveloped spirits who are attracted by your state. We urge you not at such times to place yourself in communion with our world. Be wary of the future for many reasons. Your greater development, which is rapid and progressive, will render you more and more amenable to spiritual influence of all kinds. Such spirits will endeavour to approach you, and by sitting you facilitate their entry to the circle. You need fear no evil, but you may have disturbance. It is well for all highly-developed mediums to be chary of sitting in circles where influences other than those which surround them are gathered. Danger always attends such experiments, and your present tone and temper of mind lays you doubly open to assault. Try to bring to the circle a patient and a passive mind. Your evidence will be the more readily attained if you are content so to act.

[I replied that I wished so to do, but that I must estimate everything according to my own reason. I put two or three points which seemed to me to be of crucial importance, far more than the communications given from spirits who had borne great names on earth; and who rather perplexed me than otherwise. I did not think it likely that the world's celebrities would come back for the purpose of giving me little bewildering messages. I asked for good and plentiful evidence of the return of a friend who had lately passed from among us, and who had been most deeply interested in our circle. That seemed to me to be an opportunity which might settle the identity question definitely. And I further asked very earnestly for clear and conclusive statements as to the origin, scope, and issue of the movement, specially as to spirit identity. Assuming the truth of statements already made, I pointed out that it was vitally important that the necessary proofs to withstand scoffing and sceptical criticism should be full and unmistakeable. At present I had no shred of proof of anything beyond the existence of certain phenomena, and the presence of some external intelligence. I could not act on that. Even if I were willing I was not able to go on till doubts which I could not dispel were cleared from my mind. An answer came to me, Oct. 1, 1873] :—

May the blessing of the Allwise rest upon you! If we do not follow you into all the points or discuss all the questions which you have mooted, you must attribute it to the impossibility of giving you complete evidence which shall be satisfactory to you in your present frame of mind. Though we are thankful to recognise in many particulars a fair and candid spirit in your objection, still we cannot fail to know that at the root of them lies mistrust of our statements and want of confidence in our claims. This is painful to us, and, as we feel, unjust. Doubt is sin in none. Intellectual inability to accept certain statements is not matter for blame. But refusal to weigh evidence fairly, and inclination to set up a personal standard of evidence which is fictitious and selfish, may end in grievous consequences, and this is the ground of our complaint. We respect your doubts, and shall rejoice with you when they are removed. But we blame and censure the attitude which makes it well-nigh impossible for us to remove them; which fences you in as with an icy barrier beyond which we cannot pass; which degrades a candid and progressive soul to a state of isolation and retrogression, and binds the spirit to the dark regions of the nether earth. Such temper of mind is the baleful result of evil influence, and, if it be not checked, it may become a permanent bar to progress.

We have not deserved of you that you should receive us in such a spirit, or that all our attempts at communion should be viewed with jealous and suspicious eye. You are fond of comparing the state of the world and the favoured few in Judæa with that which now obtains. We will give you a parallel from the very mouth of Jesus in His answer to those who asked of Him a sign. You know that none was given save one which He Himself selected. We care not now as to the why and wherefore. Perhaps it was impossible : perhaps it was undesirable: perhaps the very attitude of mind precluded the possibility of granting the request. Such is precisely the case with you in this respect. The temper of mind which dictates such arguments as you have addressed to us makes it impossible for us to reply to them in terms pleasing to you. The reasons which presumably operated in the one case now operate in the other. And it should scarcely be necessary to remind you that it was not to the Pharisee, the Sadducee, or the wise in their own conceit, who came to Him seeking to entangle Him in His talk, that Jesus vouchsafed either His words of comfort or His miracles of mercy, but to the humble and the meek, to the poor in spirit, the faithful, earnest souls who were too careful to gather up the blessed truths, and to reap the precious fruit, to care very curiously to inquire in what form it came or under what conditions it was bestowed. It was so throughout His earthly career : and in so doing He did but act as the Father Himself deals with man. The proud, dogmatic, haughty man who informs Omnipotence of what he wants, and murmurs if it be not instantly bestowed, is not the recipient of Divine benediction, but the humble, trustful, prayerful soul, whose cry from the depths of an earnest and loving heart is, "Father, not my will but Thine be done."

This is the law which governs all Divine manifestations. We say nothing now of the identical law which operates amongst you. But we deal thus with you; and we complain that the positive tone of your mind, and the line of dogmatic argument which you have determined to follow, is one that is little fitting in your case. We are compelled, however unwillingly, to visit it with censure. Review the past. Let your mind recur to that phase of your life which you know to have been associated with us. Of the previous care of your guardians extending throughout your life you can have no knowledge yet. The watchful care which developed in you the struggling germ of progress; the tender care of those angel-guards whose watchful protection never failed; the preservations from evil; the guidance in difficulty; the direction in the onward path; the raising of your soul from ignorance and error to knowledge of the truth—this unseen working is to you unknown. But our efforts have not been entirely secret. During the immediate past we have been around and about you day by day. You have known our words and acts; you have received from us constant messages, records of which remain with you. Did a word of ours ever strike your mind as false? Did an act ever seem to you mean, or selfish, or unkind? Have we committed ourselves? Have we spoken to you words that were degrading or foolish? Have we influenced you by wiles which were earthy, by motives that were sordid? Have we led you to a course that is retrogressive? In short, by our fruits if we are judged, has the influence on you been for evil or for good? for God or for His foes? You yourself, are you better or worse for it? more or less ignorant? more or less useful? more or less happy?

We dare any to say of us aught that may reasonably reflect on us, on our acts, or on our teaching. We assert in the face of all who hear that it is God-like, and that our mission is of and from Him.

Nor have we failed to justify our claims by signs following, even as Jesus did and said. We have placed before you a body of convincing evidence to which it would be difficult to add. We have not been chary of complying with your wishes for manifestations of power. Nay, we have even risked doing harm to you in our desire to gratify our friends by the exhibition of the more remarkable manifestations. We have cheerfully granted all requests made to us, when it was possible, and as we, in the exercise of wider wisdom, judged desirable to do so. When we have refused your requests it has been because you have asked impossibilities, or because in your ignorance you have wished for what would do you harm. It is necessary to remind you that we see from a clearer standpoint, and with a more piercing vision than man has yet attained; and we are frequently obliged to refuse requests made in ignorance and folly. But what has been refused, never without good reason, is as a speck to the mountain of evidence which has been given—evidence which is sufficient to prove over and over again the existence of a power external to earth, beneficent in its action, elevating in its operation, and blessed in its issue—a power which can come from none but God, since it is Divine in act and outcome. Yet that power, so proven, so known to you, you distrust, and seriously question the statements which we make to you as to our identity. It is to you, forsooth, a stumbling-block that names which you have exalted should stoop to concern themselves with a Divine Work, under the leadership of Divinely-sent messengers, and designed for the amelioration of man's destiny. And so you refuse credence, and, with daring ignorance, charge on us that we are, or at least may be, impostors, and that we are performing acts of beneficence with a lie in our mouths. This you do though you know that you can devise no reason why we should deceive, no source but God from which we can be derived, no errand but mercy on which we can be sent, no end but man's eternal benefit on which we can be employed.

It is this that constitutes your fault, and we are bound to censure it in you. We tell you that it is in you sin, and that we will have no dealings with you on such terms. We will give no signs so demanded. We have reached the limits beyond which we will not go, and warn you that it is at your own peril that you despise what has been placed before you. We charge you solemnly that you meditate on the past, that you ponder its lessons, weigh its evidence, and pause before you wilfully put aside such a body of teaching, and such a mass of evidence merely for an idea.

More we will not now give. We refuse to be judged as you would judge; and we appeal from yourself blind and foolish, to that calmer and truer self whom we chose originally as the recipient of our teaching. That appeal you must entertain according to the ability and honesty which is in you. By it we stand or fall as regards you. We wish you to decide fairly, and as in the sight of God—not hastily or rashly, but as one who knows the magnitude of the issues, and the vastness of the responsibility of decision.

Meantime seek not for further evidence; it will not be given. We warn you to avoid mixing with other circles. At your risk do you seek communications thus. You will but perplex and bewilder yourself, and render our task more difficult. We will afford you information on points that may arise; and we do not absolutely forbid, though we discourage the meeting of our own circle. We can give no new evidence there, and, if you meet, it must be with a desire for explanation, and for the promotion of harmonious intercourse. We hinted to you long ago that rest and reflection are needful for you. We now enjoin them on you. If our circle *will* meet, we will join them occasionally under certain conditions, which we will tell you of. But we discourage any such meetings. You will not be left alone; rather you will be doubly guarded. We leave you with our blessing, and we guard you with our prayers. May the All-wise guide you! May He direct you, for you cannot direct yourself.

✚ Imperator.

SECTION XXI.

[During this time my state was such as to preclude any sort of manifestation that could bring satisfaction to my mind. I was powerfully influenced, and all my endeavours could not bring me any satisfaction. I was forced to recur to the past, and to try and gain some coherent view of what had been said. Though I did not in the least realise what was going on in me, I can see now that this was part of the educational process to which I was being subjected. I was compelled to traverse the past again and again, to review the arguments from every possible standpoint, and to tear them to pieces again. I hardly rested day or night so vehement was the influence that dominated me. Only when at work, with which I never suffered anything to interfere, was my mind occupied with any other subject. I made a stern rule, which has never been broken in these ten years, that I would always do my daily work before I permitted myself to think on these engrossing subjects. When I did turn to them, the mind was absolutely filled by them.

As the result of all my pondering I came to the conclusion that no good end could be served by reiterating objections which I was far from considering that IMPERATOR had met. I regarded his reply as a piece of special pleading. I never denied the claims put forward by him, and he ignored utterly what seemed to me of the last importance. I considered that I had a complete right to require proof which should satisfy my own judgment as to identity, and which should establish in my mind a conviction that I was not the sport of my own fancy, or of a delusion, or of an organised attempt to deceive. So I simply stated again what my difficulty was, saying that it had not been met, and that a threat of withdrawal only made matters worse. I professed my readiness to wait, to review what had been said, and to hear and weigh anything that might be added. But I stated firmly that I could go no step further until my judgment was satisfied. I pointed out that vague denunciation was not with us considered to be reply, and that a frame of mind such as mine was not fairly described in terms that had been used. Moreover, I submitted that to tell me that Jesus Christ refused all tests save those of His own choosing—while undoubtedly a strong point—was perhaps a dangerous argument to advance. As to the threat of withdrawal, I said that it would only be to leave me in my present state of uncertainty, not to say of disbelief, and its result must be to cause me to throw over the whole matter as a tangled web which I could not unravel: which might be useful if one could disentangle it, but which might be useless and unprofitable, and which probably was not worth the trouble. The answer came at once]:—

Friend, we have weighed what you say, and we are disposed to recognise the cogency of your reply. We did not intend in the words which we felt constrained to employ to censure your desire for information, but rather the attitude of mind which seemed to prescribe to us conditions with which we felt ourselves unable to comply. And we intended to convey forcibly to your mind the impression which was made upon us by constant opposition, or at least by the perpetual presence in your mind of anxiety and mistrust. Such inharmonious conditions hamper us. We have a mission to discharge, and we are not content to wait and waste precious time and opportunity. We have a work to do, and it must be done; if not through this circle of friends, then through others. And we did but state our intention of withdrawing from you because we accepted your own statement that it was impossible for you to go forward until we had complied with your conditions. We could not do so, and felt the necessity of withdrawal. We have no wish to break the connection we have formed, and to undo the work which has been so laboriously accomplished. It may be that in the future we may influence you more fully. It may be that rest and reflection may help us and you. We urge you to ponder and meditate, and to ask only at rare intervals for communications in circle. Only when an earnest desire for communion exists will we give it. We are not desirous indeed to add anything to what has already been given. The additions to our circle which you speak of are not desirable. Every such addition involves a change of conditions which causes much anxious care and trouble to us, which we do not grudge when there is prospect of advantage. In this case there is not, and we must discourage the scheme.

All attempts at physical experiment with yourself we absolutely forbid. You are certainly unable to bear the strain which such could involve; especially now, you set too much store by mere physical marvels. They are at best subsidiary. And you run risk of injury by sitting in strange circles. We discourage all such attempts. They do but retard progress, and will end in injury and disappointment. Such a course is never beneficial to you; and though we have not interfered to prevent you from joining other circles, we tell you that we must repress such attempts now. If we are to work with you, you must seclude yourself from other influences. This is essential. If you do not, you render yourself so far the worse for our work, and run grave risk of possession by intelligences whom you would avoid, did you know more of the risk you run, and with whom we could have no part. You err in supposing that your power is of value to other spirits in other circles. We prevent that; and you will gain no proofs in that way, nor be of service in helping other mediums; rather the reverse. We cannot allow you to be so used.

For the present we do not enter further into the points raised. Did we not know integrity and truth to govern your mind, we should long since have ceased to take pains which yield so little fruit. Ignorance has caused you to do much that you would not have done had you been wiser. And though our friends have not aided us as we hoped, we have desired to do all we can to benefit them and you. But there is a limit to our power and will in such matters, and we should act unwisely did we attempt to force on you that for which collectively you are not fit. Hereafter it may be done; now we see it is impossible to do more. We shall not attempt fresh efforts. We cannot spend further time and pains on that which, you have convinced us, is useless. Your arguments prove at anyrate that your mind has not grasped the true nature of our work. We are not able, nor indeed are we willing, to comply with the suggested tests which you prescribe. It is not thus that conviction is assured, and God's messengers avouched. Compliance would but cause further demands; and conviction cannot be established by any such material means.

Meditate rather on what has been done. You have put aside what we have laid before you. We do not blame you for honestly rejecting what does not commend itself to you. But this done, we have no alternative. The choice is of eternal import, and you appear to have made it; whether wisely, time will show you; and it may then be possible for you to undo some of the effects of your choice. We would even yet hope that a careful review of your position may induce you to retreat from it.

+ IMPERATOR.

[On the following day, Oct. 4, 1873, the writing was resumed. Some of it is so purely personal that I prefer not to print it. It was couched throughout in terms of great solemnity and commenced with an invocation. The gist of it all was the reiteration of the claims previously made, and the concession of some points which I had insisted on, especially that of the threatened withdrawal. On this point the reply shows such evidence of pure human reason, and is so typical of the logical method in which this Intelligence has always dealt with my arguments, that I print it as it stands, though so personal in its nature. It was written with great clearness and rapidity, and entirely without knowledge on my part of what the substance was until it was complete]:—

I, the servant of God, the minister of the Most High, and the guide and guardian of your spirit, implore upon you the divine benediction. The Holy and Loving Father bless you.

May the influences, invisible but potent, by which you are surrounded be gracious and powerful for your good. It has been strongly urged on us that we should pause before we abandon all our efforts to act further upon you. This has especially been put forward by —— [*a friend recently dead, who had communicated with me very soon after his departure*] whose knowledge of the conditions of belief which beset you is more fresh and vivid than our own. It has been urged that, while our work must be done through others if not through you, still that time should be given for consideration, and that no one who has received the mass of evidence which you have can in the end resist complete conviction of the truth. The point of view from which you see, the mists of prejudice which enshroud even a candid mind, the influences which the adversaries are able to throw around you, the difficulties which must beset attempts at spirit intercourse—all these are points which are to be borne in mind. And while we, knowing as we do the truth and sincerity of all that seems to you dubious, can scarcely grasp your position, we are still hopeful that the earnestness and reality of your doubts will be the measure of the strength of your conviction in the future.

So long as your frame of mind did not surround you with an atmosphere in which we were not able to act upon you, we confined ourselves to replying to your difficulties. But when the circle which we had gathered with such pains and care became so broken as to be useless, and so inharmonious that it was impossible for us to establish a control in most cases, our plans were frustrated, and we were forced to consider if any good could come of further efforts. The constant repetition of physical phenomena was far from our wish. It is not for such purpose that we are with you. And even if it were, we could not use your organism for that mode of manifestation. The daily demand which you make upon your vital power, and the peculiar nature of your bodily strength, constantly fluctuating, preclude any such attempts. It needs a ruder organism on which no other demands are made to safely carry out such experiments. We have indeed successfully communicated to you in this way by writing much that we desired to say. But, after all, we found that a great part of our work was confined to answering your objections, and, as regards our circle, the great end we have in view remained unaccomplished.

It was while we were perplexed and troubled thus that you put forward a demand for certain tests which we found it impossible as well as undesirable to give. We felt that they would but be the prelude to more; and we knew that you had not sufficiently weighed the evidence already given. Moreover, we could, at our own opportunity, supply better proof than that which you ignorantly asked for. So we decided that if you were withdrawn from spirit communion, by the withdrawal of communications, your mind would probably recur to the past, and learn its lessons aright. But we have in view the alternative prospect, which is that we are unable to cut off the power which is in you, though we may refuse to use it; and so that you would run the risk of its being seized upon by others, and deceit and falsehood might find an entry, and our work be utterly set at naught. We dare not ignore this risk. Nor can we refuse to acknowledge that to leave you now might be to allow you to relapse into disbelief. From the habit of pure logical deduction, which in you supersedes intuition to a great extent, it might result that you would cease to believe what had ceased to recur daily. Impressions would fade, and gradually die out.

It seems, then, that patient waiting is the only course that does not present difficulty. We are not able to prophesy results; but we know the two roads that lie before you, and that you will pursue whichever of them your reason chooses. We have no power, even if we had the wish, to force your choice. Its responsibility rests solely on yourself. You may choose well, and your spirit be put on the road to progress and enlightenment; or you may refuse the opportunity, and find that you have thereby consigned yourself to darkness and retrogression in the future. That rests with you. We abate not a jot of our claims: rather do we magnify them. You will know in the future more clearly what they are. For the present, earnest, prayerful, and careful study is due to us, and what we have put before you. Go over the past: weigh its teachings, study its records, draw out in words your conclusions from it. Mark the progress made. Record with minute care the process by which what you admit to be a Divine Creed has been elaborated; and then carry on your mind to the future. Look down the vista of the ages yet to come; reflect that you stand but on the very threshold—that much remains to be eradicated before your spirit can progress—that much has to be cleared away before the building can be raised—that eternity is before you, and that we proffer to you the key of knowledge.

Pause, we implore you, before you reject what comes a second time to none. Rejected, it will be a curse that shall rest like a dark shadow on your soul through the ages. Accepted, it shall be a jewel that shall shine with increasing lustre, brighter and brighter yet through eternity.

Pray rather, pray to the Great Father that He will bless your work, and allow us to guide you still. Pray that your spirit may be raised from the cold, cheerless atmosphere of earth to commune with the bright intelligences that wait to instruct you. Few have been so tended; shall it be that few have so little benefited? Our prayer shall mingle with yours that such may not be, but that you may be protected from influences of ill, bodily and spiritual, and that you may be led on to higher fields of knowledge, and to clearer and more perfect trust.

Father!—Eternal, Infinite, All-wise—we draw near to Thee, and lay before thee our petitions, knowing that Thou dost hear us and wilt answer our prayers. Eternal God, remove from our path the bars and clogs that hinder and hamper us. Loving Father, shed into the doubting heart a beam of light to illumine the dark corners, and to drive out the lurking foe. Mighty Master, bear down to us that consolation which we need in our labour. Great the labour, great must be the love. Great is the work, great must be the power. Grant it, Almighty Power! and to Thee will we render our praises. Before Thee we will testify of our grateful adoration, and to Thee will we bring the free-will offering of our loving homage. Glory and blessing and honour and praise be to Thee from angel and spirit through Thy universe!

+ Imperator.

[The above communication was practically the conclusion of this phase of the argument. I did not feel immediately convinced, but the cessation of argument, and to a great extent of communication of all kinds with the world of spirit, left me free to estimate the past. I could judge more calmly when direct influence was in abeyance, and conviction of the honesty, sincerity, and truth of the communications grew by slow degrees from this date; or rather, perhaps, I should say that faith was perceptibly deepened, and doubt imperceptibly removed.]

SECTION XXII.

[IMPERATOR having been absent, I asked some questions as to the cause, and was told that he had other work, not in this world, which had detained him. He was able, he said, to influence me without actual presence with me, as I should understand the term, but that this required the direction of thought (so to say) to me. Preoccupation would prevent that. And on this and other occasions he spoke of what I may call a meeting of the spirits for solemn adoration, and prayer, and praise, and intercession. More questions elicited amongst other answers the following on Oct. 12, 1873]:—

We had betaken ourselves to prayer and intercession, and had withdrawn for awhile from the cares and anxieties which beset a mission to your nether sphere, into the peaceful seclusion and harmonious atmosphere of the sphere of adoration. It is well that we refresh ourselves at times with rest and the society of the blessed lest we fail and faint in our work; lest we grow sad and weary in spirit, and cease to labour with zeal and success.

Ah! you who in your earth-life have toiled among the lanes and alleys of your crowded cities, who have trodden the haunts of vice in the mission of mercy, who have breathed the stifling air fever, laden and noisome in its impurity; who have watched the scenes of misery and sin, and have felt yourselves powerless to alleviate, much more to remove distress and want—you may know what are the feelings with which we minister amongst you. You have felt sick at heart, or you have pondered over the ignorance and folly and vice which you have no means of removing. You have felt prostrate with association with poverty and crime, and mind and body has wavered under the thankless toil. Yet what do you see and feel compared with what we do? You are apt to think of us as mysterious far-off beings who have no interest in your lives, no knowledge of your miseries, and no share in the troubles that beset you. You do not understand that we can enter into your feelings and know the hidden griefs that vex you, even more really than your fellow man can. You think of us as dissociated from earth, whereas we have very real knowledge alike of its sorrows and its delights. And you fancy that the miseries, physical and spiritual, which crowd around the lives of some are beyond our ken. It is far otherwise. We see far more clearly than you the causes that produce sorrow, the temptations that beset the criminal, the miseries that drive to despair, the hordes of the undeveloped who throng around and tempt to vice and sin.

Our view is not alone of material misery, but of spiritual temptation; not alone of the sorrows that meet the eye of sense, but of the hidden grief of which man knows nothing. Do not fancy that we are unable to see and to know your sorrows and crimes, nor that we can mix with your people, and breathe the atmosphere of your world without drinking in somewhat of its curse.

What is the contrast from your life to that of the outcast in the noisome atmosphere of some foul den in a back alley of your crowded cities—the home of misery and crime—compared with that which strikes cold and chilling on us as we come to your lower spheres! We come from the land of light and purity and beauty, wherein is naught that is unclean, unholy, or impure—from a scene blurred with no disfigurement, where is no shadow of darkness—nothing but radiance and unspotted purity. We leave the society of the perfected, and the atmosphere in which dwells peace; we quit the light and love, the harmony and adoration of the spheres, and we descend to your cold earth, to a clime of darkness and despair—to an atmosphere of repulsion and sorrow—to an air heavy with misery and guilt—to a people disobedient, unbelieving, steeped in materialism, and dead to spirit influence—to a world crowded thick with vice, surrounded by the spirits of the undeveloped, and deaf to the voice of God. We quit the home where God's light and truth prevail, for the outer darkness of your earth, where only the faintest glimmer of spirit-truth from circles rare, and few greets our eyes. Harmony and peace we exchange for turbulence and discord, for war and turmoil; the society of the pure and peaceful for the chilling company of the sceptic and scorner, or even of the drunkard and sensualist, the outcast and the thief. We leave temples where we adore the God of heaven for your nether world, where our God is unknown, and where a being of man's own imagining reigns in His place, save when even that idol has been dethroned, and man has relapsed into absolute disbelief in all spirit and all incorporeal existence.

This we do, only in most cases to find a people who are deaf and dead to us; aye, and even those who do in a measure listen to our words so long as they please them, and coincide with what they have themselves fancied—even they will turn away from following when we would raise them to a higher level and show them a purer light. The story of Jesus is fulfilled again. The people will wonder at miraculous works; they will follow so long as personal interest is excited, and personal curiosity gratified; but when we raise them from that level, when we cut out the egoistic element, and deal with eternal and imperial facts, they turn back—they are not able to receive what is too high for them. And so the designs of God are thwarted, and the benefits which we are commissioned to bestow are cast aside with thanklessness; and the chilling sense of threatened failure is added to our sorrow. So it is; and we withdraw at times for rest and refreshment, and return with some of the harmony of the spheres to cheer and comfort us in the midst of our labours in a cheerless world, and among a thankless people.

[I had not received a communication before which so savoured of pure human weakness, almost of the tone of despair. There had before been a tone of dignity which seemed to be above that of earth. Nothing, indeed, was more striking in the presence and words of IMPERATOR than his absolute superiority to the weaknesses, the petty cares and concerns of earth. He seemed to move, as indeed he did, in another world, and to be at once careless and unconcerned by the things which filled our human gaze. He was superior to them: his views were wide, and concerned with matters of imperial significance. Yet he was always tender and compassionate to our weakness, and quite undisturbed by any gusts of human passion. He was "in the world, but not of it," a visitor from a calmer and more peaceful sphere, bringing with him somewhat of its repose. I remarked the tone of his words, and it was replied]:—

We complain, but we do not faint. Association with you and with your surroundings causes us to imbibe somewhat of the tone of your mind. We have said what we have said that you may know that we sacrifice somewhat, and that we are amenable to the same feelings which sway you. We suffer mental agony and spiritual distress. We feel pangs as real as those which wring the hearts of men. Were we not (as you say) human in our sympathies, we could not enter into your necessities. You will know, too, one day, that by a law as yet unknown to you, the spirit returning to earth takes on much of the pure human tone which it loses when absent. It becomes assimilated to earth and earthly ideas.

[The advice to refrain from seeking too frequent communication, and to ponder the past, was repeated. The production of physical phenomena in excess was said to be dangerous for me, the drain on the vital power being too great. Above all, I was warned not to join mixed circles, except in cases of necessity, as for the observing of phenomena which I wished to describe in print. Moderation in all things was urged, in work as well as other things, and reflection and rest encouraged. We did not omit sitting, but did not meet so frequently as before. It was noticeable that great efforts were made to bring home evidence of identity. One very striking case occurred (Oct. 14) thus: A spirit who had long communicated with us was cross-examined by one of our circle from a book which recorded some facts in his life. The book had lately been published, and no one of us except the questioner had seen it. The names and dates had got jumbled in his head, and it was most striking to find the unseen intelligence correcting every mistake, refusing flatly and persistently to acquiesce in an error and even spelling out words that had been mispronounced.

The sounds made were most expressive of annoyance, irritation, and vexation. The corrections were rapped out with the greatest promptness before a question was complete, and in all cases with literal exactness. It was impossible to doubt that one was dealing with an entity whose individuality was as strong as ever, whose memory was by no means impaired, and who had lost nothing of the energy that characterised him in his embodied state. I refer to that evening the growth in my mind of a strong conviction that the intelligences who communicated were really the persons they pretended to be. The accent of denial was so perfect, the irritable rejoinder and correction were so human, so natural, that I do not believe a personator could have done it, or would have thought of such a subtle trait. On the following morning I questioned on the subject]:—

I was much struck by your corrections last night.

The book was wrong, and imperfect in many ways. I did make acquaintance with —— before he became my pupil, and I told you truly that I studied at Paris.

I don't doubt it. You were evidently in earnest, and quite angry.

It is provoking to me to be questioned wrongly, and from imperfect information imperfectly remembered. I knew what I said.

I can't affect to be sorry; for it brought out the best proof of identity I have had yet. Of course we only value it as such.

Yes. But you watch for an opportunity of entangling.

Oh, no! I only want proof.

You have proof which it would be hard to increase.

[My faith in the information given, and especially in the tests furnished, though what was said was always true, suffered many relapses. I was haunted by a suspicion which, if vague, was none the less real, that what was pretended was not literally true; that the information given did not really come from those whose names were used; that, in short, there was a mystery or an allegory in all, which might be deception, or simply something which I could not understand. This frame of mind, the very worst in which to seek communion with the spheres, caused our circle to be practically broken up. We all saw, I think, the wisdom of discontinuing our sittings, and IMPERATOR strongly urged, and finally enforced, that course upon us. He left us—so far as our sittings were concerned—with an injunction to ponder over the past, and with a very strong warning as to the risk we should run by attempting to join other séances, or to ourselves meet after his withdrawal. The automatic writing continued somewhat fitfully. I made many inquiries as to what was proposed, and the answers I received showed just the same determined will working out its own purpose as I always found in IMPERATOR. The most cogent evidence was given of a clear and decisive intelligence operating in antagonism to my own mind. At no period had I more forcible evidence of external intelligence than now. Elaborate plans were made and carried out, convincing and logical arguments used to defend them, and I was forced to admit the coherence of all.

It was at this time that a long account was written out of the spiritual influence which had been brought to bear upon my whole life. The narrative startled me very much, and renewed my conviction of the sincerity and reality of the intelligence that was dealing with me. Though I am going a long way in laying bare so much that I should prefer to keep secret, I cannot bring myself to print what is of so purely personal a nature. I print personal remarks and details only so far as they tend to throw light upon the general course of teaching and proof of Spirit Identity.]

SECTION XXIII

[On Nov 2, 1873, a question which I proposed to put was set aside, and a communication was made as to the progressive revelation of God in that part of the universal Church of which we have the record in our Bible. I had been told before that this was but one of many collateral revelations]:—

We would speak to you of the revelation of God amongst men in times of old by agencies similar to those which we use now. Throughout the history of which you possess the record in the earlier part of your Bible there stand out noble spirits who, during their bodily lives, shone as lights of truth and progress, and who, when released from the flesh, inspired in their turn those who were to succeed them. Such, in the early days when God was fabled to deal with man more personally than now—such was he whom you know as Melchizedek. He blessed and conveyed to Abram the seal of Divine favour. He was the chosen vehicle of spirit power in a day when man had not cut himself off from belief in spirit intercourse. He was the light shining in darkness, the prophet of God to one section of His people.

And it is well that we warn you here, on the threshold of your enlightenment, that you must learn to discriminate in the ancient records between that which is record of fact and that which is only expression of belief. The writings which give the history of those early days are full of inconsistent statements. They were not, as we assert to you, the compilation of their reputed author, but were compiled from traditional beliefs in a far later age, at a time when history had merged into legend, and much of mere opinion and belief had become stamped with the mark of authenticity. So, though it be most true that fact is embodied in these records, as indeed in the sacred books of other faiths, you must beware how you accord implicit belief to every isolated statement contained in them. Hitherto you have read these stories from a standpoint of unquestioning assent. It is needful now that you study them in a new light—one more profitable, and not less interesting.

God did not associate with man after the anthropomorphic fashion described in Genesis; nor did He personally govern a favoured nation save through His selected instruments.

His dealings with man have been uniform through the ages —intimate in proportion as man cultivates spirituality, remote as his animal nature asserts itself, and he becomes corporeal and material in his instincts.

So, in those now distant days, it was Melchizedek who bore to the chosen Abram the Divine Benediction. He whom Christian and Mahommedan alike have agreed to exalt was not the immediate recipient of spirit guidance as was the Priest-King of Salem. Abram faded from power when he passed from the body, and in the centuries since his incarnation he has been but little concerned in influencing men. It may seem strange that it should be so; but it is so with many a spirit whose name fills a large place in your world's history. The work has been done, and the new work does not bring the spirit in contact with matter. Or, perchance, the work has been badly done, the chosen vessel has lost its perfume, and becomes in spirit-land savourless and useless.

Melchizedek returned again to influence the most powerful reformer your world then had—the leader of the Israelites out of Egypt, and the Lawgiver who framed for them their code and constitution. He was a most powerfully organised and developed instrument of spirit-power. A keen intelligence had been developed in what was then the best school, the esoteric wisdom of the Egyptians. A powerful magnetic will fitted him for the post of ruler; and a powerful band of spirits operated on the Jewish nation through him, and through them on the world. A code of religious observance was perfected, a system of government elaborated, and laws and regulations laid down which were adapted for the specific necessities of a great people in a great crisis of their history. The Jews were then passing through a phase not unlike that which has come to other people in later days—one to which the present age bears some noteworthy points of resemblance; a period of development of knowledge, when old things are passing away, and the creative spirit makes all things new.

Here again beware of false deductions. The laws then given were not meant for all time, as some of your teachers falsely pretend. They were the power of God to that distant age— so much of truth as man could grasp, inspired in the same way, and in no other, as have been all the utterances of truth which the good God permits His messengers to declare to men. They set forth the needed truth that the One Supreme God rules over His people and cares for their well-being. The love due to God and the charity and loving-kindness due to the brother were embodied for a nation which had drunk in the baser forms of Egyptian polytheistic teaching, and had had no part in the inner mysteries where alone truth dwells.

These commandments which have been perpetuated till now, embodied for a changeful age a phase of truth. They contain laws of action which are true in spirit, but not binding in literal exactness on those who have outgrown the necessity for them. They were given by the spirit-guides to Moses on the secluded top of Sinai, above the turmoil of Israel, and removed from the lower influences of earth. They knew then what man has forgotten now—how that perfect isolation is requisite for perfect communing, and that if you would have pure and unadulterated spirit-teaching, it must be communicated to one who has been removed from the mixed influences, the cares and anxieties, the jealousies and disputes which crowd the lower air. So is the message more pure, and so does the medium hear and receive with sincerity and truth.

Moses was to select seventy elders—men of spiritual development, for such alone were then chosen for offices of power —upon whom his own influence was perpetually brought to bear, and who were the channels by which that influence permeated the people. So the code was elaborated and set in operation, and when the great Lawgiver passed from his work on earth he became an exalted spirit whose name is emblazoned for all ages as a benefactor of men.

He, too, in his turn, influenced men after many generations as the inspiring guide of Elijah. We intentionally pass over the other manifestations of spirit-power which occur in other directions, in order that we may preserve intact the grand chain which stretched from Melchizedek to the Christ. Nor do we name more than it is necessary to indicate in order to show you the continuity, and to press on you the fact that these, who had been great workers for God during their lives on earth, did influence man's destinies even after their withdrawal from the body. Many other chains of influence there were, and many other centres from which truth, more or less advanced, was diffused, but you are not concerned with them. That which culminated in Jesus Christ is that with which you are concerned, though we implore you to cast aside that ignorant and selfish sectarianism which would arrogate to itself the sole proprietorship of truth.

Elijah, the great master, the grandest spirit who ever graced the nation of Israel, was in a very high degree the recipient of spiritual guidance from Him who had been the Leader of His people. The traditional reverence for Moses and Elias felt by the Jewish people is shown you in the fable that God buried the body of Moses, while he caught up Elijah in a chariot and horses of fire to the skies where the fancied heaven lay. Such was the reverence felt, that they were fabled to be singular even in death. We need not tell you that no material body was ever translated to lead a corporeal life in the land of spirit. You know that such is but an allegory to indicate the glorious translation of an exalted spirit from a sphere where his work is done, to one where his extended influence is to begin. He left to his successor a two-fold portion of his spirit, not indeed in that Elisha was endued with double virtue, for that was far from being so, but that the glorious results of Elijah's power showed with two-fold force in the days of his successor, who seconded his efforts and carried on his work.

He, too, reappeared in after ages, and exercised his great influence again, and stood, as you know, with his Master side by side with the Christ on the Mount of Transfiguration.

And in the vision of John the Divine, they are again depicted as coming to revisit the earth in still later days.

[I did not at all understand the allusion made to this return in later days when the communication was written, November 2, 1873. It has only been lately that I have been led to refer it to "the two witnesses" mentioned in Revelation xi. 3, etc. Nor should I have noticed this at all, but for a pamphlet on the Apocalypse which some unknown friend sent to me. The pamphlet deals with these witnesses, and their prophesyings, and came to me most opportunely to elucidate what I could not understand.

I asked some questions at the time, and, among others, whether there were not some before Melchizedek who were the recipients of Divine inspiration. It was replied] :—

Assuredly. We commenced with the first link in the chain which culminated with Jesus. In it we left many links unnoticed, and we expressly said that out of it there were many who were recipients of Divine inspiration. Such was Enoch, a highly-gifted spirit. Noah, in like manner, but imperfectly. Deborah was highly favoured, and all they whom history calls Judges of Israel, were chosen for the special reason that they were amenable to spirit-influence. It were long to particularise all, and we shall speak hereafter of other manifestations of spiritual power in the Jewish records. For you will see that we confine ourselves now, first, to the Jewish records ; and, next, to one particular chain in these records.

You said that the ancient records were not to be depended on for literal accuracy. As to the Pentateuch, is it the work of one author?

The Books to which you refer are the compilation of the days of Ezra. They were compiled from more ancient records, which were in danger of being lost, and some parts of which had to be supplied from tradition or memory. The original records of the days previous to Moses did not exist; and the record which you have in Genesis is partly imaginary, partly legendary, and partly the transcript of records. The account of the Creation and the story of the Deluge are legendary. The account of the Egyptian Ruler, Joseph, is transcribed from records. But in no case are the books as they now stand the work of their reputed author. They are the compilation of Ezra and his scribes, and do but embody the conceptions and legends of the period. The accounts which concern the Mosaic law are more exact, because precise records of the code were preserved as sacred books, and from thence the particulars were drawn up. We mention this to avoid at once the necessity of replying to any texts from these books which may be quoted as an argument. The records themselves are not of literal accuracy—in the earlier portions not to be relied on at all, and in the later, only where they refer to that part of the Mosaic record which was preserved.

Imaginary, you say.

It was necessary to supply lost books, and what was drawn up was from memory or legend.

Abraham. You speak slightingly of him.

No; but in comparison with the great spirit, who was to him God's messenger, he was on a lower plane. We do not show man's opinion in all such matters. His name has been widely known; but he has played no great part with us.

The translations of Enoch and Elijah. What were they?

Legendary beliefs. A halo of glory was shed around even the death of those whom men reverenced. In earliest days the man who attracted to himself the reverence of his fellows, and round whose name a certain reverential awe had gathered, was fabled to have been taken to join his God in the heaven for which his life had fitted him. Moses, the mysterious agent of Divine power, the commanding head of his people, was so fabled to be mysteriously removed from earth. He had talked familiarly with the Deity whom he had revealed, and now he was to go to join Him. Elijah, in like manner, the strange, weird, mysterious power, who came and went as with the freedom of air, who seemed to be guided by no human laws, governed by no such restrictions as fence in man's movements —he, too, it was imagined, was translated from earth to heaven in such sort as he had lived. In all cases it was the imaginings concerning an anthropomorphic God and a material heaven that lay at the root of the fancy. We have before told you that man can only receive such ideas about God and heaven as he is fitted to grasp by his spiritual development. In the early days of your world's history man pictured a God who was but an omnipotent man—a man in every respect, with certain qualities superadded, those qualities being such as man would fancy as natural additions to the being with which he was already acquainted. In other words, man took the highest ideal of humanity, and added to it certain qualities; the result he called Deity. In this he was doing only what man has always done. The human conception of Deity must ever be clouded with mortal mist, even as the revelation of God can only come through a mortal medium, and be proportioned to human capacity. This is a natural and invariable consequence of the conditions under which you exist. So, the knowledge of God being progressive, and man having grown in wisdom, he discovers from time to time that his conception of God must be revised. The need is felt, and the additional light is given. (This is the best answer to those among you who fancy that man can learn nothing from us of God and the spirit's life and progress.)

So it is with regard to heaven. You have unlearned much that previous ages have fancied about heaven. And none save the most ignorant would now imagine that a material body could find a home in heaven, as once men thought it could. The time of material heavens, into which mysterious beings who had been deified on earth were translated bodily into the society of an anthropomorphic God, is past. You do not imagine God as an omnipotent, omnipresent man, living in a place where His throne is surrounded by a throng who do nought else but worship and adore, as men would worship were they to see God amongst them on earth. Such a heaven is but a baseless dream. Into spirit-life spirit alone can enter.

You know that you have outgrown the fable of the bodily translation of a material frame somewhere into the skies, there to live as it had lived on earth, in the society of a God who was human in all respects save that He was superhuman, in a heaven which was borrowed from the images of a vision which typified under a symbol spiritual truth to John the Seer. You know that no such God exists. A translation will await each good and true man, but not of his human flesh and bones. His glorified spirit shall rise from the dead and worn-out shroud of flesh that has served its purpose, to a brighter life than man has pictured, in a brighter heaven than human seer has ever imaged.

> *No doubt there are a number of legends which come in the end to be accepted as truth. The difficulty is to know truth from legend, and the danger, to uproot the tares with the wheat. And even a myth may have a very discernible meaning, and embody truth.*

It is so. The legends of which your sacred records are full are in very many cases superstitious beliefs that have centred round great names. There is a nucleus of truth enveloped in a surrounding of myth. We have frequently told you that man has erred greatly in his conceptions of us and of our influence and work. Some causes which have produced this result are beyond his control, others he can govern. He cannot in the childhood of his intellect grasp knowledge which his mind has not the power to comprehend.

That is unavoidable. He cannot picture correctly a condition of life which is utterly different from the state in which he has lived, and with which alone he is acquainted. He must be taught by illustration and analogy. That too is unavoidable. But he heaps together words and ideas which were intended to be figurative, and constructs from them a notion which is incoherent and absurd. Each step of knowledge will lead you to see this more clearly.

Moreover, man has fancied that each revelation of God enshrines permanent truth of universal application, of literal and exact accuracy. He did not see that man is taught by us as man teaches his own children; and accurate definitions of abstract truth do not suit the comprehension of a child. With all the literalness of a child, he accepts the very words of revelation as mathematically and logically accurate, and builds upon them a number of theories, absurd in their nature, and conflicting among themselves. The child accepts the parent's word unhesitatingly, and quotes it as law. It is only later that he learns that he was being taught in parables. Man has dealt with Revelation in the same way. He has assumed literal exactness where there is only Oriental imagery, and mathematical accuracy where he has only a very fallible and frequently legendary record. So he has perpetuated ignorant ideas about a jealous God, and a fiery hell, and a heaven in the skies where the elect are gathered, and a physical resurrection, and a universal assize, and such notions, which belong to the age of childhood and are outgrown by the developed man. The man should put aside the notions of the child, and soar to higher knowledge.

But in place of that legendary belief, primitive superstitions, ignorant fancies, are perpetuated. The hyperbolical visions of an imaginative people are taken for hard fact; and a medley of fancy, folly, and truth is jumbled together, which no reflecting mind on an advanced plane of knowledge can continue to accept as matter of belief. Faith is the cord that has bound together this incoherent mass. We cut that cord, and bid you use your reason to try that which has been received and held by faith alone. You will find much in the mass that is of human invention, dating from the infancy of man's mind. You will reject much that is both cumbersome and profitless. But you will find a residue that commends itself to reason, is attested by your own experience, and is derived from God. You will gather hints of what the good God destines for his creatures. You cannot get more in your present state. Sufficient that you enter on a new phase of being free from the blunders and misconceptions too rife in the present. You will see by degrees that the past is valuable principally for the light which it sheds on the present, and the glimpses which it gives you of the future.

This, as you should know by this, is the purpose of our present work—to lead to purer and less dishonouring views of God, of life, and of progress, than have hitherto obtained among you. To this end we must first point out the errors in your creed, the human figments that have passed current for Divine truth, and the legendary fancies that have become crystallized into history, accepted by faith, but rejected by right reason. We do but require patient and honest thought on your part. Nor think that our work is all destruction. We shall be able to construct when the rubbish is removed. Till then, if we seem to be scattering destruction broadcast, bethink you that we are but gathering the rubbish in heaps, and removing it, preparatory to the erection of a nobler edifice, a holier temple to a Diviner God.

+ IMPERATOR.

SECTION XXIV.

[I asked a question as to that interval of time between the records of the Old and New Testaments of which we have no account in the Bible.]

Of that age you have no record, because the influence of the Spirit was withdrawn save in cases of rare influence rarely exerted. We do not dwell on that, because we wish to point out the grand chain of spiritual influence from Melchizedek to Jesus. Sufficient now that you know that it was a period of darkness and desolation and spiritual dearth, after which we were again enabled to awaken in the minds of men an expectation of dawning light. The first ray of light shot across the world—that portion of it with which alone we are now concerned—when men were led to feel their blindness, and to look onward to a time when the pall should be lifted, and the light should shine again.

It is ever so with the races of men. Though the corporeal may so far assert itself from time to time that the spiritual be to all appearance completely eclipsed, it is not actually so. The period of darkness gives place to dawning light, and the spiritual germ asserts its existence. The spirit-power is renewed, and man awakes to the knowledge of divine truths higher than he had before conceived. It is as with the man who has laid him down to rest, tired with the labours of the day. Darkness has gathered around him; his spirit is chafed and wearied with toil; his body tired and worn. Gloom outer and inner settles on his spirit, and he falls into sleep. Tired nature is restored, the wearied mind is recuperated, and he wakes again to find the bright sun shining with its blessed beams upon him. Elasticity returns to mind and body, and his spirit rejoices in the life and beauty that surround him. The joy of the morning is come.

Even so it is with the spiritual experiences of the generations of mankind. There come epochs when the old spirit-teachings which were so satisfying pall on the understanding. The mind of man wearies itself with questionings. The material side of humanity predominates. Doubts and difficulties creep in, take root, bear fruit. One truth after another is questioned, one fact after another denied, until man feels that the blessed sunlight of Divine truth is being veiled from his eyes. The sun sinks below the spiritual horizon, and the night of inaction, and weariness, and thick darkness begins. The Spirit of God strives not; the night of ignorance and gloomy despair reigns, and the spirit-messengers bide their time, waiting for the moment when the sleeping souls shall stir again and turn towards the light. Sure as that man's spirit is not dead but sleepeth, that moment comes, and in the dawning of the morn the messengers of God sing their anthem of praise to Him who brings light and joy out of darkness and despair.

Such period intervened between the spiritual epoch which closed with the Old Testament record and that when the voice of the forerunner sounded. Such has recurred in days immediately preceding your own. We are directing you to the dawn, and doubt not that it shall be now as ever, that the morning shall be one of increased knowledge, of extended experience, of more assured belief. The morning light shall be stronger and clearer than the twilight that has preceded it. Only wait and watch. Be ready to catch the inspiration lest it fail and pass away, and you turn again to slumber, and the opportunity be lost.

[I inquired whether such a period of darkness invariably followed one epoch of revelation and preceded another.]

It is necessary to be more precise. It is not always a period of darkness, but at times a period of rest and repose after excitement and deep stirring. To borrow again an illustration from your earth. The body needs repose for a period of assimilation. So much of truth has been given as the world can assimilate, and the process goes on till more is needed. The craving precedes the revelation.

Then revelation is more from within—subjective?

The internal craving is correspondent to the external revelation: we have said before that man cannot receive more than he is prepared for. He is gradually led by spirit-guidance to a higher plane of knowledge, and then, when the need is felt, advanced and progressive information is given to him. Those of you who have questioned whether man does not evolve for himself a theoretic or speculative system which comes entirely from within, are not informed as to the operations of the Divine messengers. At the very outset of our information to you we explained that man was only the vehicle of spirit-guidance. What he wrongly imagines to be the evolution of his own mind is in reality the outcome of spirit-teaching which acts through him. Some of your greater minds have wandered near the truth when they have so speculated. Did they but know enough of spirit-teaching to be aware of the influence that acts upon them, they would be far nearer the truth than those who have fancied that their Bible contains a complete and infallible Revelation, to which nothing will ever be added, and from which no scrap may ever be removed as useless. It is not necessary for practical purposes in your life on earth to speculate on the exact correlation between man's mental action and God's revelation. You may easily bewilder yourself by vain attempts to separate the inseparable and to define the indefinable. Sufficient that we tell you that spirit-preparation precedes your knowledge, and enables the progressive mind to evolve for itself higher views of truth, those very views being not the less the very voice of the messenger of truth. And so revelation is correlative with man's needs.

It is to us curious how perpetually man seeks to define his own part in our work. What if we use the readiest means to our hand, and instead of keeping to the sterile work of acting without human agency, influence the mind and mould the thoughts of those whom we influence? Is that a less noble and profitable work than producing some curious phenomenal action apart from human means—as the juggler who astonishes and amuses by apparently inexplicable tricks? We have done enough to show an independent action. Cease to tie down our work by confining it to so narrow a groove, and learn to receive the impressions which we can convey to the mind, and which will be all the more vivid because we find material stored up there. You need not fear that we shall find there anything which will supersede the necessity for our teaching.

> *Scarcely. But I want to keep my own individuality out of the question. And, on wider grounds, many great thinkers have doubted the possibility of Divine revelation at all. They argue that man cannot receive what he cannot understand, and that no external revelation can make a home in his mind which he could not have evolved for himself.*

They are answered in what has been already written. You will see as time goes on how wrong is such conclusion. We do but protest against the mechanical nature of the work to which you would condemn us. Even when you imagine your own mind to be most assuredly acting you err, for there is no such thing with you as independent action. You have always been guided and influenced by us.

> [Some days after the above communication, I asked as to some conclusions to which I had come in reading over the Gospels with the new light which I had received. I seemed to see them in a new light altogether. I wondered whether my conclusions were true, and whether they were new.]

The result is in the main correct. The conclusions are not new. They have been reached long ago by those who have been enabled to cast aside trammels, and pursue truth without clogs and fetters. It has been given to many.

> *Then why cannot I read their works? It would save trouble.*

Better you should arrive by your own paths at the results, which you may then compare with the conclusions of others.

> *You always work so. It seems roundabout. If this be so, why was I allowed to live so long in error?*

We have told you already that you were not fitted to receive truth. Your past life, which has not been so long as you imagine, was a careful preparation for progress. It was in its day useful and progressive, but only as leading you on to higher planes of knowledge. The time will come when you will look back on this too, which now is new and strange, and wonder how it could have seemed to you so startling.

Life, the totality of your being, is progressive throughout; and its early stages are but preparatory to its later development.

Theology was a necessary phase in your training, and we were both unwilling and unable to prevent you from taking erroneous views. Be content to pursue your present path. It has been one of our chiefest difficulties to uproot false dogmas from your mind. It has been a steady work, and now we hope that you may find out much respecting the question of revelation which will enable us to clear away false opinions and infuse true knowledge. We can do little so long as traditional reverence for any mere words, however venerable in their associations, is implanted in your mind. We must wait till you can appreciate at its real value each utterance made through man, whether that utterance be contained in your Bible or not. So long as you reply to our arguments with a text we cannot teach you. Any one who can so reply is beyond reach of reasonable teaching.

There are many points to which you may well direct your mind in the life and teachings of the Christ before we throw upon it the light which we are able to give. Your study of the records of His life may lead you to discuss the question of their reliability, the source from which they were derived, the authority which they claim. You may deal with such questions as these: the account of the incarnation; the atonement, as grounded on the words—first of Jesus, and then of those who spoke in His name; the miracles; the crucifixion and resurrection. You may ponder these points: the teaching of the Christ about man's duty to God and his fellow as compared with ours; Jesus' views on prayer, and those of His followers; the duty of resignation and self-abnegation as put forth by Him and them; charity; pardon on repentance and conversion; heaven and hell; reward and punishment.

On such questions as these you are now prepared to enter

honestly. Prior to this you would have sought only to find a preconceived conclusion. Weigh first the validity of the records. Settle the exact weight to be given to their statements; and then select the teaching of Jesus in such way as you would select the teaching and system of a Socrates, a Plato, or an Aristotle. Translate Eastern hyperbole into sober fact. Estimate the utterances of enthusiasm by calm reason. Cast aside that which is merely legendary, mythical, or traditional, and dare to walk alone, untrammelled by any bonds, and unfettered by dread of any conclusion at which you may arrive. Dare to trust God, and seek for truth. Dare to think soberly, calmly, about revelation.

To such a seeker shall come a knowledge of which he little dreams; a comfort which no creed of tradition can afford. He will know of God and of His truth as none can know who has not trodden the path of personal investigation. He will know of things Divine as the traveller knows of a far-off country when he has himself visited it and lived amongst its people. Round him will centre the ministry of enlightenment, the guidance of the spirits whose mission it is to proclaim truth and progress to mankind. Old prejudices will fall away; old fallacies will shrink from the new light into congenial darkness; and the soul will stand unbound in the presence of Truth. Be of good cheer. Jesus it was who said, "The Truth shall make you free, and you shall be free indeed."

[I said it was worth any cost, if attainable. I was not sanguine, and rather grumbled at being left to grope.]

We do not leave you. We help, but we may not save you from personal labour. You must do your part. When you have laboured, we will direct and guide you to knowledge. Believe us, it is best that you do this. In no other way can you learn the truth. If we told you you would not believe us, nor would you understand. There is much outside of this question of the Christian revelation that you must look to; other Divine words; other spiritual influences; but not yet.

Cease: and may the Blessed One illuminate you!

+ IMPERATOR.

SECTION XXV.

[Following up the investigation into the nature of the Mosaic record with the new light which I had received, I detected plain traces of a gradual evolution of the idea of God, which seemed to point to the conclusion that the Pentateuch was not the work of one author, but a compilation of many legends and traditions. I inquired as to this.]

In the investigation to which you have been directed you have arrived at correct conclusions. We have directed you to it in order that you may see how little reliance is to be placed upon isolated texts taken from books which do but embody the floating legends and traditions of an ancient people, decipherable only by those who had the key. We wish to insist on this point. The amount of credence to be placed in any statement drawn from the ancient books of your religion depends on the nature of the book from which it is taken, and on the specific nature of the utterance itself, as well as on your understanding of its true meaning. It is possible for you to select from your oldest books words which sublimely picture an elevated conception of Deity. It is possible, on the other hand, to select from other and later writings conceptions of God the most dishonouring, the most human, the most repellent. Such are they which represent the Pure and Holy One as wrestling in human form with man; as discussing with a mortal his plans for vengeance on an offending city; as a monster of cruelty and carnage, levelling in gore, and glutted with the blood of his enemies: yea, even as a man who sat at the tent door of his friend and consumed the flesh of a kid and cakes of bread. You may select conceptions the most dissimilar, and no separate utterance can be of more than the individual weight judged by the rules of right reason. And even thus it behoves you to see well that you understand aright the hidden meaning which frequently underlies such passages, lest you wander from truth and err through ignorance.

Inspiration, we again say, is not different in kind in different ages, but only in degree. The words in all cases are the words of the inspiring spirit conveyed through a human medium; and in proportion as the medium is pure and elevated are the utterances trustworthy and the conceptions sublime. The plane of knowledge of the medium is the plane of revelation through him. And we need not say at length that in the world's earlier days—such as those spoken of in the ancient records of the Jews—that plane was low, and these conceptions, save in rare instances, anything but sublime.

Man has progressed in knowledge since the days when he feigned for himself a vacillating, puny God who repented and was grieved at the failure of his plans in man's creation, and who was compelled to undo them as a failure. If you seek for conceptions more sublime and true, you will go to a later age, when man had unlearned somewhat of his folly, and had ceased to be content with a God framed after the devices of a barbarous imagination and an undeveloped mind. The barbarous age could grasp nothing nobler, and accordingly nothing nobler could be revealed. That is in accord with the universal practice, viz., that God's revelation is proportional to man's mental plane. The error has been that you have laboured to perpetuate these foolish and crude views. They have been held by your theologians to be of Divine inspiration, binding for all time. This fallacy we desire utterly to uproot.

Another error even more destructive of truth is the fable that Divine inspiration, plenarily communicated, guided all the writers of all the books of your Bible into absolute truth; and that, as God was in every case the Author, so each individual utterance of each scribe is of paramount as well as permanent authority. This error we have uprooted in your mind, for you now know that God cannot be the Author of contradictions, nor can He have said at one time what He contradicts at another. The light shone through a dark medium, and was distorted in the passage.

In place of these false views we have taught you that inspiration is the control of the inspiring spirit; of various degrees of elevation, perfection, or reliability; to be judged in each case by reason, and to be estimated in precisely such manner as you would criticise and judge works of professedly human source. You will therefore accept no text as an argument. You will deal with these ancient books as you deal with all that is put before you. And in criticising them you will find it necessary to deny much that has been affirmed and believed with respect to them and their contents.

You have asked information respecting the Pentateuch. It is, as we have before hinted, the compilation by Ezra of legends and traditions which had been orally handed down from generation to generation, and which were collected by him to prevent their loss. Some parts of the Pentateuch, especially the early portions of Genesis, are mere legendary speculations collected and arranged by the scribe. Such are the Noachic and Abrahamic legends which exist in collateral forms in the sacred books of other peoples. Such, in another way, are the statements of the book Deuteronomy, which are the direct additions of Ezra's day. For the rest, the compilation was made from previous imperfect collections made in the days of Solomon and Josiah, themselves in turn records of previous legends and traditions which again had a still more remote origin. In no case were they the very words of Moses; nor do they embody truth, save where, in dealing with the law, they draw their information from authentic sources.

We shall dwell hereafter on the notion of God which pervades the early books of your Bible. Sufficient that we now point out that the mythical and legendary sources from which most of them were compiled forbid you to attribute any weight to their historical statements or moral precepts, save when they are confirmed by reasonable evidence from other sources.

> [I found this communication to confirm my own researches. I thought I could trace the two sources—Elohistic and Jehovistic—from which the compiler drew his information: as in the account of the creation, Gen. i., ii. 3, compared with Gen. ii. 4—

iii. 24, and in the seizure of Sarah at Gerar by Abimelech (Gen. xx.), compared with xii. 10-19 and xxvi. 1-11. I inquired if I was right.]

What you have given is but an instance out of many. When you recognise the fact, you will see evidences of it all around you. The documents in question were the legendary sources of the compilation of Ezra's scribes, Elnathan and Joiarib. They were many in number, some compiled in the days of Saul, some even earlier, in the days of the Judges of Israel, and some in the days of Solomon, Hezekiah, and Josiah—crystallisations of the floating legends which had been orally handed down. We have already pointed out to you the true line of inspiration from Melchizedek. All prior to that is untrustworthy: and not all, indeed, that is recorded concerning the lives of the real recipients of spirit-guidance is accurate. But on the whole, the channel of Divine teaching was such as we have said.

[If this was the way in which the Canon of the Old Testament was settled, I inquired how far the case was the same with the Prophecies.]

The books you name were all added and arranged from existing sources by Ezra's authority, save and except those which were afterwards added—those called by the names of Haggai, Zechariah, and Malachi. Haggai was concerned in the compilation of the book Ezra, and he and Malachi finally completed the Old Testament by the addition of the later books. They, with Zechariah, were much in communion, having been the privileged attendants of Daniel when he saw his great vision and received his commission from Gabriel, the Archangel of God, the Chief of the Ministering Angels, and from Michael the Archangel, the Chief of the Hosts of the Lord against the adversaries. Of a surety Daniel the seer was a highly-favoured recipient of Divine inspiration. The great God be thanked for His mercy, and for the manifestation of His power.

Is that the vision recorded in Daniel x.?

That by the banks of the Hiddekel.

The same. Then selections only were chosen from the utterances of the prophets?

Only selections, and they chiefly for some hidden meaning, which does not lie on the surface. As the open vision was about to cease, selections were made from the records of the past, and the canon was closed until the days when the voice of spirit-teaching should sound again amongst men.

You speak of Daniel as a great seer or medium. Do you know if the gift was common?

He was a very favoured recipient of spirit power. Such became more rare as the spiritual age was about to close. But men cultivated the power more then. They valued more and knew more of spirit power and teaching.

Vast masses of trance addresses, visions, and the like, such as those preserved in the Old Testament, must have been lost?

Assuredly. There was no need to preserve them. And many that were preserved are now excluded from your Bible.

[A few days later (November 16th, 1873) I asked that the promised communication about the idea of God might be given.]

We have already spoken in passing of the conception of Deity in your Bible. We desire now to draw out more clearly this fact, that the growth of the idea of God was a gradual one: that the God of Abraham was an inferior conception to the God of Job: that the cardinal truth which we have ever insisted on is manifest in your Bible even as elsewhere, viz., that God's Revelation is correlative with man's spiritual development, and that He is revealed in proportion to man's capacity.

You have but to read, with this idea prominent to your mind, the records of the lives of Abraham, Jacob, Moses, Joshua, David, Ezekiel, Isaiah, Daniel, to see that this is so. In early patriarchial times, God, the Supreme, was adored under many anthropomorphic representations. The God of Abraham, Isaac, and Jacob was superior, in the opinion of those who worshipped him under that title, but *only superior*, to the gods of their neighbours. The father of Abraham, as you know, worshipped strange gods, *i.e.*, gods other than his son's God. Nay, this was invariably the case, each family having its own representative deity by which its members vowed and swore. The name given to the Supreme, Jehovah Elohim, shows you so much as that.

Laban, too, remember, pursued and threatened Jacob for having stolen his gods. And the same patriarch collected on one occasion the images of his household gods, and hid them under an oak tree. Here you see that Jehovah was, as he was constantly called, the God of Abraham, Isaac, and Jacob: not the *One Only God*, but a family deity.

It was only when the children of Israel grew into a nation that the idea gradually enlarged itself to that of the national God of Moses and Joshua. Even the great lawgiver, in his elevated conception of the Supreme, was not entirely emancipated from the notion of a *superior God* ; for he says expressly that there is none like to Jehovah among the gods. And many like sentiments are to be found in the recorded sayings. Indeed, in the commandments given as the very words of the Supreme Himself, it is said that the Israelites should have no other God before Him. Read Joshua's dying address, and you will see in it, too, the notion of a Superior Deity.

It was not until the development of the nation had so far progressed as to make these anthropomorphic notions repulsive, that you find truer ideas of God becoming rife. In the prophetical and poetical books of your Bible you get far nobler conceptions of the Deity than in the earlier portions.

This is assured. God is revealed in your Bible in many forms. Some are noble and elevated, as the books of Job and Daniel. Some are grovelling and mean, as the books which are called historical. In all you see an exemplification of the truth that God is revealed in proportion to man's capacity.

And it was not always a progressive revelation. As master minds stood forth so was the God-idea chastened and refined.

It has ever been so. It was markedly so when Jesus revealed to man His conception of the Supreme. It is so still, as, one by one, exalted spirits have found an aspiring soul to whom they could convey noble ideas of the Great Father, and through them shed forth a brighter beam of truth. Such have stood forth in well-nigh all your generations, and through them from time to time revealings of Deity have been vouchsafed brighter than ever were shed forth before. And an unprepared world has blinked and shielded its eyes from the unwonted glare, and has chosen the gloom, for that it was not prepared for the full radiance of the Divine truth.

> *Handers-on of the courier fire. Yes: it is easy to see in history men who were, as we say, in advance of their age. I suppse the history of the world is a mere record of development, and that man cannot grasp more of truth than his faculties fit him to understand. Otherwise, where would be the eternal growth? At any rate, little enough is known yet.*

It is well that you recognise your own ignorance. It is the first step to progress. You are but now standing in the outmost court, far away from the temple of truth. You must walk round and round, until you know the outer precincts, before you can penetrate the inner courts; and long and laborious efforts must precede and fit you for eventual entrance within the temple. Be content. Wait and pray, and keep yourself in silence and patient watching.

✝ IMPERATOR.

SECTION XXVI.

[Jan. 18, 1874. There had been a considerable lack of communication for some time past, and the work seemed to be passing into another phase, or being quenched by my inability to obtain conviction on matters respecting which I was in doubt. This retarded everything, and caused our sittings as well as these communications to be interrupted.

At this date various changes were made, fresh directions given, and a kind of retrospect written, from which I extract the least personal part.]

It may be well that we review the course of teaching by which we have endeavoured to influence your mind aright. We may at least urge you to go over in detail what has been said, and to survey the broad expanse of truth—such as is suited to your present needs—which we have mapped out for you. You will see that we have preached to you a nobler gospel revealing a diviner God than you had previously conceived. To your objections, again and again reiterated, demanding proofs and tests which it would have been vain to grant, we have replied step by step. And if we have not succeeded in effacing from your mind doubts that have lingered there, it is because the doubting habit of mind has become so natural that we have found only rare intervals during which we could penetrate through the fog. You have wrapped yourself in an impenetrable veil, and it is only now and then that it has been lifted.

We have dealt more successfully with other friends who have witnessed our dealings with you; and we thankfully look on that as proof of final success. We shall in the end prevail even over that sceptical frame of mind which is the hardest to approach. We are most hampered by the impossibility of bringing home evidence to the mind which, however honestly, is unable to accept the grounds on which we work:

more especially since it is in almost all cases impossible for us to grant specified tests imposed by you with great force of will and in total ignorance of the conditions which beset us. This is a fact which you will do well to recognise and bear in mind. The spirit of mistrust and eager desire to entrap and ensnare us by a predetermined test is one which defeats its own end. If we be such as you suspect, it would be well that you have nothing further to do with such emissaries of evil. If that be to you a position you would not assume, then we counsel you to put aside mistrust, and cultivate a feeling of frankness and receptivity. A brief time spent with such a temper would enable us to do far more than many years of such intercourse as your present frame of mind necessitates. It is not, as you imagine, that we will not, but that we cannot help you now. We treasure up, indeed, the reasonable requests of our friends, and if we cannot comply with them literally, we do so in substance at another time. The history of our intercourse with you throughout will attest this. It is, indeed, a general law of spirit-communion.

Moreover, when your demand for a prescribed test, on which your mind is strongly fixed, takes the form of a request for some special information, the answer, if given as you wish, would in most cases be imperfect and unreliable, from the admixture of your own mental action and that of the circle, so that in any case your end would be frustrated. But we have cheerfully done so much as we could. The question on which your mind has been set, that of the identity of spirits, has received more than one illustration of late, and you have been compelled to admit their strength.

We have not done more of late than we have always done, but we instance what has been done as an argument for the wisdom of our advice to you, that both in circle and in your private communion with us you seek to maintain an attitude of perfect passivity, accepting or rejecting what is offered according as reason dictates, and deferring to a convenient time your final judgment. Remember that there are degrees of proof, and that evidence very insignificant in itself may be vastly enhanced by preceding or succeeding facts or arguments.

That which seems to you vague now may be rendered precise by some further point long after; and many proofs extended over long time have a daily added weight. More especially is this the case when the general and special results show unvarying truthfulness in us who speak to you. At least you are not able to allege that we deceive you. Our influence is not for evil; our words are words of truth and soberness. We are the preachers of a Divine gospel, suited to your needs, and elevating to your mind.

It is for you, then, to accept the individual responsibility, from which none may relieve you, of deciding whether, being what we are, we are deceivers in matters of vital and eternal import. Such a conclusion, in the face of all evidence and fair inference, is one which none could accept save a perverted and unbalanced mind, least of all one who knows us as you now do. Ponder our words, and may the All Wise guide us and you.

✝ IMPERATOR.

[From this time forward repeated evidence of individuality perpetuated after bodily death was brought home to me. I do not interrupt the course of the teachings to detail them. Some were written communications, in which peculiarities of handwriting, spelling, and diction were accurately reproduced. Some were verbal communications made through my own guide. Some were laboriously rapped out in the circle. Some were corroborated by my clairvoyant vision. The ways used to convey the information were various, but all agreed in one particular. The facts given were invariably literally and exactly true. In most cases they related to persons not known to us except by name, sometimes not even by so much as that. In other cases they related to friends and acquaintances. This course of evidence continued for a long time; and collaterally I developed a power of clairvoyant vision which rapidly increased, until I was able to see and converse at length with my invisible friends. The inner faculties seemed to be opened, so that the information given received new confirmation from my clairvoyant sight. This power eventually developed to a very high degree. I had a number of extremely vivid visions in which my spirit appeared to act independently of the body. During some of them I was conscious of living and acting among scenes not of this earth; in others dramatic tableaux were enacted before me, the object evidently being to represent some spiritual truth or teaching to me. In two cases only was I able to satisfy myself by collateral evidence of the reality of my vision. I was in deep trance during each occasion, and could not distinguish between the subjective impressions of a dream and the real occurrence of what I so vividly saw before me, save that I could confirm in these two cases what I saw and heard in vision by what I afterwards discovered from external sources. The scene in these cases was real, and I do not doubt that it was so in all. This is not, however, the place to discuss such a point. I do but note these visions as a phase of the development of my spiritual education. It was always represented to me that what was shown to me had a real existence, and that my inner senses were opened for the purpose of instructing me and of confirming my faith in things unseen by the natural eye.

In the month of January, 1874, some communications were printed relative to spiritual influences which were round a son of Dr. Speer's, and which, I was told, influenced his musical powers. These were written out April 14th and September 12th, 1873. Some question which I put on February 1st, 1874, caused more information to be given on the same subject. After some personal information, it was written]:—

The conditions were bad last night for the music. You are yet to learn the conditions under which it may be had. Not until you hear the music of the spheres will you know the true poetry of sound. Music depends, far more than your wise men have dreamed, on these self-same spiritual conditions of which we say so much. The spiritual elements must be in harmonious arrangement before a good development of that which is attainable even on earth can be reached. Only then does the inspiration really flow in. The room in which the boy was rendering the thoughts of the Master was filled with an inharmonious atmosphere; hence we say that the result was inadequate. It is with the musician as with the orator. An harmonious *rapport* must exist with the audience before the words can make their mark. This the speaker feels, though frequently he knows not that his words fall dead because the spirit bond does not exist, and the inspiration cannot run on the mesmeric chain between the orator and his audience. The best results are had when the musician, the orator, is surrounded by a band of spirits who can so dispose his mind as to refine, harmonise, and spiritualise his thoughts, or the thoughts of which he is the interpreter.

Even as there is vast difference between a word coldly slurred or heartlessly spoken, and the same when it syllables the utterance of heart emotion, so is it with music. The body of sound may be there, but the soul may be absent. And, though you know not why, you mark the difference and feel the want. It is cold and trivial, and thin—mere sound; you shudder, and are not content. Again it is full, rich, the soul's voice of melody, speaking thoughts that are born in fairer spheres and purer air than earth's-spirit uttering cry to spirit. The sounds are instinct with soul; they have a language for the most irresponsive. They breathe their message to the spirit, the while they subdue the bodily senses, and harmonise the discordant jarrings of the mind. The dead body of sound is animated with the soul of music. You hear, and are satisfied. It is the whole difference between the body of earth and the spirit that soars to heaven: the gap that separates the material and earthy from the heavenly and spiritual. Hence it is that conditions under which true music is evolved rarely occur, at least on occasions of great public gatherings. It is in more harmonious air that the inarticulate voice of spirit best unfolds its story.

[The communication was signed with the autographs (exact fac-similes) of two well-known composers, as well as by some other names known to me.]

SECTION XXVII.

[I had read something about India as the cradle of races and religions, and something had been said about the subject at one of our meetings. I inquired further.]

What was said is true. India is the source from which is derived much of the religious idea which pervades your faith. From India the chain has been perpetuated through many nations of antiquity. The myths which have centred round the plain truths of revelation owe their origin to India. The Messianic legends date from the earliest days. Men have always pictured to themselves a Saviour of their race, and the best record of your gradual growth is to be found in tracing the early religious history of India. As the study of Indian lore bears much on the scientific aspect of language which you have studied and taught to others, so is the study of the religious aspect of Indian history in the far, dim past, essential for yourself now. Direct your mind to it. We have those with us who can aid you.

India, Persia, Egypt, Greece, Rome, Judea—of these and of God's dealings with them in revealing the Divine Ideal as man has been able to grasp it, it behoves you to know. You must learn how Djeminy and Veda Vyasa were the predecessors of Socrates and Plato. You will be told of this by those who know, and whose earth-life was spent at that epoch. But, first, you must labour to gather up for yourself such knowledge as is stored up. That done you will be guided further.

You must learn, too, from similar sources how that man in every age has felt his need of a Saviour outside of himself, and how the legends that cluster round these Messiahs repeat themselves from time to time. The mythic source from which many a legend sprang you will find in the story of Chrishna, the miraculous son of the pure virgin Devanagny. Hence you will get light on subjects yet dark to you. This is the special information of which we spoke long ago, but which the peculiar attitude of your mind, combined with its black ignorance on these subjects, compelled us to withhold.

We have still much to clear away before we can build safely. There is much in the mere outlines that will be strange to you, and you must be familiarised with them before we can go into detail. You must know that Egypt, Persia, Greece, Rome, the great kingdoms of the world, owed their philosophy and religion very largely to India. Manou, the great Indian reformer and teacher, reappears as the Manes of Egypt, the Minos of Greece, the Moses of Hebrew story. The name is impersonal, and is the appellative "man" in its simplest form. The great pioneers of truth to their respective peoples were called, by emphatic eminence, "The Man." They were to their fellows the highest embodiment of human power, dignity, and knowledge.

Manou of India was a learned and erudite scholar, a profound student of philosophy, more than three thousand years before the Christ was born among you. Nay, he in his turn was but a late reformer compared with those whose words are written in the ancient commentaries which belong to venerable Brahminical lore thousands of years before Manou expounded philosophically the mysteries of God, of creation, and of man's destiny.

To him Zaratushta, or Zoroaster, owed whatever of truth he taught of old in Persia. All the sublimest conceptions of God date from him. The influence of India on all ancient races, in legislation, in theology, in philosophy, in science, is as surely proven to you as the fact that the language which you use is the same tongue as that spoken by Manou himself. The adulterations of modern times have so changed it that you can hardly trace the resemblance, yet your learned philologists will tell you that it is the same. The religions of the world bear to a superficial eye no apparent identity with the ideas which are enshrined in Brahminical lore, yet they are derived frequently from those primitive teachings which Manou systematised, which Manes naturalised in Egypt, and which Moses introduced among the Hebrews.

Hindû ideas permeate all systems of philosophy and theology. The Devadassi, the holy virgins who in Hindû temples devoted themselves to the pure worship of the Supreme, according to their idea of Him, have had their successors in the consecrated virgins of the Egyptian temples of Osiris, in the inspired pythonesses of Delphi, in the priestesses of Ceres, in the vestal virgins of later Rome.

This is, indeed, but a solitary instance of what we wish to point out to you. We do but direct your mind; and our bare sketch will be plentifully filled in hereafter. You are not yet able to comprehend more than the outline.

> *Certainly I am ignorant enough. You speak as if man was a mere vehicle for spirit; more or less perfect, and so more or less instructed.*

We have told you frequently that all knowledge is from us. With us is the substance, with you the shadow only. Even as in your world, they learn most who are most teachable, so in intercourse with ours. We can teach, if you are willing to learn.

> *Not much merit in man, then?*

The merit of obedience and humility. So he best grows in knowledge.

> *And suppose his teachers teach him wrong?*

All truth is mixed with error. The dross will be purged away.

> *All spirits teach differently. Who, then, is right? What is truth?*

It is not so. We teach independently, and so details vary while the broad outline remains the same. You will know one day that evil, as you call it, is but the reverse of good. You can have no unmixed good in your present state. It is an idle dream. Truth to you is relative, and must long remain so. Be content to crawl before you walk, to step before you run, to run before you soar.

PRUDENS.

[It was at this time that there occurred that singular instance of the power of a spirit lately released from the body to communicate, which I have recorded in SPIRIT-IDENTITY. A man had met an awful death by being crushed beneath a steam-roller used for making a road near Baker Street. I had passed the spot during the day: without, however, being conscious of the event. In the evening I met the Baron Dupotet at Mrs. Mackdougall Gregory's, and the spirit manifested its presence. On 23rd Feb., 1874, I inquired about the matter, and the story told by the spirit was confirmed.]

It surprises us much that he should have been able to attach himself to you. It was owing to his being near the place when he met his bodily death. Do not direct your mind strongly to the subject, lest he vex you.

How comes it that he is awake at once, whereas our friend [who had passed away recently] is not?

He has not rested after the violent separation from the body. Well for him if he does so. If not he will remain an earth-bound spirit for long. Rest is a step to progress in the case of such a spirit. It is to be desired that the poor soul may rest and not haunt the sphere of vice in which his earth life was spent.

Is the spirit, then, unharmed by such a ghastly mutilation?

The mutilation of the body does not harm the spirit, except by the rude shock. And that would stir it into action rather than lull it into repose.

The spirit haunted the place of death? How did it reach me?

It is usual for a spirit so severed from the body to haunt the spot for long after. You passed: and being in a highly sensitive condition attracted any spiritual influences that came within your sphere, as the magnet attracts iron. This power of sympathetic attraction is mysterious to you. Yet it should not be, for you see it in action in a lower degree in your world. Attraction and repulsion operate strongly in daily intercourse. Most are unconscious of the fact, yet all especially the sensitive, act upon it. This is intensified once the body is done with. The wider methods which it supplies through the avenues of the senses are replaced by this intuitive faculty of sympathy, and its correlative, repulsion.

But do not fix your mind on the subject, or you will find that the law of attraction is set to work again, and you will have drawn to yourself the plague of an undeveloped spirit. There is no reason, seeing that you could not benefit the poor soul.

✠ Imperator.

SECTION XXVIII.

[Feb. 26th, 1874.—At one of our circles we had had a piece of direct writing of which we could make nothing. It was written in curious hieroglyphics. I inquired about it.]

The writing, though unintelligible to you, was the work of a high intelligence, who on your earth was incarnated amongst the nation who was then most spiritual, the great nation of the Egyptians. They had a more real belief in the existence and intervention of spiritual agencies than you now have. They cherished a firmer belief in immortality of the human spirit; and of the indestructibility of all spirits than your wise men have yet attained to. Their civilisation you yourself know to be vast; their erudition such that they were the depositary of the knowledge of their age.

Aye, verily; and they had knowledge which a material age has lost; knowledge which illumined the souls of Pythagoras and Plato, and which has filtered down to you only through their teachings. The ancient Egyptians were wise and erudite philosophers, and our friend may well teach you much of which you are yet ignorant. After an interval of three thousand years and over, one, who in his earth-life knew of God and the hereafter, comes to witness to the abiding nature of his faith. The time—so long in its seeming to your contracted vision—during which our friend has been a denizen of spirit-land, has served to open new vistas of truth, to remove old errors, to throw light on old speculations, but it has served also to deepen and confirm faith in the Supreme, and in the immortal destiny of man's spirit.

[I suggested that I still did not see why he should write unintelligible hieroglyphics; and asked his name.]

You shall know of him; but his earth identity is long lost

and you would know it no more than you know his signs on the paper. He knew even in the body that bodily life was but the first short stage of perpetuated existence; and he has gone onwards, as he believed, upward to Ra, the source of light, to whom his gaze was turned.

[I inquired if he believed in absorption into the Godhead after a course of progress.]

The Egyptian faith was of some such sort. Their philosophers believed in gradual progress until the dross was purged away and the spirit completely purified. His religion was one of faith in future progress, and, for the present, of high morality in life. Duty to man and to self was not forgotten, and religion was made a business of daily life. We may touch on this again as we develop in you a wider knowledge. For the present it is enough that you know that the special peculiarities of Egyptian theology—the sanctity of the body—had its true and false side.

The Great God was to them represented by every living thing, and the human body was so sacred that it was preserved from natural decay as far as might be; and so well was this done, that some still exist among you. The undue care of the body was error, but the due preservation of bodily health was true and wise. When they saw God in everything, they did well; when they reduced Him to bodily form, their care for the body misled them. Their doctrine of transmigration through vast ages and cycles was an error which symbolised and typified eternal and unceasing progress. These errors, which led to the worship of animal life in all its forms, as symbolising the Creator, and as being the future home of the spirit in its manifold transmigrations, the spirit unlearns as it progresses. But it preserves the great truth of progressive development and growth in presence of the Great Creative Force, of which they were the outward symbols.

If it seem to you foolish and unwise to worship animal life, as needs it must, remember, too, that worship may be directed through an external symbolical manifestation to that spiritual essence which it typifies; and that errors which enshrine truths are husks which die in time and leave the kernel safe. Ideas, germs of truth, never die. They may be viewed through a distorted medium, and so take a disproportioned form; but when the distorted medium is removed, the true form is seen. So our friend and his brethren see now that all nature in your world is a phenomenal manifestation of the Supreme; and that if life in all its varied forms may not be held up as an object of adoration, still the groping spirit who strives to reach up through nature to its God is not to be visited with unreasoning blame. Do you not see this?

> *In a way. I can understand the use of all helps to realising God. But I thought that Egyptian theology was material and earthy compared with that of India. The communications which you wrote out as to the religions of the world, left on me the impression that Egypt reacted from India. I suppose all error includes some truth, just as every truth has an admixture of error, both terms being relative and not absolute.*

We do not now dwell on the characteristic points of Indian theology. What you say is true. We only desire now to show you how, under forms most repulsive to your present ideas, there was a lurking germ of truth, and that such truth, known to the ancients, has in many cases perished from among you It is well that you learn to be modest in estimating both your own knowledge and that of the ancients.

> *Yes; I am not aware that I have any particular knowledge except of the prevalent ignorance touching these matters. And it is silly to laugh at any form of religion. Our friend lived long since. An Egyptian priest, was he?*

He was one of the prophets of Osiris, and was in his time learned in the mysteries esoteric and unmentionable to the vulgar. Osiris, Isis, and Horus—this was the Trinity he worshipped. Osiris, the Supreme; Isis, the All-Mother; Horus, the Child, sacrifice for human sin. He knew God as your sacred historian revealed Him, in terms borrowed from Egypt

—I am the I am—the Universal Essence; the Source of Life and Light. This title of Jehovah, Moses borrowed from the priests of Thebes.

What was the original name ?

NUK-PU-NUK. I AM THE I AM.

He who inspires this communication was Prophet of Ra, at On, the City of Light, which the Greeks call Heliopolis, City of the Sun, and he lived sixteen hundred and thirty years before the era which you call Christian. His name was Choin, and he speaks to you a witness for immortality from the ages that have long passed. And I bear him witness that his testimony is true.

+ IMPERATOR.

[I inquired if there were any available records of Egyptian theology to which I could get access.]

It is not necessary. All that remains of the old Hermaic books is little. The writings in the mummy cases from the Ritual of the Dead are excerpts from them. The care for the body, we have said, was the distinguishing mark of Egyptian religion. The funeral ceremonies were very long and minute, and the writings on the tombs and on the caskets which enshrined the bodies of the departed are the earliest records of Egyptian faith.

You will not need to dive into these matters. It is needful only that you see and grasp this great truth, that the despised knowledge of the past had its germ of truth.

Nay, more. Religion was to the Egyptian the master principle of daily life, to which all else was subservient. Art, literature, science, were the handmaids of religion, and the daily life itself was an elaborate ritual. The faith in which he lived was incorporated in every act. The Sun-God, as it arose and set typified the life which was then but beginning and which in the twin Sothriac cycles would return again after three thousand years of progressive education to earth, only to be absorbed at last in the pure beams of Ra, the source and spring of life and light.

The ceremonial purifications of worship pervaded his daily work, and gave a tone of spirituality to the businesses of life All that the Egyptian did had reference to the life hereafter on which his stedfast gaze was fixed. Every day had its special presiding spirit, or deity, under whose protection it was placed. Every temple had its great staff of prophets, priests, pontiffs, judges, scribes. These were versed in mystic lore, and spent lives of purity and chastity in penetrating into nature's hidden secrets, and the mysteries of spirit intercourse. They were a pure, learned, spiritual race, albeit their knowledge of some things known to men now was but slight. But we may say to you that in deep, philosophical knowledge, in clearness of spiritual perception, your wise men have no claim to rank with them.

Nor in practical religion can your people equal the old Egyptians. We have learned long since to estimate man's religion by acts rather than by words; and we pay little heed to the character of that ladder by which man climbs heavenward. False faiths abound still. Man now, as heretofore befogs himself with foolish imaginings which he calls Divine Revelation. And though the faith of Egypt were erroneous in much, it possessed that which redeemed its errors and en nobled the lives of its professors. They at least had not clothed their lives with a dead materialism. They had not closed every avenue to the higher life of spirit. They recognised their god in every act of daily life, even though their idea of the god-principle was crude. They would not buy and sell and trade with deliberate purpose to defraud and overreach. They would not ignore all else but dead matter, even though they did pay undue reverence to the perishable and material.

You know how far it is true of your age, that it is material, earthy, grovelling; that its thoughts and aspirations have been earth-bound; that it is unspiritual, without lofty aspirations, without deep spiritual insight, without active faith in spirit-life and intercourse. You can draw the contrast for yourself. In pointing it out we do not exalt Egyptian religion, save to show you that what seems to you so earthy and vile was, in some of its aspects, a living faith, powerful in daily life, and possessing deep spiritual wisdom.

> *Yes, in a way, no doubt. It seems that so much may be said for every form of faith. They are all man's groping after immortality, and vary in degree of truth according to his enlightenment. But you are hardly fair to this age. No doubt there is a deal of Materialism, but there is also a deal of striving to avoid it. Few are Materialists from choice. And if ever there were a time when thought about religion and God, and the hereafter, might be said to be rife, it is now. It seems to me that your strictures would suit better a bygone age of apathy than one which is at least awake and alive to the momentous questions on which you speak.*

It may be. There is, as you say, much tendency to look into these matters; and where that exists there is hope. But there is also a strong desire to exclude all reference to spirit as a factor in human existence: to refer all to matter, and crush out all seeking into spirit intercourse and the spirit life as at least unpractical, if not unreal and delusive. It is, perhaps, necessary that the temper of your age should take its tone from the peculiar religious epoch through which you are passing. The transition state that intervenes between one form of faith and its successor, is necessarily one of convulsion. The old is fading, and the new is not yet clear. Man must pass through this, and it has a tendency to distort his vision.

> *Yes. Things seem in a fluidic state, shifting, and obscure. Then, of course, there are many who do not want to be disturbed. They resent being roused from their dreams. And some have dealt with matter so long that they cannot bear to think that after all it is only the vail of spirit. But this does not affect my belief that no age that I know of, short of that grand era in old Greece, shows anything like the same active*

and intelligent seeking into deep spiritual and natural truths.

It is well that you think so; nor do we desire to shake that opinion. We have but striven to show you by a typical instance that there are truths hidden even in those faiths which to you seem most gross and earthy.

I suppose the Jewish Lawgiver, "learned in all the wisdom of the Egyptians," incorporated a good deal of it into his code.

Yes, indeed. The ceremony of circumcision was borrowed from the Egyptian mysteries. All the ceremonial purifications of the Jewish temple were borrowed from Egypt. From the same source came the linen dresses of the priests; the mystic cherubim that guarded the mercy-seat: nay, the very idea of the Holy place, and Holy of Holies, were but adaptations of the plan of Egyptian temples. But Moses, skilled as he was in the learning of the priests by whom he was trained did not in borrowing ritual, borrow also the spiritual ideas which it typified. The grand doctrines of immortality and spirit agency find no real place in his writings. The destiny of spirit, as you know, he never alluded to. The appearances of spirits are mere phenomenal manifestations incidentally introduced, and the great doctrine is untouched.

Yes. The rite of Circumcision existed in Egypt before the time of Moses?

Oh, yes. Bodies which were so religiously preserved by them at a date previous to Abraham, and which still exist among you, prove that, if you need proof.

I did not know that. Did he borrow any articles of faith?

The doctrine of the Trinity existed in Egypt as well as in India. The Mosaic code reproduced much of the minute character of Egyptian ritual without its spirituality.

How comes it that such mines of knowledge as Egypt had should be closed to us? Confucius, Buddha, Moses Mohammed live. Why not Manes?

He lives only in the effect he had on others. The religion of Egypt was confined to a favoured class, and was not sufficiently extended beyond the country to be permanent. It was a religion confined to a priestly sect, and it died with them. Its effects are seen in other faiths.

The idea of the Trinity, was it Indian or Egyptian?

The Trinity of Creative Power, Destructive Power, and Mediatorial Power, existed in India as Brahm, Siva, Vishnu; in Egypt as Osiris, Typhon, Horus. There were many Trinities in Egyptian theology. The same existed in Persia as Ormuzd, Ahriman, Mithra (the Reconciler).

Different parts of Egypt had their different theologies. Pthah, the Supreme Father: Ra, the Sun-God, manifestation of the Supreme: Amun, the Unknown God, were all various manifestations of the God-idea.

I thought you said that Osiris, Isis, Horus, made the Egyptian Trinity?

We did but put in Isis as the Productive principle—Osiris, Creator; Isis, Principle of Fecundity; Horus, son of Osiris and Isis. There were many developments of the idea of the Trinity. It is not important, save that it bears upon the broad question.

Then did Egypt get its religion from India?

Partly: but on that point we have no one who can speak.
              PRUDENS.

[The foregoing was written February 28th, 1874. On April 8th, the answer was written, much other matter having been given in the meantime.]

You inquired as to the connection between India and Egypt. The religion of Egypt was essentially a religion of body, as that of India was of spirit. Egypt had multifarious acts of external ritual; India cultivated contemplation. God to the Hindû was an undiscoverable essence; to the Egyptian he was manifested in every type of animal existence. To the Hindû time was nothing; eternity, all. To the Egyptian every passing moment had its consecrated work. Egypt was the antipodes of India. Nevertheless, it is true that Egypt received its first religious imspiration from India, even as did Zoroaster in Persia.

We have told you before that the special grandeur of Egypt's faith was the consecration to religion of daily life. It was a faith which influenced daily acts. Therein lay its power. It was a faith which recognised God in all nature, and especially in all animal life. It was the mystery of existence, the highest manifestation of Divine power that the Egyptian worshipped, when, as you imagine, he bowed down before an idol graven in the image of an ox. . . . . . It would be well that the same care for the body, the same present view of religious duty, the same perception of an all-pervading Deity which formed the creed of ancient Egypt, and which enters so largely into ours, should be again prevalent among you.

I suppose, in effect, that Egyptian theology was a reaction from Hindû mysticism. You speak as if that elaboration of ritual was a good thing. I should have thought that the Egyptian priest wasted a deal of time, and that his punctilious washings and shavings were merely silly.

Not so. The ritual was necessary for the age and people. We are not concerned with anything but the underlying idea. Art, literature, and science laboured for religion: and so far from worship absorbing the work of life, it was rather that every act of common life was raised to the dignity of an act of worship. In this sense only is it true: and a nobler truth can hardly be declared. To live in the presence of Deity—to see His image all around, to consecrate every act to His service, to keep mind, spirit, body, pure as He is pure, consecrated to Him, and to Him alone—this is to lead the godlike life, even though it contain mistaken details.

No doubt prejudice hampers us greatly. But you would not say (would you?) that a man's faith is entirely indifferent in its substance, so he honestly professes it. For instance, Egypt reproduced now would not be the ideal you seem to paint.

Surely not. The world progresses, and gains higher knowledge. It may not recur to that which was fitted for another people in an earlier stage of development. But though the world has gained, it has lost also; and among the things which it has lost is that which may belong equally to all forms of faith, the devotion of self to duty and to God. This is no inseparable quality of Egyptian faith. Rather was it amplified and exemplified in a higher degree in the life and teaching of the Christ. But you have forgotten it—you have lost that mark of true religion. It needs that you see that in this point you were surpassed by those whom you despise and contemn.

We do say, we have always said, that man's responsibility is in proportion to the light which is in him; that man's duty is not lessened but increased by the quality of the revelation of which he is the recipient. We tell you that many a soul has progressed in spite of its creed by honesty and sincerity and singleness of purpose; and that many a soul has been dragged down by the very load of that faith in which its hopes were centred. We know that it is so, and that man's faith in its external presentment—the outer shell which alone you can see—is of comparatively little moment. He must perforce take that which falls to his lot, and according to the use he makes of it is his progress. It is an accident whether an incarnated soul be Jew or Turk, Mahommedan, Christian, Brahmin, or Parsee; but it is of the essence of that soul's progress whether it so uses its opportunities as to progress, or so abuses them as to retrograde. Souls have different opportunities here, and according as they use them they have increased or diminished capacity for progress in the *after* state for which they have fitted themselves. This you know; and the chance of progress may be as great with the despised and humble soul on whom the Pharisaical Christian looks down with contempt as with one incarnated amidst every influence of good, and every opportunity of progress. It is a pure question of spirit, into which you cannot yet enter. You are concerned with the husk here; you have not reached the kernel.

> *But surely one who acts up to his knowledge as a Christian, that knowledge being high, and the acts good and complete, according to capacity and opportunity, gets a long start of the barbarous fetish-worshipper, however honest he may be.*

In this small fragment of existence it is not possible that any gain be snatched which may not be readily made up in another state. You are hampered by the limited nature of your vision and knowledge. The accidents which seem to you such bars, may be but the means selected to bring out some needed quality—endurance, patience, trust, or love; whilst the luxurious surroundings, the poisonous flattery, the complacent self-satisfaction may be the engines of the adversaries who are dragging down and stifling a soul.

You judge too hastily and imperfectly, and from external signs only. Nor are you able to see what the guardians intend, nor to make due allowance for temptation and its results. These are questions which now are beyond your judgment.

Further, as to your question, it is a bounden duty in each to accept and act up to the highest view of Divine Truth which is revealed in him, and which he is able to accept. By this his progress will be judged.

Do you teach a General Judgment?

No. The judgment is complete when the spirit gravitates to the home which it has made for itself. There can be no error. It is placed by the eternal law of fitness. That judgment is complete, until the spirit is fitted to pass to a higher sphere, when the same process is repeated, and so on and on until the purgatorial spheres of work are done with, and the soul passes within the inner heaven of contemplation.

Then, in fact, there are many judgments?

Yes and no. Many and none. Judgment is ceaseless, for the soul is ever fitting itself for its change. No such arraignment before the assembled universe as is in your mind. That is an allegory.

In each stage of probation the spirit builds up a character by its constant acts, which fits it for a certain position. To that position it goes of necessity, without what you mean as judgment. Sentence results at once; just as the total of a number of items is ascertained without argument or judgment. There is no need for the process of a court of justice as you understand it on earth. The soul is the arbiter of its own destiny; its own judge. This is so in all cases of progress or retrogression.

Is each entry into a new sphere or state marked by a change analogous to death?

Analogous, in that there is a gradual sublimation or refinement of the spirit-body, until by degrees all gross elements are purged away. The higher the sphere the more refined and ethereal the body. The change is not so material as that which you call death, for there is no corporeal envelope to lay aside, but it is analogous to it in that it is a process of development, the entry of the spirit into a higher state of existence.

And when all the gross elements are gone, the spirit enters the spheres of contemplation, and is refined till all may be refined away?

Not so. It is refined until the dross is gone, and the pure spiritual gold remains. We know not of its life in the inner heaven. We only know that it grows liker and liker to God, nearer and nearer to His image. It may well be, good friend, that the noblest destiny of the perfected spirit may be union with the God into whose likeness it has grown, and whose portion of divinity, temporarily segregated during its pilgrimage, it so renders up to Him who gave it. These to us, as to you, are but speculations. Leave them and be content to know that which is alone worth knowing. Could you penetrate all mysteries there would be no longer occupation for your mind. You can know but little here; but you can aspire, and in aspiring, raise your spirit above the sordid cares of earth to its truer home. May the blessing of the Blessed One rest on you!

✝ IMPERATOR.

SECTION XXIX.

[March 15, 1874.—We had received many warnings as to the danger of deception by personating spirits, and the warning had gained force by a particular case occurring in our experience, though outside of our circle, in which such an attempt had been made. Many very striking messages were given on the subject, of which the only one sufficiently public in interest, is the following]:—

We have been particular in our statements, because we are anxious to reiterate the warnings we have frequently given, as to the danger of attack by deceptive and personating spirits, whom you know as The Undeveloped. Of late, too, we have told you that trouble and perplexity were at hand through this same cause, and we gave you special warning lest you should fall a prey to their attacks. We have ascertained that the spirit who falsely pretended to be working with us is a personating spirit, whose aim is to injure and retard our work.

We need to explain fully on this point. You have heard of the antagonism between the adversaries and the divine work which is in process amongst you. There is direct antagonism between them and us, between the work which is for man's development and instruction, and their efforts to retard and thwart it. It is the old battle between what you call the good and the evil—between the progressive and the retrogressive. Into the ranks of that opposing army gravitate spirits of all degrees of malignity, wickedness, cunning and deceit: those who are actively spurred on by the hatred of light which an unenlightened spirit has, and those who are animated by sportiveness rather than by actual malice. It includes, in short, the undeveloped of every grade and class: spirits who are opposed, for infinitely varying reasons, to the organised attempt to lead men upward from darkness to light, with which we are associated, in company with hosts of others.

It would appear that your inability to see the operations of these adversaries renders you unable to grasp their existence, or to appreciate the magnitude of their influence in your world. Not till your spiritual eyes are open will you really understand how great it is, and how present. To those ranks gravitate, of necessity, the earth-bound and unprogressed spirits to whom incarnation has brought no gain, and whose affections, centred on the earth, where all their treasure is, can find no scope in the pure spiritual joys of the spheres of spirit-life. Hovering over their old haunts, they live over again their wretched, polluted earth-lives, by influencing congenial spirits still in the body, and so gratifying their lusts and passions at second hand.

The poor wreck whose lusts have survived the death of that body in which and for which alone he lived, have survived the means of direct bodily gratification, finds his resource in seizing on an impressionable medium, and goading him on to sin, so that he may get such poor enjoyment as alone remains for him. The debauched drunkard, who sank his body in disease, and soddened his spirit with the poisoned draughts of liquid fire, now haunts the dens where his pleasure used to be, and goads on the wretches whom it finds it possible to influence. He leers with spite as he drives one more soul to a lower state of misery, and gloats as he draws his own foul gratification, though it spread broadcast ruin and woe among innocent women and their babes, and foster in the midst of your centres of knowledge and refinement a sink of infamy and disgrace. These things go on all around you, and attract your notice scarce at all. Where are the denunciations that should ring from end to end of your world while such plague-spots linger—nay, flourish and abound amongst you? Why is no voice uplifted? Why? but that the dark influence of those baleful spirits avails to blind your eyes and to paralyse the voice of truth within you. Not in the gin-den alone, but far round it as from a centre, the malign influence radiates, and the vice perpetuates itself. The sot, dead—as you falsely think,—is a sot in spirit still, and his influence perpetuates his vice among congenial spirits yet on earth.

The murderer, again, whom your blindness has cut off from the trammels of the body, and let loose in fury on your earth, is not idle. With all his envenomed passions stirred within him, mad with wrath and sense of wrong—for his sin is frequently the result of your civilisation, and he is what you have made him—he goes forth to wreak his vengeance on those who have wronged him. He incites to rage and destruction of life. He is the prolific inciter of crime, and perpetuates the circumstances of which he was the victim. When will you learn that crimes for which you daily, hourly, visit rude vengeance are but the necessary product of those mixed conditions of life which obtain in your crowded centres of life? Why lop off an ugly branch here and there when the root is rotten? Why punish the wretch because he is what you made him? Nay, if you be but selfish, why let loose on you a wrathful avenger to your own hurt? Ah! friend, you must pass through many cycles of progress before you learn that your old criminal code is founded on fallacy, and works to mischief and perpetuation of the abuses it is intended to prevent.

These and such as these, coming from your world such as you have made them, are, of necessity, enemies of progress, purity, and peace; adversaries of ours, and leaders in the attack on the work in which we share. What else can they be? Can that spirit whose earth-life has been one long scene of debauchery and degradation become of a sudden pure and good? Can the sensualist be changed into one who lives for purity, or the degraded animal into a progressive and aspiring spirit? You know it cannot be. They are, in company with hosts of others, the foes of man and spirit so far as their desire is to thwart progress and keep down truth. Count on them as a perpetual source of antagonism, and if you cannot realise to the full their influence for evil, do not ignore their power, or invite their attacks by exposing yourself to them.

We will leave no word of warning unuttered, for the danger is all the more real that it is so secret and so far-reaching. To their efforts operating on congenial spirits in your world you must refer much of crime and misery that exists among you: war with its attendant horrors which yet disgrace and defile your world, and blots your boasted civilisation and refinement. To them attribute the fostering of the crimes that befoul your great cities, that spread a mantle of corruption over them, and make them homes of iniquity and dwelling-places of shame.

You tell of your progress in knowledge, in art and science, in culture and refinement. You boast of your civilisation, and are at pains to send to far distant peoples the religion which adorns and elevates your own country. Nay, you even force it on them as that Divinely-given panacea for human ills of which you are the favoured recipients. It would be well that you should keep silence over the fruits which religion and civilisation between them have produced among you. For your religion we have said frequently that it is a degenerate offspring of that simple and pure faith which alone deserves the name of Christianity. For your civilisation and culture they are but of the surface, and do but faintly hide festering sores, all too plain to spirit gaze, while in their ultimate effect upon the nature they are too frequently demoralising to the truest and noblest instincts, and productive of hollowness, deceit, and selfishness. The Arab of the desert, the Indian of the far west, in whom nature's instincts have not been dwarfed, distorted, paralysed by civilisation, is frequently a nobler man than the crafty trader, who thinks it clever to outwit and overreach, or than that baser product of civilised life from whose foul tongue no character is safe, and whose lustful, sensual life marks none as sacred from attack.

Foul, weltering masses of vice and cruelty, and selfishness, and heartlessness, and misery that your great cities are! In them the spirit is starved and crushed; dwelling in an atmosphere through which life-giving influence can hardly penetrate, it groans in agony as it aspires to a purer and serener air; but its groans ascend hardly above the pall of darkness that hovers round. The aspirations are crushed out by reiterated temptation; good resolves are stolen away by the adversaries nigh at hand, and the spirit cares less and less to struggle against the efforts of its foes. These are only too well seconded by the recklessness and folly which offer a premium to vice, and make virtue well-nigh impossible.

And even when the body is removed from those dens of impurity, sensuality, and woe, which are tenanted by so many of your fellows even within reach of your own homes, where riches secure exemption from bodily distress, what is the result? We do not see gross vice, shameless physical surroundings, open degradation of soul and body, but we breathe an atmosphere scarcely less spiritually bad. Money-hunting is the business of life, and pleasure is too often found in bodily gratification and sensuous enjoyment. The air is thick with the greed of gold, with lust of power, with self-seeking in all its myriad forms. The spirit—do you ever think what is the state of such a spirit? It has no food, no development, no occupation. It is dwarfed, or compelled to occupy itself in concerns which drag it back, and give the adversaries their best chance of fostering and inflaming passions and desires which are to us detestable. Hardly can we reach these more than the debased, where in the crowded alleys and lanes vice has its home—where in the thronged exchanges and marts money rules supreme, and breeds its progeny of selfishness and greed, and larceny—there the adversaries have their centres of action, from which their baleful influence radiates.

But you know it not. You are ignorant in respect of the world of causes, and foolish in respect of what you do in your world in providing conditions favourable to crime and sin. Your ignorance perpetuates these conditions, and renders it more hard for us to impress upon you the true principles which should govern the origination and development of life upon your globe, and the cultivation of spiritual progress. Some of your more advanced reformers have seen the vast importance which attaches to the subject of marriage; and we have endeavoured to put forward such views as you were fitted to receive. Much remains to be said when the world is ready, but that is not yet. We do but allude to the subject as being intimately bound up with the great questions of disease, crime, poverty, insanity, which vex and disturb us in our dealings with men. To the folly, and worse, to the criminal recklessness, and not less criminal and more foolish conventional law which governs the marriage customs among you, very much is chargeable. And this no less among those whom you call the educated and refined than among the ignorant and uncultured, rather, perhaps, does the greater sin rest with the rich. You must unlearn much that men have dreamed; you must undo much that society has sanctioned in the trafficking that goes under the name of marriage; and you must learn truer and diviner rules for happiness and progress than you now tolerate, before you wipe away the great original source of deterioration and retrogression. Mistake us not! We are no advocates of license—no apostles of social freedom so called. Liberty ever degenerates with the foolish into license. We spurn such notions with contempt, even with more than we view the infamous buying and selling, the social slavery into which you have degraded the holiest and divinest law of life.

Nor have you yet learned that the body is the avenue of spirit, and that laws of health and conditions under which bodily development are possible are essential for man incarnated on earth. We have spoken before of this. Now we only say that in this, as in the other matter, you are in alliance with our foes. Nineteen centuries have passed since the pure and refined teachings which you profess to treasure were spoken amongst men; and you are but little better in all that makes for true progress, but little wiser in real wisdom, but little advanced in pure religion; nay, you are worse than the Essenes, amongst whom Jesus lived and was trained. You are as the Scribes and Pharisees, who drew from Him his bitterest denunciations.

And you know it not. In matters of body and spirit—matters of vital import that touch both the life here and the life hereafter—you have well-nigh all to learn.

These are some of the adversaries of whom we have told you aforetime. They are massed in force, ever ready to thwart, and vex, and injure us. Their ranks are being perpetually swelled by spirits debased and degraded by human ignorance.

In all that we have said we have made no account of those who strive to do for their race and for its development what in them lies. We have said nothing of the acts of self-sacrifice and devotion, the simple noble lives, the generous acts that redeem your race, and make us hopeful of its future. Our business now is to paint the dark side of the picture: and we have so drawn it as best to attract your attention to it. We earnestly warn you that its lineaments are sketched with the pencil of truth; and we warn you in all solemnity that the great truth which underlies this message, viz., the antagonism between good and evil, and the fostering of evil by human folly and ignorance, is one which vitally concerns you and us in the future of the work which we have in charge. In what has now been said, we have but recapitulated what has been said before of the organised opposition from those who are our opponents. But one special form of attack, which will become more and more frequent, we have not yet dealt with. As objective spiritual manifestations become more and more frequent, and as the inconsiderate craving for them increases, so will it come to pass that powerful instruments will be developed through whom our adversaries may be enabled to produce their frivolous or tricky manifestations, so as to discredit the true spiritual work. This is one of the special forms of opposition, and the most dangerous: for in proportion to the undeveloped character of the spirit will be its power over gross matter, its cunning, and, in some cases, its malignity. Powerful agencies are even now at work, as we are assured, who will seize every opportunity of developing mediums through whom phenomena the most startling may be produced, so as to convince the inquirers of supernatural power so called. This done, the rest is easy. By degrees trick and fraud are allowed to creep in, the moral teachings are allowed to appear in their true light, doubt is insinuated, and the uncertainty and suspicion which have become the fixed attitude of the mind regarding phenomena which at first seemed so surely spiritual, gradually extend to all manifestations and teachings.

No more sure means of discrediting the teaching of those who are sent to instruct, and not merely to astonish or amuse, was ever devised by cunning. For men say: We have tried, we have tested for ourselves, and we have found it out. Either it is connected with fraud, or it teaches base and immoral doctrines, or it is full of falsehood; in short, it is diabolical. It is no use to appeal to such, and tell them that they must discern between the true and the false, for their shaken faith will not allow of this. They have proved what they trusted to be false, and the whole edifice of their belief lies in ruins around them. The foundation is not secure, and will not support the building.

We say again that no more diabolical device for paralysing our work was ever planned. We solemnly warn you of it. See to it that you act upon our warning. Beware of encouraging the promiscuous evolution of violent physical power. Such comes generally from the lower and more undeveloped; and its development is frequently attended by spirits for whose absence you should pray. In the encouragement, especially in newly-formed circles, of undue care for physical marvels is a great risk. Such are necessary to the work, and we do not in any degree undervalue their importance to certain minds. We desire to bring home evidence to all; but we do not desire that any should rest in that material form of belief, in an external something which is of little service to any soul. We labour for something higher than to show curious minds that we can do badly under certain conditions what man can do better under other conditions. Nor do we rest content even with showing man that beings external to himself can interfere in the order of his world. If that were all, he might be so much the worse for knowing it. We have before us one sole aim, and that alone has brought us to your earth. You know our mission. In days when faith has grown cold, and belief in God and immortality is waning to a close, we come to demonstrate to man that he is immortal, by virtue of the possession of that soul which is a spark struck off from Deity itself. We wish to teach him of the errors of the past, to show him the life that leads to progress, to point him to the future of development and growth.

It is not with such an end before us that we can tamely allow our work to be set aside for the development of any strange phenomenal power that spirits may possess over gross matter.

If we use such power at all it is because we find it necessary, not because we think it desirable, save always as a means to an end. Were it harmless we should say so much. But being what it is, an engine of assault from the adversaries, the worst we have to dread, we are urgent in warning you against promiscuous seeking after these physical marvels, and against resting in them as the end and aim of intercourse with us.

Regard them only as means of conviction, as so many proofs to your minds of actual intervention from the world of spirit with the world of matter. Look upon them as such only, and use them as the material foundation on which the spiritual temple may be built. Rest assured that they of themselves can teach you no more than that; nay, if the operating spirits find in you no capacity to grasp more, they will gradually give way to those who can do such work better than they can and so the means of further knowledge will pass away. From that basis you must go on to further steps. You must seek to know of the nature of the agency, of its source and intent. Surely you would desire to be assured that it is of God, beneficent and pure in origin and intent. Surely you would seek to know how much the visitors from beyond the grave can tell you of that universal dwelling-place of your race; how they can satisfy you of your own soul's destiny, and of the means by which you may best fit yourself for the change which you call death. For if we be not as you, how is our experience fruitful to you? If we cannot tell you of your own immortality, what profits it that we prove to you never so conclusively that we ourselves exist? Such may be a curious fact; it can never be more.

When you can reach out beyond the phenomenal to the actual investigation of Truth for its own sake—when, in short, you can believe our pretensions—then we can open out to you a realm of which you are yet ignorant, and which has been far more fully revealed to earnest seekers in other lands than yours. To few only in your land have the higher revealings of spiritual truth been vouchsafed. Even this means of communing by writing, which seems to you such an advance on the clumsy rapping out of messages and such material means of communication, is as nothing, compared with the inner communing of spirit with spirit without the intervention of material signs. In America, the land from which dates this movement in your days, there are many who have been so far developed as to lead a dual life, and to hold face to face intercourse with us. We have even now a band of workers there who are achieving results which we cannot command here through faithlessness of mind, materiality of interests, and even grossness of atmospheric surroundings. It is not with our work as with your mundane affairs. We read the heart, and it is useless to feign interest which you do not feel—that you would not do—or to proceed on our way while faith is lacking. It has been so in all ages of the world. Efforts have been made from time to time to pour in advanced knowledge; it has been found that the time was not come, and the effort has been withdrawn. But this is not what we wish to say. We desire only to warn you against a danger, and to encourage you to rise above the material to the spiritual plane. Receptivity must precede higher development: but we yearn and pray for the time when you shall have shaken yourselves free from earthly trammels, and seek only after the higher revealings of Truth. To that end you must have singleness of purpose: you must have shaken yourselves free from human opinion, and have dissociated yourselves from the material plane, so far as an occupant of earth may do so.

Eternal Father! Thou in Whose Name we work, and for the revealing of Whose Truth we are sent to earth, enable us to elevate and purify the hearts of those to whom we speak, that they may rise from earth and open their spiritual senses to discern the things which we reveal. May Faith grow in them, so that they may aspire to Truth, and, leaving earthy interests behind, press on to learn the Revelation of the Spirit.

+ IMPERATOR.

[I remarked that I had no doubt that all that was said was true, and I added that I had difficulty in understanding why some law and order did not obtain on the spiritual side, so as to curb those unruly spirits. They seemed to do what they pleased, and to be under no governance. Also I expressed my wonder at their false statements. I could not see why a spirit should take pleasure in personation.]

You err in supposing there is no law and order with us. It is that the neglect of conditions on your part frustrates orderly effort. You must learn to fence your circles round with proper conditions, and then you will eliminate half the trickery and contradiction. The time will not come when all that you call evil will be wiped out; for this is a matter of spiritual training, and we have no power to save you from the process, which is for your progressive development. It is necessary that you pass through it. You have much to learn, and this practical experience is one of the ways of learning.

As to personation you will learn more hereafter. For the present, we tell you that there are spirits who delight in such personation, and who have the power, under certain conditions, of carrying out elaborate deception. Such take names which they see to be desired, and would reply equally to any name given them. They may usually be excluded by a careful attention to conditions, and by the efforts of a strong guardian who is able to protect the circle. Those who sit frequently and in open circles, where no care is taken of the spiritual conditions, and who have no powerful spirit friends to protect them, are in danger of incursion from these. In most circles, as far as we know, every facility is given for the intervention of tricky spirits. The phenomena are sought after in a spirit of mere curiosity. Personal friends are greedily summoned, and no pains taken to ascertain whether the spirit answering be indeed a friend or a deceiver. Foolish queries are addressed, and foolish replies eagerly swallowed. What wonder that such are the sport of the undeveloped!

> *How is one to know that this personation does not extend to all? and that what in Spiritualism appears good and coherent, will not in the end prove to be only a cleverer trick? If such powers are behind, who is safe?*

POSSIBLE DANGERS. 241

We can but give you the answer you have had before. We have proved to you our good faith, our truth, our external individuality. We have given you proof upon proof. We have shown our moral consciousness by consistent truthfulness in all things—by the presence of a tone in our teachings to you, which you must estimate for yourself. When complete they shall stand forth to all as pure and good. Even now you admit them to be elevated and good in tendency. Your knowledge of us, of our work, and of our aims, must lead you to a judgment such as you would frame of a fellow-man under similar circumstances.

> *Yes. This personating spirit, by speaking of whom I commenced, would upset one's faith very soon, if it had got access.*

It might have been so; we cannot tell how far we could have counteracted the effort; but we do not wish to run the risk. For contradicting statements would surely have been made, personation carried on, and in the end the scanty faith you have would have sustained a rude shock. This is a real danger to you; for the introduction of false and contradictory statements would do more to foster a suspicious feeling in your mind than anything. In the end it would undermine us and drive us away.

> *Really the subject seems to be a most dangerous one to meddle with.*

The abuse of everything is bad; the use, good and commendable. To those who in frivolous frame of mind place themselves in communion with the spheres; to those who force themselves from low motives in that which is to them only a curious thing; to the vain in their own conceit, the triflers, the untruthful, the worldly, the sensual, the base, the flippant there is doubtless danger. We never advise any of unbalanced mind to meddle with the mysteries of mediumship. It is direful risk to them. Those only who are protected and guarded round, who act from no inner motive, but in obedience to the impulse of the guardians, who are wise and powerful to protect, should meddle, and they carefully and with earnest prayer. We deprecate always any unlicensed meddling. Nor can any safely mingle with the spirit-world, and so introduce one more disturbing element into his earth-life, except he be of even mind and steady temper. Any unhinged mind, spasmodic temperament, fitful, purposeless character, becomes the ready prey of the undeveloped. Doubtless it is perilous for such to meddle, more especially if their interest be only in the marvellous, to gratify an idle curiosity, or to solace their own vanity. The higher messages of the Supreme are not audible to such. Would that they who can hear them would forsake the trifling of the lower spirits, and, leaving the inferior planes, press on to the purer atmosphere of the higher spheres of knowledge.

But all this is caviare to the world. They think far more of a good thump on the head, or of a floating chair, than of all your information, which, by-the-by, is hard enough to get.

True, we know it only too well. The present phase of our work is one that must be passed through. The physical accompanies, but is no real part of our work. It must, as we say, precede the real development for which we wait. It will go on all around you with increasing development; and while we warn you against the dangers which accompany it, we do not disguise the necessity for it in the present material state of your knowledge. While we deplore we acknowledge the necessity. We have more to add to what has been said, but not now. For the present, cease.

[After a short rest, this addition was made to what had been said.]

We have told you of the operations of the adversaries, and of the danger to be apprehended from them. But others there are who, without being malignant foes, are nevertheless a cause of trouble to us. Many of those who are withdrawn from earth are not, as you know, very progressive, nor, on the contrary, very undeveloped. The majority of those who pass from the body is neither very evil nor very good in spirit.

Such, indeed, as are so far progressive as to gravitate rapidly through the spheres nearest the earth, do not return unless called to a special mission. The earth-bound we have already told you of.

It remains to speak of the agency of a class of spirits who, from mischievous design, or from pure sportive fun, or from love of mystification, frequent circles, counterfeit manifestations, assume names, and give erroneous or misleading information. Such are not evil, but unbalanced, spirits who lack even balance, and who delight in plaguing mediums and circles: in giving exaggerated tone to communications, in introducing false elements, or in personating friends, and reading in the thought the answer which they give to a query. The work of such is that which causes you to say that Spiritual manifestations are frequently foolish or silly. This is due to the efforts of these spirits who, from fun or mischief, counterfeit our work, and play on the feelings of those who trust them. These are they who personate relatives whose presence is desired, and answer to their names. These are they who make true identification of friends in mixed circles impossible. Most of the stories current of such return of friends are due to the work of these spirits. These are they who infuse the comic or foolish element into communications. They have no true moral consciousness, and will pray readily, if asked, or will do anything for frolic or mischief. They have no aspiration beyond the present: no desire to injure, but only to amuse themselves.

These are they who allure to wrong paths, and suggest wrong desires and thoughts. They secretly influence mediums much, and prevent noble aspirations. They view with impatience noble and elevated aims, and suggest the material. They act as bars and clogs. They are greatly concerned with physical manifestations. They are usually shrewd and clever at such work, and they delight in presenting bewildering phenomena for the purpose of disturbing the mind. They victimise mediums in divers ways, and find a pleasure in the bewilderment of mind which they cause. Obsession and possession, and the various forms of spiritual annoyance, pro-

ceed very frequently from such. They are able to psychologise a mind over which they have gained influence. . . . .
These again are spirits who befool inquirers who have asked for personal information. They return plausible answers, and bewilder the deluded inquirers, or if a personal friend have once appeared, and given a good test, his or her place on the next occasion may be filled by one of these spirits, who takes the name and replies to queries, giving vague and unsatisfactory replies, or telling false stories. It is always well to put the personal element as far from you as possible, lest you open the way to deceit.

• • • • • • • •

✚ Imperator.

SECTION XXX.

[The fondness of spirits for anniversaries has led to my receiving a number of special teachings on Church Festivals. As a specimen I give the Easter Teachings for three consecutive years. It will be seen that the words written in 1875, and signed by another name to those who have given other teachings, breathes a different spirit, and is conceived from another standpoint.]

[Easter Day, 1874. I referred to a communication given on the corresponding day of the year previous from DOCTOR and PRUDENS.]

It may serve as a landmark for estimating progress, if you review your feelings then, and contrast them with what you now know. You will see how much you have both learned and unlearned on matters all-important. We taught you then of the resurrection of the soul, in opposition to the resurrection of the body. We explained the true theory of the rising of the spirit, not in a far distant hereafter, but at the moment of bodily dissolution. This was new to you; it is not so now. You have now knowledge of what then seemed unintelligible to your mind. We have told you too of the mission of Jesus, and of His present work among you through His messengers. We have shown to you the true Divinity, the real grandeur of the Lord whom you had ignorantly worshipped. We have shown Him to you as He was, as He always described Himself, a man like yourselves, only the noblest of the children of men, the likest God, the truest and purest ideal of man's perfection. If we have taken from the Christ the halo which a foolish and human creed had spread around Him, we have shown you the man Christ Jesus in divinest form, the full realisation of human perfection on this earth.

His body has not indeed been raised, but He has never died, and in spirit He manifested to His friends, walked with them, as we may one day walk with you, and taught them of the truth.

What you are now witnessing are the signs and wonders that prelude the opening of a new dispensation, the advent of the Lord, not as man has fancied and as your teachers have vainly taught, in bodily presence to judge an arisen humanity, but in His new mission (the fulness of the old), through us, His messengers and ministers, in the declaration of a new evangel to your world. In those events which even now transpire among you we bear our part. It is our mission, under the sacred guidance of Him in whose name we speak, to tell to a world only partly able to bear it a new Gospel which, in after ages, shall take its place among the revelations of the Supreme to man, and shall be valued as the outcome of the past.

We have lately been able to act more directly on you, because of your increased passivity, and more receptive frame of mind. We earnestly encourage you to prayerfulness and stedfastness, together with patient watching. Be not diverted from the purpose for which we labour. Meditate long and frequently on the sacred message which God now sends to earth. Strive to throw aside obstacles and bars to progress. We would not have you neglect your daily work. The time will come when we shall be able to use you more frequently. That time is not yet come. It is necessary that you go through this additional trial and preparation; meantime, dear friend, remember that you need training, even as by fire . . . you must endeavour to rise above the plane of earth to the higher spheres, where the higher spirits dwell. This is our Easter message to you. Awake and arise from the dead. Cast aside the gross cares of your lower world. Throw off the material bonds that bind and clog your spirit. Rise from dead matter to living spirit; from earthly care to spiritual love; from earth to heaven. Emancipate your spirit from earthly cares which are earth-born and unspiritual. Cast aside the material and the physical which have been the necessary aids to your progress, and rise from engrossing interest in the worldly to a due appreciation of Spiritual Truth. As the Master said to His friends, "Be *in* the world, but not *of* the world." So shall those other words of your Sacred Records be fulfilled in you: "Awake thou that sleepest, and arise from the dead, and Christ shall give thee light."

You speak as if I wasted time on worldly things.

No; we have said that it must needs be that your earthly work must be accomplished even at the risk of preventing the education of your spirit. But we would have you to devote your care to higher spiritual teaching, and to leave the lower planes of objective evidence, which should no longer be required. We would have you to progress. And what we say to you we say to all.

> [After some further questions I suggested that development might go on till one became quite unfit for work in the world; so sensitive as fit only to be shut up in a glass case; so absorbed in spirit-land as to be useless for a workaday world: that indeed being the perfection of mediumship.]

Doubtless it might be so with another type of spirit placed in other circumstances and under other guardianship. We shall see to that. We have made our choice with a view to it, and have preferred to risk delay rather than to choose an instrument who would be ill-regulated in mind, and a prey to the fantasies of every vagrant spirit. We have trusted that the fulness of time will lessen the weight of doubt and difficulty, and that assured confidence being established, and over-carefulness diminished, we may progress with speed and safety. We cannot hasten that time; we would not if we could. But we shall not cease to urge on all our friends the necessity for higher aspirations; nor to impress on them that the physical foundation having been laid it is time to raise the spiritual superstructure.

> [I repeated what I had before said, viz., that I would go where I saw my way; but that I thought much that passed current for Spiritualism to be unworthy and even mischievous; that mediumship was anything but an unmixed blessing, and, when exercised in mixed circles, a very dangerous thing. I added that faith was no doubt necessary, but that I had about as much as I ever should have. And quite certainly no amount of physical proof beyond what we had received would add one iota to it.]

You are mistaken in supposing your faith to be as strong as it will be. When enlarged and purified it will be a vastly different power from that cold, calculating, nerveless assent which you now call Faith. The faith you now possess would pale and fade away before real obstacles. It has no hold upon your mind, is no factor in your life. In one way it would be strengthened by opposition, but a severe spiritual attack from the adversaries would well-nigh extinguish it. Faith to be real must be outside the limits of caution, and be fired by something more potent and effective than calculating prudence, or logical deduction, or judicial impartiality. It must be the fire that burns within, the mainspring that regulates the life, the overmastering force that will not be at rest. This is that faith that Jesus spoke of when He said of it that it was able to move mountains. This is that which braves death and torture, braces up the feeble knees for long and hard endurance, and conducts its possessor safe at last through any perils that may assail him to the goal where faith finds its reward in fruition.

Of this you know nothing. Yours is not Faith, but only logical assent; not spontaneous living faith, but a hard-wrung intellectual assent weighted always with a mental reservation. That which you have would move no mountain, though it might suffice to select a safe way round it. It would be powerless to animate and stir the spirit, though it would be fitted to estimate evidence and weigh probabilities. It would suffice for purposes of intellectual defence, but it is not the faith that springs unceasing in the innermost soul, and becomes, by virtue of its power, an over-mastering leader, a mainspring of action, of high and holy purpose, at which the world may sneer, and the wise may scoff, but which is the central spring of all that is best and noblest in man's life.

Of this you know nothing. But, mark us, the time will come when you will marvel how you could have ever dignified this calculating caution by the name of faith, or have dreamed that to its hesitating knock can ever be unbarred the portals of Divine truth. You must wait, and when the time comes you will not set up that pale marble statue in place of what should be a living body, instinct with conviction, and energised by the loftiest purpose. You have no faith.

> *You have a way of putting things, which, however true, is slightly discomfiting. However, since " Faith is the gift of God," I can't see how I am to blame. I am as I was made.*

Nay, friend, but you are what you have made yourself through a life which has been moulded both from within and from without. You are what external circumstances, and internal predilections, and spirit guidance have made you. You misunderstand. We did but rebuke you for your vaunting that as faith which has no claim to the name. Be content. You are on the road to higher knowledge of a nobler truth. Withdraw (so far as may be) from the external, and cultivate the interior and spiritual. Cease not to pray for faith, that what you well call, "the gift of God," may be poured into your spirit, and energise through it to a higher knowledge. You retard us by your very anxiety.

✝ IMPERATOR.

[Easter Day, 1875. I had been conscious of the presence of a great number of spirits in the morning. After some reference to this, it was written under an entirely new influence, though by the usual amanuensis]:—

We have told you that we always celebrate anniversaries, and Easter is with us a festival as well as with you: though we celebrate it from other reasons, and with a higher knowledge. Easter is to us the Festival of Resurrection, but not of the body. To us it symbolises not Resurrection *of* matter, but Resurrection *from* matter, the Resurrection of Spirit: and not this alone, but Resurrection of Spirit from material beliefs and surroundings: the emancipation of the soul from the earthy and material, even as the spirit rises from the dead body with which it has done for ever.

You have learned that there is a spiritual significance in everything, even as there is a spirit underlying every material object. So the dogma that Christendom celebrates to-day is to us of special significance. Christians keep festival in memory of the rescue of their Master, the Lord Jesus, from the grasp of death : and though they erroneously believe that the material body was revived, they do in ignorance celebrate the great spiritual truth that there is no death. The festival to us is one of joy over the partial recognition of a truth divinely seen by men: and of still greater rejoicing over the mighty work consummated on this day. It is not that death was vanquished, as you say, but that man began dimly to see a vision of eternal life.

[I enquired as to the character of Christ's human body, and the spiritual significance of his life.]

It is sufficient to say that the Incarnation of an exalted spirit for the purpose of regenerating mankind is not confined to a single instance. The special salvation which mankind derives from these special Saviours is that of which at the time it stands in need. These special Incarnations you will know more of hereafter. For the present we say only that they are in degree different from that of ordinary men, even as among men there is every grade of nationality in the body: some gross and sensual, others refined and ethereal. The human body of Jesus was of the most ethereal and perfect nature, and it was trained and prepared during thirty years of seclusion from the three years of active work that the spirit had to do.

You err in supposing [*the thought had crossed my mind, How disproportionate the preparation to the work!*] that the work done by an incarnated spirit is to be bounded by the span of earthly existence. It is very frequently, as in the case of Jesus of Nazareth, the after effect of the life that is the truest part of the work. So, though the work was begun during these three years, it has been carried on ever since.

It was the union of the majestic with the humble that was the note of his life. Majesty and meanness combined. The majesty shone out at seasons—at his birth, at his death, at intervals during his life, as at Jordan when the attesting voice of spirit sanctified his mission. Men knew of him, all his life through, that he was not as other men: that his life was not to be bound by social or domestic ties: though the harmony of the social circle was pleasant to him. Men knew this: and your Bible gives you, in this respect, a most imperfect idea of the influence he exercised on all who came near him. It dwells too little on the moral effect his words and actions caused, and too much on the ignorant misconceptions of the learned and respectable classes who then, as always were, the bitterest foes of new truth. The Scribes and Rulers, the Pharisees and Sadducees, were the ignorant foes of the Christ, even as your learned men and doctors, your theologians and men of science so-called, hate, and would persecute, the mission that springs from Christ now.

When you come to write the story of our work, you would not seek for its records among such classes of men; and the fault is, that those who have given you the only record you have of the life of Jesus have insisted too much on his persecution by learned ignorance, and too little on the moral dignity of his life amongst those who lived with him. They had not access to the original recipients of his teaching, and borrowed at tenth hand stories that were rife. It is as though, centuries hence, men should compile a history of these days from the current stories of society. It is important to mark this.

The life of the Christ, so far as it was public, was comprised within three years and a few months. For that the previous thirty years had been a preparation. During all that time he was receiving instruction from those exalted angels, who inspired him with zeal and love for his mission. He was a constant communer with the world of spirit; and was the more able to drink in their teachings that his body was no bar to his spirit.

In the case of most incarnate spirits, who have descended to minister on earth, the assumption of corporeity dims spiritual vision, and cuts it off from remembrance of its previous existence. Not so with him. So little did his ethereal body blind the sense of spirit, that he could converse with the angels as one of their own order, who was cognisant of their life, and remembered his own part in it before incarnation.

His remembrance of previous life was never blunted, and a great part of his time was spent in disunion from the body, and in conscious communion with spirit. Long trances, as you call the interior state, fitted him for this, as you may see in some distorted passages of your records, the supposed Temptation, for instance, or that which speaks of his habit of meditating and praying alone on the mountain-top, or in the Garden Agony.

You may also detect by the light we now give you flashes of recollection of his state before incarnation, even, as he is recorded to have said, in the glory of the Father before the world began. There are many such.

His life, but little hampered by the body—which, indeed, was but a temporary envelope to his spirit, assumed only when it was necessary for the spirit to come in contact with material things,—was different in degree, though not in kind, from the ordinary life of man—purer, simpler, nobler, more loving, and more loved. Such a life could never be understood aright by those who were contemporary with it. It is of necessity that such lives should be misunderstood, misinterpreted, maligned, and mistaken. It is so in a degree with all that step out from the ranks, but especially with him.

Prematurely was that Divine Life cut short by human ignorance and malignity. Little do men grasp the significance of the truth to which they carelessly give utterance when they say that Christ came into the world to die for it. He did so come: but in the sense of these enthusiasts, he came not. The drama of Calvary was of man's not God's devising. It was not the eternal purpose of God that Jesus should die when the work of the Christ was but just commencing. That was man's work, foul, evil, accursed.

Christ came to die for and to save man in the same, though in a higher sense, that all regenerators of men have been their Saviours, and have yielded up bodily existence in devotion to an over-mastering idea. In this sense He came to save and die for men: but in the sense that the scene on Calvary was foreordained to occur when man consummated his foul deed, he came not. And this is a mighty truth.

Had the full life of Jesus been completed on earth, what vast, what incalculable blessings would men have reaped? But they were not fitted, and they pushed aside the proffered blessings, having but just tasted them. They were not prepared. So with all great Lives. Men take from them only that which they can grasp, and leave the rest for after ages: or they push them impatiently aside, and will have none of them: and after ages worship and revere a spirit incarned too soon. This too is a mighty truth.

It is not permitted us, nay, it is not in the counsels of the Supreme Himself, to force on man a truth for which he is not ripe. There must be, throughout God's universe, orderly progression, and systematic development. So it is now. Were men fitted to receive the truths we tell of, the world would be blest with a revelation such as it has not had since last the Angels shed on it the beams of Divine Truth. But it is not prepared: and only the few who have learned wisdom will receive now what future ages will drink in with gladness. In this sense the Christ life was a failure during his existence on earth, and a potent vivifying influence among men afterwards.

Guided by angel-influence, the Church, that bears his name, has gathered up the germs of truth that that life typified, though now, alas! long custom has familiarised men too much with the old ideas, and they have lost their chief power.

You know that the three branches of the Church of Christ are agreed in celebrating certain festivals in memory of events in the life of Jesus. They who, outside the Church, have refused to keep fast and festival are not wise. They cut themselves off from a portion of the truth. But the Christian Church keeps in memory of its Head, Christmas, Epiphany, Lent, Easter, Ascension, and Whitsuntide. Those are the landmarks in the Christ life, and each represents an event in his life with a hidden spiritual significance.

The Christmas Festival of the Birth of the Spirit on the plane of Incarnation typifies Love and Self-denial. The exalted spirit tabernacles in flesh, abnegates Self, animated by Love. It is to us the Festival of Self-denial.

The Epiphany, the Festival of the manifestation of this new

light to the world, is to us the Festival of Spiritual Enlightenment: the shining of the True Light that lighteth every one that is born into the world: not the carrying of it to men, but the uplifting of the Light so that they who can see may come to it.

The Fast of Lent typifies to us the struggles of Truth with darkness. It is the Wrestling with the Adversaries. The recurring season shadows forth a constantly recurring struggle. It is the Fast of Conflict: of wrestling with evil: of the endeavour to overcome the world.

Good Friday typifies to us the consummation of the struggle, the end that awaits all such conflicts in your world—Death: but Death in Life. It is the Festival of Triumphant Self-sacrifice: the realization and consummation of the Christ Life. It is to us no Fast, but a Festival of Triumphant Love.

Easter, the Festival of the Resurrection, typifies to us the perfected life, the risen life, the glorified life. It is the Festival of Spirit, conquering and to conquer: of the risen life, enfranchised and set free.

Whitsuntide, which Christendom associates with the baptism of the Spirit is to us a Festival of great import. It typifies the outpouring of a large measure of spiritual truth on those who have accepted the Christ-life. It is the Festival which is the complement of Good Friday. As human ignorance slays the truth that it cannot receive: so, as a consequence, from the higher realm of spirit comes a blessing on those who have embraced what the world has crucified. It is the Festival of the outpoured Spirit, of increased grace, of richer truth.

Ascension, lastly, is the Festival of the completed life, of the return of the Spirit to its home, of the final sundering from matter. It is the end as Christmas was the beginning: not of life but of earth life: not the end of existence but of that span consecrated by love and self-denial to mankind. It is the Festival of the completed work.

These are the spiritual ideas which underlie the Festivals of your Church. It is not because she has not fully grasped their meaning that she has not done well to celebrate them. And as the spirit who has charge of us and of our work has broken down for you the wall of dogmatism and has shed light on the superstitions of the Church, so it is permitted to us to show you that beneath all lies enshrined the germ of truth: and when man's error is removed, God's truth is more plainly seen.

We have desired to complement the teaching you have received. As it was necessary to destroy, so is it to conserve. Even as He, the Lamb of God, the Saviour of men, rescued Divine Truth from Jewish ignorance and superstition, so do we rescue Divine Verities from the crushing weight of man's theology. As He, the great Healer of the nations, unloosed the struggling souls, and released them from the dominion of spiritual evil: so do we set free the spirit from the bonds of human dogma, and bid the enfranchised Truth to soar so that men may see it and know that it is of God.

CRUCIFIXION AND RESURRECTION.—SELF-SACRIFICE AND REGENERATION.

An Easter Message, 1876.

[I asked for further teaching on the subject of Death and Life, especially in the symbolic aspects in which they present themselves to Spirit.
In the question put by me, I alluded to the spiritual symbolism between the Death and Resurrection, and suggested that it typified death as the portal of life; and spiritual death as the road to spiritual regeneration.]

Refer to what we wrote for you on the last Festival of Easter. The symbolism to which you allude was then explained: viz., resurrection *from* matter, not *of* matter. We explained the spiritual significance of the various Festivals which the Christian Church has always kept. Refer.

[I referred to the message which immediately precedes this; in the course of which the Church Festivals are symbolically explained; Christmas, self-denial; Epiphany, spiritual enlightenment; Lent, spiritual conflict; Good Friday, triumphant love; Easter the risen life; Whitsuntide, the outpoured spirit; Ascension, the completed work.]

So it is. The whole course of the typical life of the Pattern Man is emblematic of the progressive development of the life begun on earth, completed in heaven (so to use your terms), born of self-denial, and culminating in spiritual ascension. In the Christ-life, as in a story, man may read the tale of the progress of spirit from incarnation to enfranchisement. Thirty years and more of angelic preparation fitted the Christ for His mission: three short years sufficed to discharge so much of it as man could bear. So man's spirit in its development progresses through the course covered by the Festivals of the Christian Church, from the birth of self-denial to the festival of the completed life. Born in self-denial, progressing through self-sacrifice, developed by perpetual struggles with the adversaries (the antagonistic principles which must be conquered in daily life, in self, and in the foes), it dies at length to the external, and rises on its Easter morn from the grave of matter, and lives henceforth, baptized by the outpoured spirit of Pentecost, a new and risen life, till it ascends to the place prepared for it by the tendency of its earth life.

This is the Spirit's progress, and it may be said to be a process of regeneration, shortly typified by crucifixion and resurrection. The old man dies, the new man rises from his grave. The old man, with his lusts, is crucified; the new man is raised up to live a spiritual and holy life. It is regeneration of spirit that is the culmination of bodily life, and the process is crucifixion of self, a daily death, as Paul was wont to say. In the life of spiritual progress, there should be no stagnation, no paralysis. It should be a growth and a daily adaptation of knowledge; a mortification of the earthy and sensual, and a corresponding development of the spiritual and heavenly. In other words, it is a growth in grace, and in the knowledge of the Christ; the purest type of human life presented to your imitation. It is a clearing away of the material, and a development of the spiritual—a purging as by fire, the fire of a consuming zeal; of a life-long struggle with self, and all that self includes; of an ever widening grasp of Divine truth.

By no other means can spirit be purified. The furnace is one of self-sacrifice: the process the same for all. Only in some souls, wherein the Divine flame burns more brightly, the process is rapid and concentrated; while in duller natures the fires smoulder, and vast cycles of purgation are required. Blessed are they who can crush out the earthy, and welcome the fiery trial which shall purge away the dross. To such, progress is rapid and purification sure.

Yes; the struggle is severe, and one hardly knows what to fight against.

Begin within. The ancients were wise in their description of the enemies. A spirit has three foes—itself; the external world around it; and the spiritual foes that beset the upward path. These are described as the World, the Flesh, and the Devil.

Begin with self—the Flesh. Conquer it, so that you are no longer slave to appetite, to passion, to ambition: so that self can be abnegated, and the spirit can come forth from its hermit-cell, and live and breathe and act in the free scope of the universal brotherhood. This is the first step. Self must be crucified, and from the grave where it lies buried will rise the enfranchised spirit untrammelled, free from material clogs.

This done, the soul will have no difficulty in despising the things which are seen, and in aspiring to the eternal verities. It will have learned that truth is to be found in them alone; and, seeing this, it will maintain a deathless struggle with all external and material forms, as being only adumbrations of the true, too often deceptive and unsatisfying. Matter will be regarded as the husk to be stripped off before the kernel of truth can be got at. Matter will be the deceptive, fleeting phantasm behind which is veiled the truth on which none but the purged eye may gaze. Such a soul, so taught, will not need to be told to avoid the external in all things, and to penetrate through the husk to the truth that lies below. It will have learned that the surface-meanings of things are for the babes in spiritual knowledge, and that beneath an obvious fact lurks a spiritual symbolic truth. Such a soul will see the correspondence of matter and spirit, and will recognise in the external only the rude signs by which is conveyed to the child so much of spiritual truth as its finite mind can grasp. To it, in veriest truth, *to die has been gain.* The life that it leads is a life of the spirit; for flesh has been conquered, and the world has ceased to charm.

But in proportion as the spiritual perceptions are quickened, so do the spiritual foes come into more prominent view. The adversaries, who are the sworn enemies of spiritual progress and enlightenment, will beset the aspirant's path, and remain for him a ceaseless cause of conflict throughout his career of probation. By degrees they will be vanquished by the faithful soul that presses on, but conflict with them will never wholly cease during the probation-life, for it is the means whereby the higher faculties are developed, and the steps by which entrance is won to the higher spheres of bliss.

This, briefly, is the life of the progressive spirit—self-sacrifice, whereby self is crucified; self-denial, whereby the world is vanquished; and spiritual conflict, whereby the adversaries are beaten back. In it is no stagnation; even no rest; no finality. *It is a daily death, out of which springs the risen life.* It is a constant fight, out of which is won perpetual progress. It is the quenchless struggle of the light that is within to shine out more and more into the radiance of the perfect day. And thus only it is that what you call heaven is won.

> Sic itur ad astra. *That is very much the central idea of Christianity, and also of Buddhism, as well as of the Occultists. Christ's sayings teem with the notion which animated his own life. The great difficulty is to carry out such an abstract system into operation in the world.*

Therein is the struggle, as He himself said, to be *in* the world, but not *of* the world. The high ideal is well nigh impossible for those who have upon them the care of daily toil. Hence it is that we have striven to withdraw you, so far as we can, from the objective side of spirit-intercourse, foreseeing that it would be hurtful to you. You must strive to rise above the material, and to leave it behind. Such intercourse is fitted only for those who can be secluded from the cares of daily life.

I said long ago that I believed mediumship, if carried out, to be incompatible with daily work in the world. The very development of sensitiveness, which grows so rapidly, is quite enough to unfit the medium for rude contact with the world: or, at any rate, to encourage in him moods, and draw round him influences, which make him unfit for work.

To a great extent it is so: and, therefore, we have withdrawn the more material side of mediumship from you, and that should develop the spiritual, in which no such danger lurks. At any rate, you may trust us to do what is wise. The danger is when they who guide are unfit for the work. It is then that risk becomes serious. Be content; your course is clear. Only remember that now is the hour and power of darkness. Be patient.

+ IMPERATOR.

[Easter Day, 1877.]

May the blessing of the Supreme and All-good be on you! We have somewhat to say to you, as our habit is at this season, of resurrection and renewal of life.

We will leave the plain symbolism of the Christian festival, of which we have before discoursed. We have told you of conflict followed by victory. You have learned how the life of the Man Christ Jesus was a symbolic representation of the progress of spirit. It may be well that we remind you here of this symbolism.

Descending from His spiritual life in the spheres of bliss, the Anointed One came to your earth to fulfil His Divine mission. Vailing in human flesh the radiance of His pure spirit, He took a body in the manger of Bethlehem, and became man, with all the imperfections and frailties of humanity, subject to the sorrows, the temptations, the discipline through which alone progress is gained.

In this read a type of the descent of spirit into matter as its sole means of progress. Spirit, existent in the ages past, having won for itself the requisite development, descends to incarnation, so that by conflict and by discipline it may be purified and made fit for the progress it cannot otherwise gain.

Born thus into the sphere of humanity, the Anointed One became subject at once to persecution and assault from a Prince of the world. The powers of the sphere into which He came were arrayed against Him, and sought to try and prove Him. The word went forth to slay the Anointed One because His royal claims were thought to be in conflict with the pretensions of the earthly monarch.

A type this of the conflict that besets the incarnate spirit from the moment of its entrance into the sphere of earth.

At the threshold of every new sphere of development stand, as we have told you, the guardians from whom the benefits to be gained by entering it are won only after wrestling and agony [*i.e., as afterwards explained, conflict*]. These blessings are not to be gathered idly and dreamily, without risk and strenuous labour. Were it so, the benefit would cease to be. It is in the conflict that the blessing lies, in overcoming the foes, in victory after the battle is over. Lay it to your account that this is so, and that for the incarnate spirit there is always a persecutor who seeks to slay.

Threatened by these enemies the young child was withdrawn to Egypt, where He was safe, and where from a full storehouse He gathered in a rich store of knowledge. Egypt had been, since earliest days, the receptacle of mystic knowledge, and there was derived much of that mystic knowledge that the Anointed One displayed in after years.

You will not need to seek far for the significance of this type. Where shall the spirit, beset and threatened by the foes that throng around it, find its sanctuary at once and its armoury more surely than in the mystic lore stored up for it by those who have preceded it in trial, and have left for it records of their experience? In the Egypt of esoteric lore is that armoury whence the militant spirit may find power to overcome, thoroughly furnished and equipped for the conflict, instructed and edified by what it has learned. For, be it known to you, the withdrawal to Egypt has a double significance. It is not only a retreat to a place of safety, but a sojourning in a school of instruction. The spirit that seeks to withdraw into the esoteric sphere of instruction, so as to be edified there, draws from that edification its spiritual weapons of conflict, the while it rests and refreshes itself in an atmosphere of comparative peace. Meditation, edification, growth to the full stature of the warrior—even as the Anointed One grew from puny childhood to the vigour of youth, and was edified in mind by the knowledge He acquired in proportion as His body increased in strength. He increased, as it is said, in wisdom and stature.

This closes a typical epoch in the symbolic life of the Anointed One. The seed-time closes with the commencement of the public life. The spirit that has nerved itself for the life of progress and for development during the time of incarnation beyond what is sought by the mass of its fellows, is permitted to pass through a process of preparation, during which it receives so much of truth as it can assimilate, prior to the second period, the missionary period, as we may call it, of its life on earth. You do not need to be told that it is an essential condition of spiritual progress that selfishness in all its forms be crushed out, that no gift be kept for private and isolated use, but that in all things the precept be obeyed, Freely ye have received, freely give.

So that which has been given must be shared with those who seek to partake of it. The truth, in its exoteric form at least, must be proffered to the world, while the inner and diviner secrets must be cherished and kept pure, so that the soul may refresh itself in the intervals of conflict, as the Anointed One retired to the solitudes of the mountain-top, that he might commune with himself in lonely meditation, and be refreshed by association with those who were not of earth. For him no companionship then. His spirit soared too high, his associates were too exalted for the gaze even of his nearest friends, save one, who on many occasions was privileged to see the glories that surrounded the chosen Messenger of the Most High in his moments of chiefest exaltation.

[This was afterwards explained as referring to Saint John, who, on many occasions not specifically named, enjoyed a near view of the glory of his Master.]

Blessed in this respect are they who can journey with a kindred soul, and derive mutual support and joy from an earthly as well as a heavenly communion. The esoteric truth loses no bloom by such handling. The lamp sheds no less light, and that light no less pure, because another eye beholds it, if only the eye be single and the sympathy sincere and perfect. But it is rare that two can walk thus, even if they be agreed, and there must always be, for those who aspire, the mountain-top of silent reverence and prayer, to which they resort alone, knowing that for each there is the peculiar path which it is necessary for his feet to tread.

The life of instruction, complemented by the life of aspiration, prepares for the public life of ministration.

When the Anointed One came forth from the seclusion of His preparatory training, instructed in the wisdom of Egypt, and nurtured in silent meditation, clothed in purity, animated by charity, instinct with zeal, He went forth to His people to preach the gospel He had learned. There glowed within Him a holy boldness for the truth, but He was no iconoclast. Not to destroy, but to fulfil, was His aim. Not to lay desolate and to waste, but to plough, and to till, and to sow the seed, so that the crop might spring up, and the desert and the waste place might blossom and be glad. The materials ready at hand were used, the dross was purged away, and the lifeless ceremony, touched by the magic of His word of truth, was transmuted into the symbolism of a living verity. The dry bones lived, the spirit returned to the corpse, the dead arose and stood upon their feet.

In all this, be it observed by the faithful watcher, there was no rude severance, no harsh closing of an epoch, no gulf between the present and the past. All was transition and gradual awakening, just as it is in Nature now. There is no rude severance between the death and resurrection of the year. You hardly know what power has rolled away the stone from the sepulchre in which the year lay buried. One day all is cold, lifeless, cheerless, and you mourn over the glories that seem to be past and gone for ever, replaced by abiding gloom. But, by-and-by, the change comes, not by might, nor by power, as man sees, but by the potent spirit. The sun shines forth, and his rays unlock the prison-house in which the dead year has lain, and buds begin to peep, and flowers to lift their heads shyly and half in fear, and the emerald carpet grows beneath your feet, and the mantle of tender green is spread around, and behold! the dry bones live. The season of resurrection has burst upon you, or rather has grown upon you silently, a development of the dead past. It is Nature's yearly parable of regeneration.

Read the lesson in the life of the Anointed One. When he came forth to teach His people wisdom, the whole of the spiritual life of the Jewish nation was cold and bare as the leafless tree in winter. The sap had ceased, it seemed, to flow. The branches were bare and gaunt, devoid of their seemly covering of leaves. The weary traveller should look in vain for fruit, or seek a stray flower to gladden his eyes. The death-plague was on all. He came, the Anointed Messenger of God, the chosen Messiah, on his missionary labours, the Sun of Righteousness and Truth—the Son who was also the Sun, for there was no difference there—shed his beams of enlightenment and warmth on those dead, dry, naked branches, and see the change! Empty formalism glowed again with spiritual truth, cold precepts were vivified again into exuberant life. What had been said by them of old time gained a new and extended significance. Social life was elevated, reformed, ennobled. Religion was raised to a pitch of spirituality it had never reached before. In place of selfishness there was taught charity; in place of formalism, spirituality; in place of ostentatious ritual, silent, secret prayer; in place of open parade of religion—the seeking to be seen of men—the seclusion of the secret chamber, the lonely communing between self and God. In a word, vulgar, empty, proud, unreal externalism was abolished and replaced by the meek, spiritual, aspiring life of the soul, the truest exemplification of which was not in the market-place, but in the silent chamber; not in the Pharisee, but in the Publican; not in the eyes of men, but before the searching scrutiny of the Supreme.

The parable of Nature and of the Pattern Life, runs through the life of spirit too. Duly prepared, educated, edified with such knowledge as it has been able to acquire, the spirit that has passed its probation goes forth on its journey in the new life. The dead past of formalism, of externalism, is transmuted by the touch of spirit, and a new life opens. The veriest physical fact gains a new significance as the spiritual meaning that underlies it becomes plainer to the purged eye of faith. The bare boughs are clothed with living green: the dry bones of externalism that lay apparently dead, arise under the quickening touch of spirit, and live a new life. It is not that the old is abolished; it is that it is transmuted. It is not that the duties of life are neglected: rather are they discharged with a quickened zeal, and a more loving care. It is not that the weary round of toil is shortened: it is that its lengthened path is cheered and dignified by the spiritual significance of even the meanest act.

Those dry and sapless forms of devotion that seemed so cold and dead that the soul has often cried in despair, "O Lord! can these dry bones live?" are found to be touched with life, and warmth, and reality, as the resurrection spirit quickens them. The old forms that have served their purpose are regenerated into a life more suited to the new conditions. They live again with more than the old vitality, with a loveliness more spiritual than that of the past. They have renewed their youth, and it is seen by the spiritually-enlightened that no atom of truth can perish, but is renewed and re-combined as there is need of it in the laboratory of the Master.

And so the spirit shares in the general resurrection that surrounds it. It renews its life, soars to higher planes of knowledge, learns deeper truths, and goes forth, in the might of that knowledge, to teach to others the Divine methods of enlightenment, development, and growth. Not as man sees does it see: not as man acts does it act. Beneath the most unpromising exterior it sees Divine possibilities. The veriest cumberer it would not cut down, save in so far as pruning may facilitate growth, and the lopping off of dead wood may allow the young and living branches to find place. Side by side with this public work is the unceasing esoteric life of growth in spirit, a life of aspiration and development, of communing with the spirit of truth, of rising more and more above the material and the earthy, to the measure of the stature of the fulness of the Anointed One.

Silent spiritual growth is the source of public spiritual teaching.

The closing scenes of the earth life of the Anointed One carry their symbolic meaning too. It is the lot of a teacher who combats the prejudices of an age, to incur the enmity, the scorn, the persecution, that is the world's requital for unwelcome truth. You, who regard these records of the Pattern Life as matter of history, can see now how impossible it was that teaching such as His should meet with other fate than it did. That prosperous shams should have been laid bare without those who made gain by them being arrayed against the daring innovator—that pompous and pretentious Pharisaism should have been denounced in terms more vigorous than were bestowed on the Magdalene and the Publican without setting the Pharisee in outraged wrath against his accuser—that the national religion, with its cheap ceremonialism, and its easy path for those who could pave it with gold, should be reformed, and the path made easier for Publicans and harlots than for Scribes and Pharisees, without bringing down the wrath of those in place and power on the despised Nazarene, who dared to lay his impious hand on God's own ark—this you can see to be impossible.

He was too pure and good to escape envy, too uncompromising and earnest not to provoke jealousy. His doctrines were too searching to be popular; His life precepts too spiritual to suit an age of luxury and ease. And so the age that could not receive the advanced truth, crucified Him who taught it. The age of hollowness and impurity revenged itself on the pure and holy Son of Truth by hanging Him on the tree of shame between the representatives of crime.

So it was. So in many cases it is still in intent, if not in deed. There have been reformers who have meted out to an age, over which a wave of Divine enthusiasm has just passed, that aspect of truth which commends itself to them, and so have found acceptance for their message, and have won honour and renown in its preaching. There have been others, too, who have had more of the world's wisdom and discretion, and so have been of higher service. But these are rare. To most, as to the Anointed One, death comes with contumely and open shame as the reward of truth. Death to the Teacher, but resurrection and new life to His teaching. It is not till the instrument is lost sight of that the value of the message is realised. We need not draw out the parable at length.

Hanging on the cross, the friends of the Christ were few indeed—a few women whose readier instincts and affections were true and firm in the hour of deepest darkness; and two of those who should have been nearest at hand, Joseph and Nicodemus, the two, be it known, who had made least open profession, and had even seemed most cowardly. All the rest were fled. The teacher of new truth, the preacher of a new dispensation, where was He? Dead. And where was His gospel? Dead, too, to all appearance. None remembered, none heeded it or Him. But men judge hastily. None knew who rolled that stone from the tomb's mouth, save that it was done by that might of Spirit wherewith ever and anon your world is regenerated, and death turned into new life. An angel did it; and the same power that opened that tomb and stirred its occupant whom men thought dead and buried out of sight, availed to vivify His message, and to nurture it through evil and good report, until it dominated the nations, and became in its age a mighty engine of spiritual truth.

Turn now to the individual soul. Its lot is much the same. Whether its message of what to it is Divine truth is one that makes its impress on the age or not: whether, if it do, it be received as the needful word in season, or as the impertinence of a meddling innovator, it will, almost surely, have to make its way through conflict to acceptance. Such is the Divine method of sifting. And in proportion to the severity of that conflict will be the vigour with which it will be found to have taken hold of men. The roots will be all the deeper and firmer fixed in proportion as the ground above has been trampled down by contending feet. Whether the life of conflict end, as did the life we contemplate, or whether feebler zeal or larger discretion preserve the teacher from the same fate, matters little. The word of truth must pass through the conflict to final victory, even as the soul in its solicitude and isolation must contend with tempters and with foes till it becomes perfect through suffering, and wins the crown by the cross.

The life of the Christ during such time as He remained on it after His resurrection was symbolic of the change that passes on the risen life of spirit. *In* the world, but not *of* it: moving in it as a visitor who conforms to but does not belong to it. He was animated by that most potent law of spirit which you may trace in all the ways of spirit-influence—the law of love. Whenever He appeared, whatever He did, this was the motive. The records left to you, both meagre and erroneous as they are, are yet sufficiently full to show this. He fulfilled the law of love, and then ascended to His own proper sphere: no longer seen, but felt: no longer a personal presence, but an effluence and influence of grace.

So the souls who voluntarily linger around your earth are those whose motive-spring is love, or they whose mission is animated by the same master principle. Personal affection or universal love are the motives that draw the higher spirits down to you. And when the duty is discharged they too will ascend to the common Father and the Universal God.

Be of good hope! You are too apt to fancy that truth is dead. When the cold dark days of winter are with you, you are chilled. You forget the spring that has dawned on many a winter past. You forget that death leads to resurrection, and on to regenerated life—life in a wider sphere, with extended usefulness, with nobler aims, with truer purpose. You forget that death must precede such life—that what you call death, so far as it can affect Divine Truth, is but the dying of the grain of seed which is the condition of abundant increase

Death in life is the spiritual motto. Death culminating in a higher life. Victory in the grave, and through death. In dealing with spiritual truth do not forget this.

In times of brightness and calm you may fear. When the air is stagnant and the heat scorching, when the moisture is dried up, and the fierce sun beats down with untempered splendour, the tender plant may wither and fade. And so in days of ease and smoothness, when all goes swimmingly, when all men seem to speak well of the Word of Truth, you may with good reason fear lest it fade, and its outlines be blurred, and its tone assimilated to the conventional fashion of the world. You may settle with yourselves that if all accept unquestioned the truth presented to them, then that phase of truth needs changing, and some stronger form is requisite. But when it is born in conflict be of good cheer, for by such birth-pangs man-children are brought forth, whose vigour and energy shall suffice to resist attack, and to carry on the Divine standard to a further vantage-ground.

It was in some such sort that the life of the Anointed One began and ran its course to the final consummation. It is a parable for all time.

✝ Imperator.

SECTION XXXI.

LIFE AND DEATH: PROGRESS AND RETROGRESSION.

[April 28, 1876.—The following message relates to a case in which the personal identity of the communicating spirit was established by very strong evidence. Among many such this seems to me to stand out prominently, and, making all allowance for willingness and ability to deceive, I find it impossible to understand how so coherent and complete a series of proofs can be explained away by any theory of personation or self-deception. The messages relate to the death, under melancholy circumstances, of a friend whom I had known intimately all his life. A sitting at Mr. Hudson's had resulted in his image appearing on the photographic plate, and I have since seen and known the presence of the spirit about me continually. When the photograph was taken I was entranced, and the name of the spirit was given to me, another spirit at the same time describing the position in which the figure had placed itself. The development of the plate showed this description to be correct, and I have no difficulty in recognising a bad image or *simulacrum* of my friend who had been specially brought before my mind before going to Hudson's. There was another and more striking point connected with this matter which I cannot print: it must suffice that I state that identity, both of external form and of mental characteristics, is distinctly made out to my mind. The first message I received respecting this photograph related to the method of its production. It was said that a spirit who just then was very active about me had directed Hudson's invisible operators. The shroud-like drapery which characterises all Hudson's pictures was described as an expedient for saving time and power: the head being fully formed, the rest "sketched in," as one might say. There were a number of these spiritual operators who did the mere mechanical work of partial materialisation as they had learned to do it. Hence there is a family likeness in all the pictures produced by a particular photographer.

The whole manifestation was described as being contrary to the wish of IMPERATOR who "did not wish that I should be brought again within the physical phase of manifestation." "It was only when we found that we could not prevent that we aided."

The spirit had been in my company: there had been special reasons for his being attracted that day, and so it was easier to produce his image than that of any other spirit: though I went with two friends in the hope of securing some evidence for them and not for myself.

This being so, he was taken in hand by M., who directed Hudson's spirit-people to mould a representation of his face and to sketch drapery. The *simulacrum* was made of spirit-substance, actually posed, and photographed.

After this IMPERATOR said]:—

We would speak with you of your friend. But first, we wish to explain that we prevented, so far as we could, any return of physical manifestations to you. We did not wish the medial power to recur to that phase. Hence we have prevented you from being placed in circumstances where it would be likely to be encouraged. We have explained before that we do not wish you to remain on the physical plane, and have therefore discontinued our meetings. Nor did we wish that your friend should become attached to you. His spiritual state is low, and it would have been well that you had not attracted him. Since you have done so you must now help him to progress. M. has rightly told you that you had entered into his sphere from association and conversation with ——, and from your thoughts being directed towards him strongly. That is the law of attraction of spirit to spirit. You know this?

> *Yes; but it does not always act, or rather its results are seldom manifest to us. Is he unhappy?*

How should he be blest? He lifted sacrilegious hands against the shrine in which the All-Wise had placed his spirit for its progress and development. He wasted opportunities and destroyed, so far as he was able, the temple in which dwelt the Divine spark, which was his portion. He sent forth his spirit alone and friendless into a strange world where no place was yet prepared for it. He impiously flew in the face of the Great Father. How should he be blest? Impious, disobedient, wilful in his death, heedless, idle, selfish in his life, and yet more selfish in bringing pain and sorrow on his earthly friends by his untimely death,—how should he find rest? The wasted life cries out for vengeance. The fostered self-hood dominates him still, and makes him ill at ease. Selfish in his life, selfish in his earthly end, he is selfish still. Miserable, blind, and undeveloped, there is no rest for such as he till repentance has had its place, and remorse leads to regeneration. He is outcast.

What hope of progress?

Yes; there is hope. Already there stirs within him the consciousness of sin. He sees dimly through the spiritual gloom how foolish and how wicked was his life. He begins to wake to some faint knowledge of his desolation, and to strive for light. Hence he remains near you. You must help him though at your own cost.

Willingly; but how?

By prayer first. By fostering the dawnings of the higher life. By allowing the unhappy spirit to breathe the higher atmosphere of work. His spirit knows not what that pure and bracing atmosphere is. You must teach him, though his presence be unpleasant to you. You have summoned him, and he comes obedient to your call. You must bear with him now. You cannot undo what you have done in spite of us and of our wishes. Your consolation must be that you will be engaged in a work that is blessed.

It is not fair to say I summoned him; but I will do anything. He was mad and not accountable.

He was and is accountable, and he begins to know it. The seeds of his final sin wherewith he has cursed himself were sown in a life of idle uselessness. He fostered and encouraged morbid self-introspection. He brooded over self, not for the purpose of progress and development, not to eradicate faults and foster virtues, but in selfish exclusiveness. He was enwrapped in a cloud of distorted selfishness. This bred in him disease, and in the end he fell a prey to tempters in the spirit, who fastened on him and drove him to his ruin. He exposed himself a prey to those who are always ready to seduce to ruin, and so far he was mad, as you say; but the mad act was the result of his own acts. And now he throws the same influence around those whom he wounded in his death. A curse to himself he becomes a curse to those he loves.

Horrible! That seems to me the very bitterness of retribution. I can understand how an idle, selfish life breeds spiritual disease. Selfishness seems to me to be the roo sin.

It is the plague-spot of the spirit, that which wrecks more souls than you dream of. It is the very paralysis of the soul. And when to it is added this moreover, that the selfishness is passive, it becomes more fatal. There is a selfishness which is far less baleful in its poison, and which finds its counteracting power in activity, and which even becomes the spring of actions which have in them a form of good. There is a selfishness which causes a spirit to do well that it may have the good report of its fellows: and there is a selfishness which is content to do good so it be not vexed or troubled, which will yield to any influence, so it may escape anxiety. These are faults which hold the spirit back from progress; but they are not the baleful plague which ate into this spirit's life, and drove it to despair and death. That was the meaner selfishness which stirred him not to any deeds or to action of any kind. It was idle and useless, no less than self-pleasing; nay, it was not even self-pleasing, for the whole life was blurred and blotted with morbid scrutiny of self, till its very lineaments were eaten out. This selfishness was cruel alike to himself and to his friends. There are grades of sin, and his was deep. Listen while the story is recounted for your instruction. But rest awhile, and we will remove the disturbing influence from your mind.

[I was a good deal disturbed: but I fell into a deep trance-like sleep, during which I had a soothing vision and from it I awoke refreshed.]

It is not necessary to go through in detail the story of that wasted life. Its spirit was eaten out with cruel selfishness, and its end was destruction of self-consciousness. Mad he was, as you estimate madness. None lifts the hand of the suicide against himself save when the disordered mind has lost its power of judgment. The balance is destroyed, and the spirit has fallen a prey to the tempters which surround it.

But your estimates of sin are rude. The state was self-induced. The spirit delivered itself over to the foes, and wrought its own ruin. This was not one of the cases where hereditary conditions of disease unfitted a spirit for judgment and right action. The suicide was the outcome of the selfish idler. It was an access of temptation that withdrew the power of reason, and caused the crime. In others the temptation might have taken other forms; but whether it led to destruction of self, or to ruin or hurt of others, to whatever gratification of self it tended, the root is the same.

That spirit which neglects to use its powers, which acts not, but morbidly dwells on fancied ills or sufferings, assuredly breeds in itself disease. The law of existence is work—for God, for brethren, for self; not for one alone, but for all. Transgress that law, and evil must ensue. The stagnant life becomes corrupt, and acts as a corrupter of others. It is vicious and noisome; hurtful to the community, in that it defrauds it of its due from one of its members, and sets up a plague spot of infection which becomes a fertile centre of mischief. It matters not what course the evil takes, its source is still the same. In this case the evil eventuated in personal harm, and in the wrecking of a wasted life. It has tended in sorrow and shame to the injury of all who were associated with him.

When the cord of earth-life was severed, the spirit found itself in darkness and distress. For long it was unable to sever itself from the body. It hovered round it even after the grave had closed over the shrine which it had violated. It was unconscious, without power of movement, weak, wounded, and distressed. It found no rest, no welcome in the world to which it had come unbidden. Darkness surrounded it, and through the gloom dimly flitted the forms of congenial spirits who had made shipwreck of themselves, and were in unrestful isolation. These drew near, and their atmosphere added vague discomfort to the half-conscious spirit.

It was not till the first shudder of awakening conscience attracted the ministering spirits, that anything could be done to palliate the misery, not yet half felt or acknowledged, or to minister healing to the soul. When it stirred amid the darkness, the ministers drew near and strove to quicken the seared conscience and to awaken remorse. In seeming cruelty they strove to bring home a knowledge of its state, and to paint before it a picture of its sin. Only through the portal of remorse could it enter into rest; and so the conscience must be quickened at the cost of pain.

For long their efforts availed little; but by degrees they succeeded in awakening some measure of consciousness of sin, and the spirit began to grope blindly for some means of escape from a state which had become loathsome to it. Frequent relapses dragged it back. The tempters were all around it, and no effort of theirs was spared to mete out to the spirit the full measure of its lawful penalty. They know it not; they do but gratify their debased instincts, but they are the avenging ministers of doom.

The hope for the spirit is that it may be nerved to occupy itself with some beneficent work, and so to work out its own salvation. To this end it must journey on through remorse and uncongenial labour: for by no other means can it be purified. Selfishness must be eradicated by self-sacrifice. Idleness must be rooted out by laborious toil. The spirit must be purified by suffering. This is for it the only upward path of progress; a path that its past has made it difficult, nearly impossible, for it to tread. Reiterated efforts must secure each onward step, and frequent slips and backslidings will try endurance to the utmost. Step by step the way must be won in sorrow, remorse, and shame, with faintings and cries of the despairing soul; won, too, against temptation all around, against the suggestions of the foe who will not fail to goad the aspiring soul; won as through a baptism of fire. Such is the penalty; such the road to the heaven that can be won in no other way.

Such help as the ministers can give will not be withholden. It is their glorious mission to help on the aspiring, and to cheer the fainting soul. But, though they may comfort, they cannot save one pang, nor palliate by one jot the penalty of transgression. No vicarious store of merit can avail; no friend may bear the burden, or lift it from the weary back. It must be borne by the soul that sinned, though helps and aids be given to strengthen and support the failing energies.

This is the inevitable penalty of a wasted life. It may be that the half-quenched spark may be quickened again, and be fanned into a flame strong enough to light the spirit onward. It may be that the spirit may wander in gloom and desolation, deaf to the voice of the ministers, and groaning in lonely unrest, nerveless for the struggle, till the sin through cycles of purgatorial suffering, has eaten out its virulence. It may be that the time consumed in such purgation may seem to you an eternity; or the soul may wake and stir before its condition has become fixed; and so by an effort of despairing energy may struggle up to light, and may welcome the suffering that leads to purification, and may have strength not all sapped to cast off the habits of earth, and wake to newness of life.

It may be; but such are rare cases. Characters are not so easily changed; nor does the fire of purification work so rapidly. Too frequently he that died selfish or filthy is selfish or filthy still, and the present proves only a perpetuation of the past. Pray for strength to minister to him who has in him the first faint dawnings of progression. Pray that his darkness may be enlightened, and his unrest soothed by the angelic ministrations. Such prayers are the most potent medicine for his disease.

> [On reading over what had been written, I suggested that the picture was one to strike dismay into a man, however much he strove to progress. I said the ideal was too high for earth.]

Nay! We have not painted the picture in all its details; nor have we overdrawn or overcoloured it in any way. We are not able to bring home to you the full horror of the desolation and misery of such a wasted life. No words that we can write would express the full measure of the woe felt by a soul that has awakened to remorse after a life such as this of which we speak. For the rest, we are not responsible for any ideal. We put forward none, save that which exists in the eternal and unalterable sequence of events. Selfishness and sin bring misery and remorse before they can be purged away. It is not we who laid down that law, but the Eternal and All-wise. We have but pointed out to you once again the operation of a law the working of which you may see all around you. We desired to point out what men are apt to forget, that though there be no formal judgment such as has been imagined, at a far distant day, in presence of an assembled universe, when the Recording Angel shall produce the Books of Doom, and the Christ shall sit in judgment, and shall condemn the sinner to an everlasting hell: though there be none of this, yet that every act is registered, every thought recorded, every habit known as a factor in the future character. We would show you that the judgment of condemnation needs no paraphernalia of assize, but is conducted in the silent recesses of the soul itself. No judge is there but the voice of Spirit communing with itself, and reading its own doom. No books but the records of conscience; no hell but the flame of remorse that shall eat into the soul and purge it as by fire.

And this, not in a far-off future when the arisen myriads of humanity shall all have been gathered up, but instant on death, quick as consciousness awakes, sure as the soul stirs in the new life. This too, not subject to a faint perhaps, in a dim and hazy light seen far off down the vista of the future, but sure and certain, instant and inevitable. We would teach you this. For it has been said of us that our Gospel removes the terror from religion, by which motive alone the most of men may be governed and restrained, and substitutes for it a faith which teaches salvation for all, whatever their deeds may be, whatever creed they may profess. We do not teach any such insensate creed. You know it; but you need to have repeated again and again the truth on which we have been insisting: *Man makes his own future, stamps his own character, suffers for his own sins, and must work out his own salvation.*

We did but dwell on this side because the story of that wasted life invited by its example. We have dwelt often enough on the lighter side of grace and beauty and angelic ministration. You need not to be told of the abounding mercy and love of the Supreme, nor of the tender watchful care which is ceaselessly exercised by those who minister between Him and you. It is well sometimes to show the dark side of loneliness and desolation, and temptation by the foes.

The ideal was not high: and if it were, high ideals serve only to brace the aspiring soul: they are too high for those only who have no ambition to ascend: not for those whose lives have not been eaten out by selfishness and sin, whose energies are yet strong, and will grow stronger by the exercise of them. Be assured, good friend, that the grand truth can never be escaped. Life is a journey, a conflict, a development. The journey is up-hill, and the way is thorn-beset and difficult. The conflict is unending till victory crowns the final effort. The development is spiritual from a lower to a higher plane, from the child of earth to the measure of the stature of the Christ. You cannot change the unalterable. You cannot reach the Perfect Good, save after a conflict with evil. It is an eternal necessity that you be purified through struggles with the evil that surrounds you. It is the means by which the spark once struck off from the Divine Soul wins back its way to Him and enters into its rest.

Do you need to be told that true happiness is to be had only by living up to the highest ideal? That the idler and the sluggard know it not? That the vicious man and the evil-doer, *who sins of choice and by preference,* have no part in it? That peace on earth springs up only in the soul that soars heavenwards, and finds its happiness in viewing the dangers and difficulties that have been overpassed? Do you need to be told again that the angels watch over such to bear them, up—that the ministers count it honour to support them, and that no final harm can fasten on the spirit which keeps a high ideal before it? Victory is assured: but it would not be victory were it found without a struggle in selfish and inglorious ease, by those who would not value what every idle hand might pluck. Victory comes after conflict: peace after tribulation: development after steady growth.

> *I replied that this seemed to me matter of course; and that in the seed time of life man must get as much knowledge, do as much work, and enjoy such peace as he can. But the work and the knowledge (especially of God Himself and His future) must precede Peace, or Rest. Perhaps too little room was left for meditation.*

No; the life is threefold: of meditation and prayer: of worship and adoration: and of conflict with the threefold enemy. The meditation is necessary to self-knowledge. It is an element of steady growth. With it goes prayer, the communion of the prisoned soul with the Father of spirits, and with us His ministers. Worship and adoration, in any of the countless phases that the soul seeks out for itself, whether in silent solitude beneath the heavens that speak to him of his God, or in communion with Nature, the external and material manifestation of Deity, or in the solemn service of song within some stately temple which man has separated for God: or in the upward aspiration of the heart unuttered and unheard of man—in any or all of these ways the instinct of adoration divinely implanted may find its vent. These are the necessary helps for the sustained conflict. We do not undervalue them: rather do we insist on them. We tell you that it would be well if you devoted more time to peaceful thought. Your life lacks quietness.

As to the accountability of this spirit for its rash act, surely you admit some cases where the spirit is not accountable.

Assuredly. The human instrument may be jarred and out of tune, and so may faultily transmit the will of the spirit within. There are many cases in which madness is the result of bodily disease. For such the spirit is not blameworthy. Accidental injury may derange, or congenital defect, or overstrain of trouble and distress. For such causes the spirit is blamed by none, least of all by the Holy and Just One, who deals not with body but with spirit, and who judges according to spiritual motive and intent. We reprobated the case on which we spoke, because the end was the result of life-long sin. He was and is responsible, and he begins to know it.

May the Allwise foster and increase the knowledge.

✝ Imperator.

SECTION XXXII.

[As a specimen of a message written at a later period, I append the following. It is a fair sample of some of the more elevated teaching. It was written with vast rapidity, and is printed precisely as written. There was no need to alter a word. As it was being given, I was conscious of a most powerful and elevating influence which permeated my whole being.]

TRUTH.

The blessing of the Blessed One rest on you. We have opportunity now which may not recur of answering some of your inquiries, and of conveying to you some necessary truth. From letters which you have received of late you will be led to see that the times of trouble and distress which we have warned you of are expected by others as well as by us. Be prepared for trouble: it will assuredly come. It is necessary that afflictions come. Jesus knew and taught that. It is necessary for the training of the soul. It is as necessary as physical discipline for the body. No deep knowledge is to be had without it. None is permitted to scale the glorious heights but after discipline of sorrow. The key of knowledge is in spirit-hands, and none may wrest it to himself but the earnest soul which is disciplined by trial. Bear that in mind.

Ease and luxury are the pleasant paths in which the soul lingers and dreams away the summer day. Self-denial, self-sacrifice, self-discipline are the upward tracks, thorn-vext and rocky, which lead to the heights of knowledge and power. Study the life of Jesus and be wise.

Moreover, the present is a time of hard and bitter conflict between us and our foes. We have told you that you feel the reflex of that struggle. It accompanies every great development of Divine Truth. It is, as it were, the darkness that precedes the dawn: the gloom which is the pre-requisite for growth: the period of trial wherein the earnest soul is purified. "Your hour and the power of darkness," said Jesus as he agonised in Gethsemane. It is so now: and it will not pass lightly. The cup must be drained.

As each revelation of the Supreme grows old, it is overlaid by man's errors, and loaded with his inventions. It dies gradually, and loses its hold on men. Bit by bit human error is pared away, unable to stand the shock of criticism, and men's faith is shaken, and they ask with old Pilate—What *is* truth? Then comes the answer in the new birth of a higher revelation. The throes of its birth shake the world, and around its cradle the powers of the Spiritual world contend. Great is the dust and din of the contention.

As the light dawns upon the world, and the clouds lift, the watchers, whose eyes are spiritually opened to discern the signs of the times, they who stand on the watch-towers to catch the first gleams, these are ready and welcome with joy the break of day. "Joy comes with the morning." "Sorrow and sighing flee away." The terrors of the night, "the powers of darkness," are past. But not for all. Full many there will always be for whom no ray of light is visible till the sun has gained his meridian and splendour. They slumber on, heedless of the light that is breaking on the world.

Hence the days will never come to your world when all equally will know of the truth. There will always be many for whom it has no charms, for whom it would be fraught with danger to tread the upward paths of progress, and who prefer the beaten track worn by the feet of those who have trod it through the ages past. There will be such always, even as there will be souls who catch the foregleams that herald the dawn. So do not hope that the open vision will ever be the same to all. No such dream of equality is possible. Nor is it more desirable than possible. To some are given powers that can safely pry into mysteries which others must perforce avoid. These must be the leaders and guides among men. And those who are so called, are they on whom lies the most solemn duty of personal preparation and earnest, life-long struggle with self, until it is dominated and subdued, and the free soul soars untrammelled. We have long since told you of this. See you heed it.

Do not be discouraged that so much of what most believe as truth seems to you hollow and uncertain. It is so. There are divers degrees of truth. From the many-sided crystal gleams are shot off in many directions. And it is not every soul that can receive even one ray unclouded. To few, very few, comes more than a stray glimpse, and even that is filtered through many a medium, until its clearness is all dimmed. It must needs be so. Hence the varied views of truth. Hence the divergent notions, the errors, the mistakes, the fallacies that pass current among you. Men think they see a momentary gleam. They grasp some view, enlarge on it, add to it, develop it, until the tiny light is quenched, and what was a ray of truth is distorted and destroyed. And so the truth is maligned, whereas it should be the imperfection of the intervening medium that is blamed.

Or, to take another view. That which came as the answer to the yearnings of some aspiring soul is deemed to be of universal application. The truth was so beautiful, so ennobling, so pure and holy in its essence, that it must surely be so to all. And the jewel is dragged out from casket, and prepared for open exhibition. The lily is plucked from its stem, and paraded before men. And it loses its purity; its vitality diminishes; it withers and dies; and he to whom it was so fair, so lovely, wonders to find that it loses its freshness in the heat and dust of the world's busy strife. He marvels that what was so pure and true to him in the heart's secluded temple should seem tame and out of place when advertised to the world. He learns, if he is wise, that the dew of Hermon is distilled in the silence and solitude of the heart; that the flower springs up in the gloom of night, and withers beneath the noon-day beams; that truth, the holiest and purest, comes direct from spirit to spirit, and may not be proclaimed on the world's house-top.

Doubtless there are coarse views of truth, rude blocks which man has hewn, and which all may use alike. These are the foundation stones which every builder must use. But the richest and purest gems must be preserved in the spirit-shrine, and be gazed upon in silence and alone. So when John the

Seer told of the jewelled walls and pearly gates of the Heavenly City, he spoke of the outer truths which all must see; but in the inner temple he placed nor jewel nor purest ray of light, but only the Presence and the Glory of the Lord.

Marvellous it is that you do not see this. That which to you is Divine Truth is only that atom, that speck of the whole unbroken circle which has been cast off in answer to your cry. You needed it, and it came. To you it is perfection; it is God. To another it would be incomprehensible, without a voice to answer to his cry, without any beauty that he should desire it. You cannot parade it if you would. It would die, and its hidden charm would make no convert. It is yours and yours alone, a special creation for a special want, an answer from the great Spirit to the yearning aspiration of your soul.

This Truth will always be esoteric. It must be so; for only to the soul that is prepared can it be given. Its fragrance is too evanescent for daily common use. Its subtle perfume is shed only in the inner chamber of the spirit. Remember this; and remember too that violence is done to Truth by forcing it on unprepared minds, while harm, great and far-reaching, is done to those who cannot receive what is a revelation to you but not to them.

Moreover, remember that the pursuit of truth for its own sake as the altogether lovely and desirable end of life is the highest aim of spirit on your plane of being, higher than earth's ambitions, nobler than any work that man can do. We do not now take note of any of the vulgar aims that fill up human life. The struggles and ambitions that exercise mankind, born of vanity, nurtured in jealousy, and ending in disappointment—these are plain to view as Sodom apples. But there is a subtler temptation to more refined souls—that of doing good to their fellows and adding another stone to the cairn that the pioneers of the past have raised. To them comes the desire to proclaim in accents of enthusiasm some truth which has taken hold upon their lives. They are possessed with it; the fire burns within them, and they speak. It may be a noble word they utter, and, if it meets the needs of men, it is re-echoed and taken up by other souls like-minded, and developed till men are stirred and benefited by it. But it may be the reverse. The Truth, so true to one, is true to him alone, and his voice is the voice of one crying in the wilderness, a proclaimer of idle tales. He speaks in vain, and it had been well that he had saved his energies for the quest of truth, and have learned more before he spake to men.

It is well to teach, but better still to learn : nor is it impossible to do both. Only remember that learning must precede teaching: and be sure that the truth is one that man needs. The student who dives deep into the mysteries that enshrine Truth will not recklessly violate the seclusion in which alone she dwells at ease. He will tell of her beauties, and proclaim to those who have ears to hear the words of healing which his inner sense has caught from her lips : but there will always be to him a sacred reserve, a holy silence, an esoteric revelation too pure, too dear for utterance.

[In answer to some unimportant question it was written] :—

Nay : you will be informed in time. We may not save you the exercise which is part of your discipline. Be content to walk in the path. It leads direct to truth ; but you must tread it in care and pain. We have directed you to it because it is well for you to garner up the wisdom of the past, and to learn of those who are gone before you. We foresaw long ago that those who should faithfully pursue the study of the intercourse between our world and yours, would receive rude shocks from the follies and falsities that cluster round the subject in its most exoteric aspect. We looked with confidence for the time when these should force themselves into prominence, and we prepared for it. We would teach you that there are, and ever must be, two sides to this science, as there were in the mysteries of the ages past. Having passed the one, it is necessary that you penetrate the other.

To this end you must learn who and what are those who do communicate with men. Not otherwise can you read aright the riddle that now perplexes you. You must know how and under what conditions truth can be had: and how error and deceit, and frivolity and folly may be warded off. All this man must know if he is safely to meddle with our world. And when he has learned this, or while he is learning it, he must see, too, that on himself depends most or all of the success. *Let him crush self, purify his inmost spirit, driving out impurity as a plague, and elevating his aims to their highest possible: let him love Truth as his Deity, to which all else shall bow; let him follow it as his sole aim, careless whether the quest may lead him, and round him shall circle the Messengers of the Most High, and in his inmost soul he shall see light.*

✠ Imperator.

SECTION XXXIII

{In Section IV. reference is made to some extremely minute particulars which were written concerning the life of Arne, the musical composer. On Sept. 12th, 1873, a number of other facts and dates equally minute and accurate were given respecting other composers, Dr. Benjamin Cooke, Pepusch, Wellesley Earl of Mornington, respecting whose very names I was ignorant. The details are absurdly minute, comprising just such a brief record as would be found in a Biographical Dictionary. They were described by DOCTOR, in whose writing they appear, as "worthless, save for your conviction. That is the end we have in view. Details of earth life are of little interest to us now."

On July 16th, 1874, being then confined to my room by illness, I received a further communication respecting these musical spirits who were so completely outside of my own personal interests, and yet so intimately connected with one with whom I was brought into daily contact. This time it was John Blow, described as "pupil of Christopher Gibbon, and the successor of Purcell in the Abbey, Westminster: a composer even as a boy." Further inquiry elicited his date, 1648-1708. This was the result apparently of a chance visit to my room, when I was in a supersensitive condition, of the link between me and these spirits.

On October 5th, 1873, more personal evidence was brought. The same spirit who, in Section IV., was described as being able to write out an extract from a book, transcribed some particulars about ancient Chronicles, which in their broad outline would not be unfamiliar to my mind, since the subject came within the scope of my study. In the extremely minute and precise manner in which they were given, they are quite out of my mental scope: seeing that it is a peculiarity of my mind to be unable to retain and reproduce minute and precise facts, and especially dates. Both from natural inability to use such facts, and from a belief that wide views, and a general grasp of a subject in its broad bearings are most serviceable, I have always endeavoured to cultivate such a habit of mind.

It is a singular fact in this connection that almost all the communications written through my hand are distinguished by microscopic minuteness of detail, and by a general absence of breadth and diversity of view, except in the case of those proceeding directly from IMPERATOR.

At this same time twenty-six lines from the works of Norton, an old Alchymist, were written out in a curious archaic hand, quite different from any that had been used before. The extract I afterwards verified with difficulty, for the book is scarce, and little is known of Norton, his very date being involved in obscurity. It was said of him that he was an old student of the occult: a medium in his life, and so more able to return to earth. His poem was called "The Ordinal or Manual of Chemical Art," and was written for his patron, Archbishop Neville of York.

I might adduce other cases, but they would prove no more than those already adduced. I have selected almost at random a few cases out of a great number.

One more, however, I will quote, because of the remarkable manner in which the communication was verified. It seemed that the same power that gave the fact pointed to its method of verification, and it has the merit of being absolutely external to the knowledge of any person present. I quote from my records.

March 25th, 1874.—A spirit communicated through the table, name and particulars both unknown to any member of the circle. I inquired on the following day about the circumstance.]

The spirit said truly that she was named Charlotte Buckworth. She has no special connection with us, but was permitted to speak as she chanced to be present, and for evidence to you. The conditions were unfavourable for our work; we were not able to harmonise the conditions, which were disturbed. It is always so after such a day as you passed. The different influences of those with whom you were thrown would introduce elements of disturbance which we could not harmonise.

> *I had been with four persons all more or less mediumistic. I always am affected by being in the society of such.*

You do not know how much you are sensitive to such influence. The spirit who came to you was one who has passed from among you now for more than a hundred years, having made a sudden and unprepared entrance into spirit-life in the year 1773. She passed away at the house of a friend in Jermyn-street, whither she had gone on a party of pleasure. She will probably be able to say more to you; but we have no control over her.

> *I asked that she should be fetched, but was told that the communicating spirit had no control over her. I then inquired if anything more were known about her.*

Yes. She was very anxious to say more, but the power was exhausted. She has been occupied in her special sphere of work after awaking from a long sleep, and has not been brought within the atmosphere of earth until lately. She is attracted to circles where harmony prevails, being herself of a loving nature. Her departure from your earth was instantaneous; for she dropped down at a party of pleasure, and at once passed from the body.

> *I inquired the cause of death.*

Weakness of the heart, increased by violent dancing. She was but a thoughtless girl, though of a gentle and loving disposition.

> *I asked what house and where?*

We cannot say. She will probably be able to say for herself.

[Other subjects were then written about, and no more was said of this. In the afternoon of the same

day a brief communication was made. Though I
resisted the impression to write, being busy and
not at home, I was compelled to allow the message
to be given.]

We have ascertained that it was at the house of one Doctor
Baker that Lottie departed. The day was the fifth of
December. We are not able to tell you more; but enough
has been said.

RECTOR.

[The verification of this statement was as unexpected
as was the message itself. We had decided that no
means of verification was open; and the matter
passed from our minds. Some time after, Dr. Speer
had a friend at his house who was fond of old
books. We three were talking in a room in which
there were a number of books rarely used, arranged
in shelves extending from floor to ceiling. Dr.
Speer's friend, whom I will call Mr. A——, mounted
a chair to get at the topmost row, which was composed entirely of volumes of the Annual Register.
He took one down amid a cloud of dust, and com-
mented on it as a valuable record of events from
year to year. Almost anything, he said, could be
found in it. As he said this, the idea flashed into
my mind at once most vividly that there was the
place to verify the information that had been given
about this death. It was one of these utterly un-
accountable impressions, or rather communications
with which those who commune with spirits are
familiar. It was as if a voice spoke to my inner
sense. I hunted out the volume for 1773, and there
I found, among the notable deaths, a record of this
occurrence, which had apparently made a sensation
as occurring at a festivity in a fashionable house.
The volume was thickly covered with dust, and had
lain undisturbed in its place since it had been put
there some five years before. I remember the books
being arranged, and they had never been disturbed
since; nor, but for Mr. A——'s antiquarian tastes,
would it ever have occurred to any of us to pull
them down.

I may add in this connection, that on March 29th,
1874, a communication was written out in my book,

of which at first I could make nothing. The handwriting was like none I had seen before, very shaky and tremulous, like that of an extremely old and feeble person. Though a name was apparently signed, I could not read it at all until it was deciphered for me by the spirit-amanuensis. The message was from a very old woman, of whom I had never before heard, who passed away at upwards of 90 years of age at a house not far from the place where our circle meets. For obvious reasons I am unable to print the name and address. I have neither authority nor wish to seek it from friends still living. But the name, place of residence, both in earlier years and at the time of death, age, and date of decease, were given with exact accuracy. The remarkable fact, for which (apparently) the message was given, was that the time of departure from earth was in the month of December, 1872, since which time, as was said, "the spirit being full of years in its earth-life had rested from its earthly toil." On awaking it had been attracted to its old home, and thence to the circle in the immediat neighbourhood.

I believe that in this, as in all cases of identity, the information was brought at the instance of IMPERATOR, and for the definite purpose of supplying to me evidence which I very much desired of spirit-identity, or rather of individuality perpetuated after bodily death. The cases were apparently selected by design, and I have never been able to procure evidence suggested by myself, or to interfere successfully with this apparently pre-arranged plan.

Here the continuity of the messages is broken, and the series may well terminate. The power recurred at times, but never with the sustained vigour manifested in the mass of these Teachings. The end in view had been obtained, and though much was written afterwards, the periods of intermission became more frequent until, about the year 1879, this method of communication was practically abandoned for an easier and simpler one. It would be easy to select from my various books other striking teachings. Hereafter I may possibly do so. For the present, this series complete in itself so far as it goes, may suffice as a specimen of a unique experience.

In concluding, I may venture to say that I propound these Teachings as specimens of influence brought powerfully to bear upon an independent mind from without. The opinions expressed may be dismissed or accepted by each reader according as they commend themselves to him. But he will miss the true significance of this volume if he does not recognise a sustained and successful effort of intelligence apart from a human brain to influence one who claims for himself no other merit than that of having honestly and very laboriously endeavoured to arrive at truth.

THE END.

www.ingramcontent.com/pod-product-compliance
Lightning Source LLC
Chambersburg PA
CBHW030749230426

43667CB00007B/895